Faculty Fathers

Faculty Fathers

*Toward a New Ideal
in the Research University*

MARGARET W. SALLEE

SUNY PRESS

Published by
STATE UNIVERSITY OF NEW YORK PRESS
Albany

© 2014 State University of New York

All rights reserved

Printed in the United States of America

For information, contact
State University of New York Press
www.sunypress.edu

Production, Laurie Searl
Marketing, Fran Keneston

Library of Congress Cataloging-in-Publication Data

Sallee, Margaret, 1977–
    Faculty fathers : toward a new ideal in the research university / Margaret
W. Sallee.
        pages cm
    Includes bibliographical references and index.
    ISBN 978-1-4384-5389-7 (hardcover : alk. paper)
    ISBN 978-1-4384-5390-3 (pbk. : alk. paper)
    ISBN 978-1-4384-5391-0 (ebook)
    1. College teachers—United States—Leaves of absence—Case studies.
2. College teachers—Family relationships—United States—Case studies.
3. Male teachers—United States—Leaves of absence—Case studies.
4. Male teachers—Family relationships—United States—Case studies.
5. Parental leave—United States—Case studies.   6. Sex differences in
education—United States—Case studies.   I. Title.
    LB2335.8.S35 2014
    378.121—dc23   2014002122

10 9 8 7 6 5 4 3 2 1

For my parents

Contents

List of Tables   ix

Acknowledgments   xi

1.   Introduction   1

2.   Conflicting Roles: The Ideal Worker or the
     Ideal Father?   29

3.   Family-Friendly or Father-Friendly:
     Institutional Culture and the Ideal Worker   57

4.   Disciplinary Culture and the Ideal Worker   97

5.   How Family Life Affects Faculty Life   133

6.   The Ideal Worker Inside or Outside the Home?   155

7. Tenure versus Fatherhood: How Generation X
Faculty Eschew the Ideal Worker   181

8. Redefining the Ideal   205

   References   227
   Index   237

Tables

Table 1.1   Number of Children by Faculty Rank   25

Table 3.1   Artifacts, Values, and Assumptions Across
the Four Universities   92

Table 4.1   Artifacts, Values, and Assumptions Across
the Disciplines   128

Acknowledgments

So many people were involved in helping this project come to fruition. Although I recognize some in the following pages, countless others have helped me along the way. I appreciate each of them deeply. I am particularly grateful to Mary Lucal and Joanna Kidd who, after I had collected all of the data and written several articles, both encouraged me to write a book exploring the experiences of faculty fathers more deeply. They knew that I had this project in me and encouraged me to make it happen; I'm grateful to both of them for the encouragement.

I owe my gratitude to numerous other people: mentors, colleagues, friends, and family. Although I began this project well after finishing graduate school, I will forever be grateful to my dissertation chair, Bill Tierney, who equipped me with the skills and confidence to undertake such a project. I'm grateful for the support of colleagues around the country, including Julia Colyar, Becky Cox, Ronn Hallett, Jeni Hart, Jaime Lester, Corrie Stone-Johnson, Kelly Ward, and Lisa Wolf-Wendel. Many of them read drafts of chapters and provided intellectual support as I have thought about and worked on this project over the past several years. Their work has helped make my own stronger.

I am thankful to many friends, including Kerry Buchholz, Jenny Buddenhagen, and Hilary Welty, who have all provided support, even from afar, and listened throughout this project. These friendships have enriched my life. I am also grateful to my parents, Joan and Tom Sallee. My father was the first faculty father I knew and my mother was working before all mothers did. They both challenged traditional gender roles and their fingerprints are all over this project and the way I approach my work. To my sisters, Claire and Kristie, who inspire me daily with the ways that they balance their families and work. To Mary and Simon, although neither was in my life when I collected this data, they were an important and constant presence as I wrote this book. I am so grateful to them for enriching my life and helping me understand the importance of balancing work and family.

This project would not have been possible without the research funds I received as a new assistant professor at the University of Tennessee. The funds allowed me to travel to the campuses to collect data and pay for transcriptions. There is no doubt in my mind that I would not have been able to do this project without such support. I hope that this serves as a reminder to all universities that providing even modest funds of support to faculty can lead to important outcomes. Thank you to the campus and all who supported me while I was there.

Portions of this book have previously been published in *Research in Higher Education* and the *Journal of Higher Education*. I am grateful to both journals for allowing me to reproduce some of the material here. With kind permission from Springer Science+Business Media (*Research in Higher Education*, "The ideal worker or the ideal father: Organizational structures and culture in the gendered university," vol. 53, 2012, 782–802) for allowing me to reproduce parts of this article here. Similar thanks to the Ohio State University Press for allowing me to reuse portions of the article "Gender norms and institutional culture: The family-friendly versus the father-friendly university," which appeared in vol. 84 of the *Journal of Higher Education*, published in 2013.

I am very grateful for the assistance of all of the people at SUNY Press for their help guiding me through this process. Beth Bouloukos, Ryan Morris, Laurie Searl, and many others helped shepherd this project from idea to fruition. I am grateful to each of them for their help. Therese Myers, copyeditor extraordinaire, deserves significant thanks for her meticulous attention to detail. I learned a tremendous amount by reading her suggestions and developed more as a writer throughout the process. Tremendous thanks also to the two anonymous reviewers of this manuscript; their feedback has made this book so much stronger. I am grateful to my graduate assistants, Rebecca Borowski and Maigen Sullivan, for their research assistance in the final stages of this process. Last but in no way least, I owe thanks to the 70 fathers and handful of administrators who participated in this study. I appreciated each of them sharing their experiences with me and helping me to understand just how difficult navigating the demands of work and family can be for any parent—father or mother. I learned a great deal from their experiences and appreciate that they took the time to teach me, and others, how to craft a meaningful academic and personal life.

CHAPTER I

Introduction

One of the benefits of being a dad who is involved is you get much more credit than the mom does. Like, "Oh, what a great dad—like you're doing x, y, z," and that's great because you can sit by yourself and say, "Look at me! I'm an all like liberated man or whatever!" But the downside to that, it's like this expectation is somehow that it's unusual or that I'm doing something more than I might be doing. I don't—I look at me doing what I ought to be doing. . . .

Someone's like, "Oh, well you're doing such a good job with him!" Well frick of course I am lady! I spend all the time with him! . . . I get angry where there's this expectation that I'm getting a bonus or anything or extra credit brownie points. . . . I just find it annoying, patronizing, and condescending to have this sense for me as like I'm babysitting my kid on the weekend or "Oh, Daddy's day out with your son." No it's not, "Daddy's day with my son." I'm parenting right now.

—Assistant Professor, Midwestern University

I think it would have been a problem if I had said, you know, I'm going to take six weeks off to spend with my wife and my newborn. I think there would have been some people going, "Why do you need to take time off? You know, you're the man." . . . So it's definitely different. There's almost like . . . a gender bias against males taking time off to be with their newborn. Whereas, you know, if a woman did that, they'd be like "Oh yeah, of course, you know that's what's expected."

—Assistant Professor, Southern University

These excerpts from interviews with faculty fathers at two of the four research universities highlighted in this book point to the tensions inherent for men negotiating the demands of work and family. As the Midwestern University assistant professor pointed out, men are praised for being involved parents. A father parenting his child is regarded by many as exceeding what is generally expected of fathers. In contrast, a woman is generally expected to engage in the same behaviors as a natural part of mothering. Yet, as the Southern University assistant professor suggested, while men might be praised for being involved fathers, they are simultaneously regarded with suspicion, as if they are violating assigned roles in the workplace. This father discussed his decision not to take an extended leave of absence following the birth of his child; doing so would challenge gender norms that prescribe work for men and caregiving for women.

It is this tension that this book explores. Men are praised when they are involved parents, yet simultaneously penalized if they prioritize family over work. Traditional gender norms remain entrenched in the structure and culture of many organizations, including research universities, which are the focus of this book. And, to a certain extent, men cannot challenge these norms without risking being penalized in the workplace and by others in society.

Work/life balance is nearly always framed as a woman's issue. As I will discuss, ample evidence suggests that women experience both personal and professional consequences for becoming mothers. The stakes are compounded for female academics because faculty work places heavy expectations on those forging careers in the academy. However, simply because women experience pressure does not mean that men do not. And yet, despite the significant attention given to the challenges that women face in the academy (Armenti, 2004; Comer & Stites-Doe, 2006; Fothergill & Feltey, 2003; Liston, Griffin, & Hecker, 1997; Ward & Wolf-Wendel, 2004, 2012; Wolf-Wendel & Ward, 2006a, 2006b; Wolf-Wendel, Ward, & Twombly, 2007), few studies have focused explicitly on the challenges that male academics face. This book aims to fill that gap.

Focusing on the experiences of faculty fathers is important for three reasons. First, although women may face several burdens navigating family and career, continuing to focus solely on mothers perpetuates the notion that parenting is only a woman's concern. However, it should not be—and is not—just women who worry about how to be successful employees and successful parents; men have these same concerns. One study of faculty at a research university in the South found no differences in the degree to which men and women reported feeling conflict between their work and home responsibilities (Commission for Women, 2010). Put another way, men and women reported equal senses of conflict over work and family.

Findings from a study of faculty at another research university echo these results; women and men were equally likely to report experiencing work/life conflict (Elliott, 2003). Of particular interest in this study, whereas both groups were equally likely to report work/life conflict, women were more likely to report that that their sense of conflict was affected by their familial responsibilities while men reported that work/life conflict stemmed from criticism at work. While both groups might feel equally conflicted, men's stress resulted from factors in the workplace. This conflict may not come as a surprise, given that men have typically derived their identities from their occupations, a topic to which I return shortly.

In addition, evidence suggests that men are spending more time with their children than ever before. Using data from four time-diary studies between 1965 and 1998, Sayer, Bianchi, and Robinson (2004) found that the proportion of fathers engaging in care had increased along with the amount of time spent with their children. In 1985, only one third of married fathers engaged in some form of child care; by 1998, more than one half of fathers reported engaging in child care. In 1985, fathers spent an average of 26 minutes a day with their children, but by 1998 that number had climbed to just under 1 hour a day. A subsequent study found that in 2012, the average father spent nearly 1 hour and 45 minutes per day engaged with his children (U.S. Bureau of Labor Statistics, 2013). Together, these studies suggest that fathers' time spent with their children is increasing and that they feel conflicted about meeting their responsibilities in the workplace and in the home.

Second, a study of faculty fathers is also needed to understand the ways in which gender norms dictate acceptable behaviors that individuals might adopt. Gender norms trap both men and women into fixed roles. Would men spend more time with their children if gender norms embraced active fathering as a part of masculinity? For decades, women have received a great deal of attention for being forced to make choices between their careers and child rearing. Inside the academy, there has also been attention to the fields that women might pursue. Women are still grossly underrepresented in many sciences and in engineering. These barriers are real and persistent. However, the same concerns arise about the ways that gender norms dictate acceptable male behavior. Men are encouraged to stay out of the home and avoid caregiving professions, such as nursing and elementary school teaching. Just as women need to feel free to explore traditionally masculine roles and fields, men need not be penalized for seeking more involvement with their children's lives. This study aims to explore how gender norms in the academy influence faculty fathers' personal and professional behaviors.

Finally, fathers in academia need to be studied to better elucidate the role that organizations play in their personal and professional lives.

As I suggested earlier, gender norms have dictated the types of acceptable behaviors for men and women to adopt, including norms around child rearing. While these norms have influenced behaviors in the home, they have also influenced the attitudes of organizations around work and family. Historically, organizations were more likely to provide accommodations to new mothers than to new fathers because women were expected to be the primary caregivers. Although workplaces are becoming more accommodating to fathers and beginning to recognize work/life demands placed upon them, men are less likely than their female colleagues to use the policies. In a study of companies in Sweden—arguably one of the most gender-equitable countries in the world because it provides state-funded leave dedicated to fathers' use—Haas and Hwang (1995) found that only 30% of employers reported that men taking leave following the birth of a child would lead to few to no problems. If 70% of men might experience penalties for taking leave in a country where leave for fathers is state-supported, imagine the consequences to men who take leave in a country such as the United States, which offers no paid federal leave for either parent.

Universities have a unique opportunity to be catalysts in changing these dated and constraining gender norms. In the United States, universities have frequently been pioneers in adopting values more progressive than those of the country as a whole. For example, although African American men and all women were not given the right to vote until 1869 and 1920, respectively, both groups attended colleges and universities far earlier, from the founding of the earliest historically black colleges and universities (HBCUs) and women's colleges in the 1830s. In that same decade, Oberlin College became the first institution to admit African Americans and White women. Although the U.S. government failed to provide rights to these populations, colleges and universities provided opportunities to marginalized groups, thereby playing a part in challenging and shaping society's values.

As the civil rights protests of the 1960s illustrate, higher education institutions continued to serve as sites of revolution and change throughout the 20th century. In the 21st century, the trend continues. Although same-sex marriages do not yet have complete recognition under federal and state law, many colleges and universities have found ways to provide partner benefits to employees in same-sex relationships, demonstrating their commitment to creating an equitable environment. The increasing emphasis on work/life issues and family-friendly campuses once again provides opportunities for higher education institutions to focus on equity and promote societal change. Many campuses have established themselves at the forefront of the movement by providing an array of policies for faculty and staff that far exceeds what is available at the federal level. Whether these actions are motivated by a concern for challenging societal norms about balancing work and family or are simply a recruitment and retention tool to compete with their peer institutions, the result is that some institutions are more pro-family than U.S. society as a whole.

Colleges and universities need not stop with simply providing family-friendly policies. They can go further in making inroads for women and men struggling to be committed professionals and involved parents. As I discuss throughout this book, the current culture of many higher education institutions remains thoroughly gendered. This manifests itself in several ways—from the composition of majors and departments to the allocation of funds to men's athletics. Institutions are also gendered in the type of attention often provided to work/family issues. Although policies exist for men and women to use, men are not expected to avail themselves of institutional resources. In short, different cultural expectations exist for mothers and fathers in the workplace and in the home. Universities are in a position to challenge these entrenched norms by creating a culture that encourages men and women to be active employees and active parents. Implementing policies and programs coupled with changing employee attitudes and expectations can help create a culture in which traditional gender roles are challenged, building opportunities for women in the workplace and men in the home. Although navigating work/life concerns is increasingly becoming an issue for men, prioritizing familial responsibilities remains fraught with professional complications. These challenges might be due in part to the conflict between the norm of the ideal worker and the ideal father along with notions of the gendered university, concepts to which I return shortly.

In the remainder of this chapter, I consider the expectations of faculty careers and why they create unique demands on those balancing work and family. I then review the theoretical constructs that I use to understand how the gendered culture of the academy operates to keep men in the workplace and out of the home. I discuss the disproportionate burden that female faculty face balancing personal and professional responsibilities and the related, yet more veiled, consequences born by men in the academic workplace. The last part of the chapter sets the stage for the rest of the book. I begin with an overview of the types of family-friendly policies that universities typically offer to provide some context for the family-friendliness of the four universities at the focus of this book—referred to as Eastern University, Midwestern University, Southern University, and Western University. I then introduce the universities and fathers profiled in the book before concluding with an overview of the chapters to come. My aim in this chapter is to provide an introduction to the theories along with the campuses and fathers that I will consider throughout this text.

Navigating Parenthood at the Research University

Although all employees contend with navigating their personal and professional responsibilities, the components of faculty work distinguish it from employment in other fields in three major ways. First, faculty work is never finished. In addition to teaching responsibilities, professors on many campuses are expected to engage in a significant amount of research as well as campus and professional service. In addition to preparing class lessons, grading papers and exams, and holding office hours, professors are also expected to conduct research, write articles, apply for grants, supervise and mentor graduate students, and engage in a host of other responsibilities. Although a faculty member may leave campus for the day, she or he always has projects that require attention. Second, faculty can perform their work nearly anywhere. Although the rise of technology has led to some shifts in other sectors as well, faculty members need not be on campus to work. Save for teaching classes or perhaps running experiments in a lab, faculty can perform a large portion of their work off campus. Such flexibility can provide both tremendous opportunity and tremendous challenge. Third, the structure of faculty careers puts significant pressure on new professors. Most new faculty have six years to earn tenure from the date of hire, which implies that assistant professors are supposed to work tirelessly in order to achieve often unarticulated goals. This stressful period demands remarkable commitment from faculty members who will find themselves out of a job if they fail to earn tenure. Few other careers place the same sorts of demands and penalties on new hires in the way that academic work does.

This book concerns the experiences of an even smaller percentage of faculty: those employed at research universities, which now account for about 6% of more than 4,000 institutions of higher education in the United States (National Center for Education Statistics [NCES], 2010). Of all the institutional types, research universities place the greatest expectation on their faculty to engage in high-level and funded research. As others have written, recent transformations in the academy have led faculty to face additional pressure to conduct externally funded research, particularly as a way to bring additional income into the institution (Bok, 2003; Mohrman, Ma, & Baker, 2008; Slaughter & Rhoades, 2004). Faculty at research universities are more likely to face greater pressure to publish than their peers at liberal arts colleges who tend to be rewarded more for teaching.

While one might debate whether pressure to publish or pressure to grade is more intense, faculty at research universities face additional issues that their peers employed at other types of institutions do not: many are forced to move away from families and support networks in order to take tenure-line positions. Although there are 1,085 community colleges and 726 comprehensive colleges in the United States, there are only 273 research universities (NCES, 2010). Most states have fewer than half a dozen research universities; many only have one. Given the competitiveness of the job market, an individual who is interested in pursuing a career at a research university has to be willing to move across the country. Such relocation removes the faculty member from his or her support network. Those who are married may find that their partner is out of a job in the move. Few other professions require their employees to change geographic locations simply to start work. While employees in other professions might choose to apply for jobs in different states, faculty work at research universities nearly always requires it. As a result, work in research universities places significant personal and professional burdens on faculty. While faculty have great flexibility as to where they can perform their work, many are under pressure to bring in grants and all are under significant pressure to publish or risk losing their jobs. Most will have moved a significant geographic distance to take their job. Simply to become professors at research universities, faculty are expected to put their professional lives ahead of their personal lives. Often, their partners also are expected to prioritize the faculty member's career over their own. As I now discuss, this expectation continues with employment.

The Ideal Worker in the Gendered University

Given significant shifts in the past few decades, few contemporary families mimic the traditional structure of a working father and a stay-at-home mom. According to the 2010 Current Population Survey, only 11% of all U.S. households comprise an opposite-sex married couple in which the father works and the mother stays home with the children. Among married couple households, 12% consist of families with children where only the father works; 28% are dual-income families with children; and 27% are dual-income families without children. The remaining 33% comprise other types of families including those headed by women as single earners and families where neither partner is in the workforce (U.S. Census Bureau, 2010). This shift in labor trends extends to the academy as well. A survey of more than 9,000 faculty at 13 research universities found that 72% of full-time faculty have an employed partner, 14% of faculty are single, and 13% have a stay-at-home partner. Disaggregating the findings by gender reveals that 20% of the male faculty surveyed have a stay-at-home partner (Schiebinger, Henderson, & Gilmartin, 2008). These data suggest that faculty may have more traditional family structures than society at large. As I discuss in a later chapter, regional differences point to disparities between employment statuses of couples. The majority of faculty at Southern University were the primary breadwinners for their family whereas faculty at the other campuses were more likely to be in dual-earner couples. Return-ing to the argument at hand, national employment trends, both inside and outside the academy, underscore that the male breadwinner/female caregiver dichotomy is an anachronistic model that applies to only a slim majority of the U.S. population.

And yet the university and many other organizations continue to oper-ate as if families still adhere to such a traditional division of labor. The workplace expects employees to be ideal workers—or those who are able and willing to work long hours in the office with no other demands on their time (Acker, 1990; Bailyn, 2003; Ely & Meyerson, 2000). Such an arrangement suggests that the worker is either single or has someone else to take care of children and other nonwork-related demands. Organizational structures in ideal worker environments exclude participation from those with signifi-cant responsibilities in the home. As Williams (2000) pointed out, jobs that require excessive overtime are frequently not viable options for those with caregiving responsibilities. Individuals typically establish a regular childcare schedule; jobs that require additional labor on little notice are simply not possible for many parents. In addition, academic positions may require indi-viduals to move frequently for advancement. Both of these examples operate on the assumption that the employee either has no children or has a spouse at home in charge of domestic responsibilities. When both individuals in a couple are in the labor force, the man's career often takes priority. Inherent in the definition of the "ideal worker" are notions of appropriate gender roles.

The ideal worker depends on the existence of a division of labor at work and at home. Traditionally, men have been expected to be the bread-winners while women were expected to be caregivers. In fact, research sug-gests that many men derive their identities from being the breadwinner for their families (Doherty, Kouneski, & Erickson, 1998; Emslie & Hunt, 2009; Marsiglio, Amato, Day, & Lamb, 2000). Being a good father is equated with being a productive member of the workforce. Men have traditionally been allowed to assume this role due to the fact that they had a wife to care for the children at home (Ely & Meyerson, 2000; Emslie & Hunt; Smithson & Stokoe, 2005). Recall the quote from the Midwestern University assistant professor that opened this chapter. Men who are involved fathers are often praised for their actions whereas a woman who performed the same work would receive nary a second look. Such praise stems from the fact that when men take care of their children, they are engaging in work outside their traditional responsibilities.

At the root of these gender roles are definitions of masculinity and femininity. What roles are men and women supposed to assume? As Kimmel (2001) and Connell (1995) argued, masculinity is typically defined in oppo-sition to femininity. A man strives to be everything that a woman is not.

If women are expected to be caregivers, men are expected to be providers (Connell & Messerschmidt, 2005; Lorber, 1998) and, by extension, ideal workers. Similarly, women are expected to be nurturing and empathic while men are expected to be aggressive and emotionless. Other features associated with masculinity include presumed heterosexuality and accompanying homophobia, physical strength, competitiveness, and being a father (Bird, 1996; Carrigan, Connell, & Lee, 1985; Connell & Messerschmidt; Kimmel, 2001; Martin, 1998). Multiple types of masculinity exist in every society, yet one particular masculinity is valued above all others; Connell (1995) labeled such a masculinity "hegemonic masculinity," which represents the type of masculinity to which all men are expected to aspire.

Although this particular configuration of masculinity might be most highly valued by society, few men actually embody such characteristics (Connell, 1995; Connell & Messerschmidt, 2005). For example, in American culture, sports stars are often idolized for their wealth and athleticism. Although few men ultimately achieve the same levels of success, many still measure themselves against this impossible standard. Although most men do not embody the characteristics of hegemonic masculinity, many still profit from patriarchy. As Connell and Messerschmidt argued, such men embody a complicit masculinity, wherein this group "receive[s] the benefits of patriarchy without enacting a strong version of masculine dominance" (p. 832). While a select group of men may actually fulfill the characteristics of hegemonic masculinity, the majority of men try actively to meet those standards and, in the process, profit from doing so.

Whereas the ultimate aim of hegemonic masculinity is the domination of women and perpetuation of patriarchy (Connell & Messerschmidt, 2005), hegemonic masculinity also makes distinctions between and perpetuates hierarchies among men (Connell & Messerschmidt; Demetriou, 2001). In fact, as Demetriou suggested, "hegemonic masculinity refers to a social ascendancy of one group of men over others" (p. 341). This other group of men is typically referred to as embodying subordinated or marginalized masculinities (Connell & Messerschmidt) and may include men of color, men with physical disabilities, and gay men (Carrigan, Connell, & Lee, 1985; Lorber, 1998). These groups of men are labeled as subordinate because the masculinity that they embody "is inconsistent with the currently accepted strategy for the subordination of women" (Demetriou, p. 344). As both Connell and Messerschmidt and Demetriou noted, domination and subordination among groups of men does not seem to be a goal in and of itself, but rather a means of achieving domination over women.

However, subordinated masculinities are not always rejected outright. Rather, the dominant group often appropriates behaviors of the subordinate group into accepted definitions of hegemonic masculinity (Demetriou,

2001). The example of the metrosexual may be instructive. Over the past decade, definitions of masculinity have shifted to incorporate characteristics that were once solely associated with gay men, such as careful attention to grooming and a particular style of dress. Appropriating such behaviors into mainstream definitions of masculinity means that the boundaries between hegemonic and subordinated masculinities have become less clear (Connell & Messerschmidt, 2005; Demetriou, 2001). Rather than leading to a more egalitarian masculinity, Demetriou suggested that such practices "render the patriarchal dividend invisible" (p. 354). In other words, patriarchy and other forms of domination are not disappearing, but are simply taking on new, and less recognizable, forms.

As this discussion should make clear, hegemonic masculinity is not a static construct. In fact, masculinity, and indeed, all gender is created and sustained through interaction with others (Bird, 1996; Connell, 1995; Connell & Messerschmidt, 2005; Demetriou, 2001). Men and women may police each other's behaviors to ensure that each is enacting the appropriate form of gender. Because gender is created through interaction, definitions of hegemonic masculinity change over time (Connell; Connell & Messerschmidt). The characteristics that were most valued in men in the 1950s are different than those valued today. The mutability of gender suggests the possibility of change toward a masculinity that does not oppress and marginalize groups of men and women. Just as definitions of hegemonic masculinity shift across time, so too do they differ across cultures (Connell & Messerschmidt). One can certainly agree that definitions of ideal masculinity are different in the United States than they are in Russia, but even within the same country, hegemonic masculinities differ by context. The image of the ideal male academic differs from the image of the ideal male auto mechanic. Each trade takes different skills to be successful and ultimately rewards some behaviors over others. Academia has the potential to shape organizational culture in such a way to encourage a new definition of masculinity to bloom—one that rewards men for being involved parents, or at the very least, does not punish them. Although gender norms may be slowly shifting, being a father who spends any time with his children outside of the socially prescribed roles violates gender norms and the characteristics of the ideal worker and is therefore punished personally and professionally.

The Gendered University

As I suggested earlier, definitions of masculinity and femininity are crafted within specific historical and cultural contexts. Organizations play a role in shaping the behavior of their workers, including rewarding or sanctioning workers for adhering to or violating gender norms. And yet much of organizational theory operates as if organizations are gender neutral. As others have pointed out over the past several decades (Acker, 1990; Collinson & Hearn, 2005; Connell, 2006; Ely & Meyerson, 2000), organizations are not gender neutral, but are gendered organizations that perpetuate distinctions between workers as well as laud hegemonic masculinity. Acker, one of the earliest theorists in this area, proves particularly useful in unmasking how gender operates within organizations.

Acker (1990) suggested that organizations are gendered in five ways. Organizations are gendered in the constructions of division along lines of gender, including through divisions of labor and the allocation of power. In many organizations, men occupy positions of leadership while women comprise the ranks of the clerical staff. Second, organizational symbols and images exist to perpetuate these divisions; for example, the ideal business leader is assumed to be both aggressive and competitive—qualities not commonly associated with women. Third, organizations are gendered in the way in which those within them interact. In a meeting with male and female employees, who is more likely to speak and who is more likely to be spoken over? Fourth, organizations are gendered in the way in which these processes reinforce differences in individual identity. As others have suggested (West & Zimmerman, 1987), gender does not exist on its own, but rather is created through repeated interactions with others. With repeated interaction, differences between genders and power imbalances are reinforced. Finally, Acker (1990) argued that organizations are gendered in that all of these processes also reinforce organizational structures. In addition to reinforcing individual identity through repeated interaction, organizational identity is also shaped.

Much of the early work on gendered organizations sought to introduce gender into organizational analysis, an arena from which it had been profoundly absent. As Acker (1990) pointed out, "Since men in organizations take their behavior and perspectives to represent the human, organizational structures and processes are theorized as gender neutral" (p. 142). In short, the ideal worker was assumed to be male, which led to significant consequences for women or others who differ from the norm. Typically theories of gendered organizations are used to interrogate the ways in which organizational structures discriminate against women and perpetuate male-dominated cultures (Britton, 1997; Erickson, 2012; Manville, 1997; Martin, 1994; McBrier, 2003; Smith-Doerr, 2004; Williams, 2000). However, the gendered organization has significant consequences for men and women alike. Whereas some might suggest that men profit from gendered structures that favor them over women, men are also constrained by these same structures. The gendered divisions, symbols, and interactions within organizations all reinforce individual identities that do not reward men who differ from the norm. I am interested in understanding the ways in which organizational culture might discriminate against men who do not fit the norms of the ideal worker or seek to redefine masculinity. Given that this framework highlights the interaction of organizational structure and culture, it is particularly helpful in shedding light on the ways in which universities continue to discriminate against the involved father. Gendered universities trap men and women in stereotypical gender roles. Just as the gendered university punishes women in the workplace, so too does it punish men in the home. It is important to understand how organizational structures and culture influence all members of the organization, both those who hold power and those who are marginalized. However, as I hope to make clear, many men do not feel as if they are rewarded for their behaviors.

Throughout this book, I use theories of the gendered university, ideal worker, and hegemonic masculinity to understand the challenges that faculty fathers face as they navigate the demands of parenthood and the academy. My ultimate contention is that the culture of the academy coupled with gender norms—present in both universities as well as society—creates an environment that discourages many men from being involved fathers and punishes those who are. Understanding how these cultural norms operate—and the consequences that they have—is the first step toward dismantling them.

However, Acker (1990) is not the only scholar to point to the important role of culture in shaping the experiences of those within an organization. For decades, scholars have examined the role of culture in shaping organizational life (Bergquist, 1992; Martin, 2002; Masland, 1985; Tierney, 1988). However, most of these scholars have not used a gendered lens to understand culture and simply have sought to understand culture from a less critical perspective. For example, many studies of organizations have used Schein's (2004) cultural framework of analysis, which focused on an organization's artifacts, values, and assumptions. Schein contended that organizational culture can be analyzed via its artifacts, which include such items as the physical environment, behavior, and symbols, among others; values, which are reflected in organizational artifacts; and assumptions, which are unconscious and deeply embedded in organizational structure.

Schein's (2004) and Acker's (1990) frameworks share many similarities. For example, both scholars contended that the behavior of those inside an organization reflect cultural norms. The two theories have two significant differences, however. First, while Schein examined culture more broadly, Acker, instead, focused on how such behaviors might reflect a gendered culture. In essence, theories of gendered organizations focus the lens of analysis on a particular aspect of identity and culture. In addition, while Schein's analysis of organizational culture suggested that artifacts merely are reflections of values and assumptions that compose an organization, Acker's theory of gendered organizations suggests that artifacts help to create a gendered culture. In other words, Schein's theory assumes that organizational culture is static whereas Acker's theory suggests that organizational culture, much like gender, is constantly created and re-created through individual interaction. Theories of gendered organizations point to the role that organizational members play in preserving the status quo, but also in pushing for change. However, while theories of gendered organizations bring many strengths, particularly to a project on the experiences of fathers facing organizational norms in the university, Schein's theory offers a more detailed set of tools to analyze organizational culture at the artifact level. While Acker's theory of gendered organizations uses divisions along lines of gender, symbols and images, and interactions to understand organizational culture, Schein's framework identifies six types of artifacts that might be used to analyze culture. As a result of this greater specificity, I use Schein's framework in conjunction with gendered organizations in chapters 3 and 4 to understand how culture operates at the campus and disciplinary levels.

To sum up, universities are not gender neutral; rather, their structures, culture, and practices perpetuate gender norms. Who has power? What behaviors are valued? Part of any organization's success is due to its employees. The conventional wisdom is that the more hours an employee works, the more productive he or she will be and, thus, the more the organization will profit. Being this ideal worker necessitates that the employee have no responsibilities outside of the workplace. The employee might be married and have children, but the structure of the workplace assumes that someone—read, the wife—can attend to all domestic responsibilities. Inherent in that definition of the ideal worker are traditional gender roles of men as breadwinners and women as caregivers. All of these forces—the ideal worker, gender norms, and the gendered university—come together to have personal and professional consequences for men trying to balance work and family. As I suggested earlier, although few have examined the experiences of men balancing work and family, a considerable body of scholarship on work/family challenges for all faculty and female faculty in particular exists. In the next section, I provide a brief overview of this literature and point to the ways in which it has frequently, and perhaps unintentionally, perpetuated the myth that work/family issues remain a woman's concern.

WORK/LIFE ISSUES AND THE FACULTY CAREER

A significant body of literature has examined the challenges that women and, to a lesser extent, men have faced navigating personal and professional demands. Although both genders incur penalties, past research is fairly clear that women face penalties that men do not. I briefly discuss the types of issues that both men and women face in their personal and professional lives and point out the ways in which one gender might experience a greater burden than the other.

Numerous studies have found that female faculty routinely perform more work in the home than their male counterparts (Elliott, 2003, 2008; Mason & Goulden, 2004; Misra, Lundquist, & Templer, 2012; Nakhaie, 2009; O'Laughlin & Bischoff, 2005; Sax, Hagedorn, Arredondo, & Dicrisi, 2002). In her survey of 288 faculty at one U.S. research university, Elliott found that women reported doing more housework, engaging in more elder-care, and being responsible for childcare arrangements. Similarly, in their study of faculty in the University of California system, Mason and Goulden found that while men and women reported spending nearly equal amounts of time on housework, women spent nearly twice as many hours per week engaged in childcare as men. Women reported spending 35.5 hours per week with their children compared with men's 20.3 hours per week. While this discrepancy is unsettling, note how many more hours per week the average faculty father spends with his child than the data presented earlier from time diary studies of the U.S. population. While the average American father spends about 12 hours per week with his children, the average faculty father reports nearly double that number. As I will discuss in later chapters, the flexibility of the faculty career is one possible explanation for this increased time spent with children.

In addition to shouldering more responsibility inside the home, many studies have found that female faculty have to consider carefully the ramifications of having a child. Often this takes the form of delaying or forgoing having children or avoiding taking leave after the birth of children. Many (Armenti, 2004; Drago et al., 2005; Ward & Wolf-Wendel, 2004, 2012) have documented the ways that female faculty have delayed or timed the births of their children in order to be minimally intrusive on their professional careers. In her study of 19 Canadian academics, Armenti found that the older generation of women aimed to have "May babies," timing the births of their children to coincide with the summer months to reduce the disruption to their careers. While the author found that the women in younger generations were less likely to time births for the summer, considerable evidence suggests that female faculty still carefully consider when to have children.

Timing children's births is more frequently reported as an issue that affects female faculty while men's experiences are nearly absent from the discussion. In part, this makes sense as the woman carries the child and is often the primary caregiver after the child's birth. However, both male and female faculty report minimizing the amount of leave taken following the birth of a child, frequently out of fear of career repercussions (Colbeck & Drago, 2005; Drago et al., 2005; Finkel, Olswang, & She, 1994). Although both men and women might be likely to minimize the amount of leave taken following a child's birth, Drago and colleagues found that women are considerably more likely to engage in such behaviors. The authors found that only 14.4% of fathers but 51.1% of mothers came back to work earlier than they would have liked following the birth of a child out of concern for their professional reputation. Note that their findings do not suggest that women took less leave than men, only that women were likely to feel that they returned to work too soon after the birth of a child.

In addition to facing penalties with their personal lives, many women have similarly found themselves penalized in their professional lives due to their status as mothers. Several scholars have found that being married or having children impacts female faculty more than men. For example, Perna (2001) found that being married increased women's likelihood of holding a part-time, non–tenure-track appointment. That is, married women were less likely to be employed in tenure-track positions. Perna also found that having children reduces men's likelihood of being in a part-time, non–tenure-track position. Stated differently, men with children are more likely to be in tenure-line positions while married women are more likely to be in non–tenure-track positions.

Additional scholarship has found that having children affects women's—but not men's—achievement of tenure. Using data obtained through the Survey of Doctorate Recipients, a national study of postgraduate careers from 1973 to 1999, Mason and Goulden (2002) found that women who had babies within five years of obtaining their Ph.D. (defined by the researchers as "early babies") were consistently less likely to earn tenure than men in the same situation. In contrast, women with "late babies" (defined as those babies born five years postdoctorate) and women with no children had remarkably similar rates of earning tenure as their male counterparts. The authors hypothesized that the women with late babies waited until they had obtained tenure to start their families, thus removing the major obstacles to job security. The study found no similar impact on men. Perhaps one might assume that men's wives were performing more of the work in the home, thereby freeing the men to concentrate on their careers. Research suggests that having children negatively impacts women's career trajectories, but past studies have not found the same penalties for men.

Although evidence exists that being married and having children has an impact on a faculty member's employment or tenure status, the evidence is less convincing whether having children impacts a professor's productivity. Previous research confirms that women tend to spend less time engaged in research than men (Park, 1996; Tierney & Bensimon, 2000). Often, female faculty work as many hours as men, but spend their time on teaching and service. Although women and men spend their time differently, there is less evidence that suggests an individual's marital or parental status shapes the types of work performed. For example, Sax and colleagues (2002) found that having children appeared to have little effect on a faculty member's productivity once typical variables such as rank and department were taken into account. Although preliminary analysis pointed to differences between men and women's productivity, controlling for significant variables indicated no difference between men and women. In other words, a faculty member with kids and one without kids appear to produce the same amount of research. Similarly, Bellas and Toutkoushian (1999) found that being married and having children affected neither teaching nor research. The authors found that faculty members with more children worked fewer hours per week, yet produced more research than faculty with fewer dependents. Their findings suggest that faculty with more children have learned how to use their limited time efficiently to maximize their productivity. The evidence is mixed with regard to the effects having children has on a faculty member's career. Some studies suggest that women are penalized; others suggest that men profit; and still others suggest that children have no effect on a career. In chapter 5, I discuss how the experiences of fathers in this study reveal similar ambiguity about the impact of children on productivity. Although there is some ambiguity on effects on career, the evidence is less mixed as to the impact of family responsibilities on a faculty member's home life.

As the literature suggests, men are more likely than women to accrue advantages or at least experience minimal penalty following the birth of a child. However, accepting these differences without exploring the nuances of men's experiences is problematic. The majority of work/life literature in the academy has focused primarily on the concerns of women. This book serves to fill the gap and represents the experiences of another segment of the population. The chapters that follow illustrate how men struggle with their competing demands. Many fathers discussed the fact that they felt like they failed to achieve in multiple domains; they felt that their professional lives suffered and that they were unable to be involved in the home. Simply saying that women shoulder a greater burden than men may be true, but it also suggests that men's experiences are not worth exploring. This book sheds light on how men navigate their personal and professional demands and the ways in which institutional cultures and gender norms shape their identities as professors and fathers.

Accommodating Family Demands at the Research University

While all types of colleges and universities have responded to work/life needs of faculty, research universities are more likely than others to offer accommodations to faculty. A survey of 255 colleges and universities found that, on average, research institutions offered the greatest number of policies, with the 73 responding institutions averaging 2.99 policies per campus. In contrast, doctoral granting institutions offered 1.38 policies, master's institutions offered 1.29 policies, baccalaureate institutions offered 1.09 policies, and associate granting institutions offered 0.80 policies per campus (Hollenshead, Sullivan, Smith, August, & Hamilton, 2005). Institutional resources may determine a college or university's ability to provide accommodations to faculty; providing a paid term off from teaching brings considerable cost to the institution. The institutions profiled in this book are all research universities and therefore more likely to offer policies to help faculty and staff with work/life responsibilities. Research universities also serve a special function in that they frequently play a particular role in shaping the higher education landscape and society at large. By introducing policies and practices that promote gender equity in the workplace and the home, these institutions have the potential to shift the practices of all colleges and universities as well as those of society.

Since Stanford University implemented the first tenure-clock extension policy in 1971 (Manchester, Leslie, & Kramer, 2010), colleges and universities have increasingly offered several policies for faculty use, including parental leave, a release from teaching duties following the birth of a child, on-site childcare, emergency backup childcare, tuition remission, lactation rooms, eldercare, and other policies and programs. In this section, I review the types of family-friendly policies that many research universities offer, including the four campuses—referred to as Eastern University, Midwestern University, Southern University, and Western University—profiled in this book. It is important to keep these policies in mind since in later chapters I discuss many fathers' hesitation to use them, despite their availability.

TENURE-CLOCK EXTENSION

The tenure-clock extension is perhaps one of the easiest policies for an institution to provide its faculty because it brings no additional cost to the institution. Basically, the tenure-clock extension allows faculty members who have a child to add an extra year to the time granted to earn tenure. When a professor goes up for tenure, he or she is supposed to be evaluated on work produced during the standard six-year tenure period—and not assuming extra productivity for that additional year. Campuses differ in the provision of this policy. Some institutions require that the recipient provide a substantial portion of childcare in order to be eligible. In addition, some campuses limit the number of times that an assistant professor can extend the tenure clock for family reasons; on some campuses, faculty can extend their clock only once, despite having multiple children in the pretenure period. Colleges and universities have different procedures for activating the tenure-clock extension. At some institutions, the extension is automatic; once the faculty member adds his or her child to health insurance, the tenure clock is automatically extended. At other institutions, faculty members need to request the possibility of the extension, generally within one year of the birth. Requesting the possibility of the extension does not mean that faculty are required to use the extension, but rather that they have the option to do so. All four campuses profiled in this book offer a tenure-clock extension to their faculty.

PREGNANCY LEAVE, CHILDBEARING LEAVE, AND PARENTAL LEAVE

Some campuses also offer faculty leave following the birth of a child. On some campuses, such as Western University, leave is reserved for childbearing mothers or adoptive parents. Other campuses might offer parental leave to faculty of either gender. However, on many campuses, faculty are far less likely to be offered a paid leave than those working in staff positions. In part, this stems from the flexibility that is associated with the faculty career. One might assume that since faculty have few fixed demands on their time, aside from classes they teach, they should be able to find ways to accommodate new children without taking leave. And, indeed, historically, many female faculty timed the births of their children to coincide with summer to avoid interfering with their academic responsibilities (Armenti, 2004). Today, parental leave or pregnancy leave is often framed as a medical issue to accommodate the demands that pregnancy places on a woman's body. Of the four institutions profiled in this book, only Western University offers a childbearing leave for which fathers are not eligible.

Importantly, all employees of colleges and universities are eligible to access the provisions of the Family and Medical Leave Act, passed in 1993, which offers any employee who has worked for an organization for more than one year up to 12 weeks' unpaid leave for several life events, including childbirth or significant illness. However, because this leave is unpaid many employees cannot afford to benefit from this federal policy.

RELEASE FROM TEACHING DUTIES (ACTIVE SERVICE/MODIFIED DUTIES)

While a true leave is rarely granted to faculty, research universities are more likely to offer a release from teaching duties for one term to faculty mothers and fathers. Often termed "Active Service/Modified Duties," such leave typically releases faculty from some or all of their teaching responsibilities for one quarter or semester, which allows them to maintain their research agendas while also caring for the new addition at home. Often these leaves are framed as being available to faculty with substantial caregiving responsibilities. Three of the four institutions—Western, Midwestern, and Southern universities—offer a release from teaching duties to faculty of either gender.

Although becoming more common at research universities, there is often less support for implementing such a policy, primarily because of the cost associated with it. When a faculty member is granted a release from teaching duties, his or her department often needs to find someone to teach the courses for which the professor was responsible. Departments that opt not to cancel the courses typically have two choices: ask a full-time faculty member to step in (perhaps on an overload basis) or hire an adjunct. For small departments, neither option is ideal because they have neither the human capital nor the financial capital to cover a faculty member's absence. Institutions that provide a centrally located fund to hire adjuncts, which Western University does, are more likely to have cultures in which taking a parental leave is accepted and valued by those on campus. I discuss the role of institutional culture in detail in chapter 3. While these three policies are those that are most common on campuses, some campuses offer other policies and programs to faculty parents.

PART-TIME TENURE TRACK

Some campuses provide a part-time tenure track option for faculty, although such positions also come with part-time pay. Typically, in such arrangements, the faculty member is expected to teach half of the standard number of courses and produce half the publications per year to make progress toward tenure (that is, one semester per calendar year would count toward the tenure clock). Under these arrangements, faculty often maintain full benefits and retirement. The drawback of such an arrangement is the financial penalty that comes with a faculty member only earning half of his or her income. Yet, such an arrangement allows faculty contending with a major life issue—such as a child's illness—a little flexibility with their professional lives. Eastern University proudly publicized the existence of this policy as one of the cornerstones of its family-friendly initiatives. Western University also offers a part-time tenure track option.

BACKUP CHILDCARE

Most campuses now offer on-site childcare to faculty and staff (and, in some cases, students). Indeed all four of the campuses profiled in this book had either standard childcare centers or lab schools to which many of the fathers sent their children. And, of course, the perennial complaint was that there was never enough availability in any of the childcare centers. In addition to providing standard childcare, some campuses provide emergency backup childcare, designed to be used in unexpected emergencies. Say, for example, that a faculty member has to teach class, but his child is sick and not at school. Backup childcare services send a licensed and bonded professional into the home to provide care for short periods of time. Midwestern University is the only institution of the four profiled that provides such a program, which is available to faculty, staff, and students on a sliding-scale basis. The most affluent of faculty pay $20 per hour for the service and students can pay as little as $2 per hour. (The institution subsidizes the cost of the service for those lower on the scale.) While such a resource is not frequently used, it indicates that the institution aims to help faculty attend to their personal needs in unexpected situations.

MISCELLANEOUS INSTITUTIONAL PROGRAMS

Many campuses provide a variety of other policies and programs to faculty and staff. Some campuses provide lactation rooms and breastfeeding support programs to new mothers. Western University has 37 lactation rooms on its campus and employs a part-time lactation consultant. While such a program is of limited use to the faculty fathers profiled here, the existence of lactation rooms signals the degree to which the campus supports employees contending with a significant personal event. Many other campuses offer eldercare services, most frequently in the form of referrals to community providers. Another popular program that institutions offer is a spousal hiring program. As I pointed out earlier, given that two out of every three professors is married to someone who is also in the workforce (Schiebinger et al., 2008), many families need employment assistance. In recognition of this fact, all four institutions profiled here offer either official or unofficial spousal hiring assistance. Some of the campuses, such as Western University, have a website on which they advertise their policies. Other campuses, such as Eastern University, acknowledged that the policy was unofficial. On each campus, a partner or spousal hire typically worked in the same way. Imagine that a dual-career academic couple—one chemist and one historian—was hired at a university. The chemist was lucky enough to get the tenure-track job while his partner was hired as a full-time lecturer in history. Spousal hiring programs typically call for the historian's salary to be split in three ways—between the sponsoring department (in this case, chemistry), receiving department (history), and the provost's office for a fixed period of time. At the end of this period, the historian would be expected to find more permanent employment. While such a program is helpful in that it provides an immediate position for many faculty partners, it often delays the "two body problem" (Wolf-Wendel, Twombly, & Rice, 2003) for several years until funding runs out.

Other programs that institutions might provide are less formal. Some campuses, including Western University and Midwestern University, have selected faculty to serve as ambassadors for work/family programs on campus. At Midwestern University, faculty ambassadors attend department chair and search committee trainings to discuss the importance of valuing work and family issues. At Western University, faculty ambassadors receive quarterly training and are expected to serve as advocates for other faculty who approach them with work/life concerns. As this review has suggested, institutions have taken a variety of steps to incorporate attention to work/life issues for faculty through the provision of standard policies as well as by incorporating other initiatives into their institution. With this review of national policies in mind, the following provides an overview of the four campuses and the 70 fathers at the heart of this study.

Methodology

I framed this study as a comparative case study which involves the collection and comparison of data across two or more research sites (Stake, 1994; Yin, 2009). There are two particular hallmarks of case studies. First, case studies are defined by a "bounded system"—that is, the object of inquiry has defined boundaries in terms of space or time (Merriam, 1998; Stake). In this study, each institution serves as the bounded case. Second, at least two methods of data collection must be used in a case study. I chose to learn more about faculty fathers and their campuses through interviews and document analysis.

Campus Profiles

I collected data at four public research institutions in distinct regions of the United States. Three of the four institutions are the flagship universities for their states. In addition, three of the four universities are members of the Association of American Universities (AAU), an elite body of 62 institutions that are recognized for high-caliber research and scholarship. According to the association's website, "the 60 AAU universities in the United States award more than one-half of all U.S. doctoral degrees and 55 percent of those in the sciences and engineering" (AAU, n.d.). As should be clear, all four of the universities profiled here belong to an exclusive group of higher education institutions that place a strong emphasis on research. Two institutions were selected based on their reputation as family-friendly campuses and the other two institutions were selected based on a dearth of family-friendly policies; the two family-friendly institutions had each received national recognition for their efforts in helping faculty and staff balance work and family. I made sure to have a geographically diverse sample because I was interested in regional differences. While I provide detailed portraits of each of the campuses in chapter 3, I provide a little more information about each of the four campuses here.

Western University is a public research university located in a college town on the West Coast of the United States. Despite its growing size (the campus currently boasts 32,000 students and 2,500 faculty), the campus still maintains a community feeling. The campus frequently partners with the local community to host a variety of events throughout the year. Many of the fathers spoke of their appreciation for the local community as an ideal place to raise a family; they reported loving that their children could bike to school or downtown with friends. The town was known for strong public schools and both the town and nearby cities hosted many family-oriented activities. Western University is well known for its family-friendly policies for faculty and staff. Sample policies include a paid term off for childbearing faculty mothers, another term of teaching release for faculty mothers and fathers, and a tenure-clock extension.

Midwestern University is a public flagship institution with approximately 42,000 students and 3,500 faculty located in a college town in the Midwest. One of the top public universities in the United States, Midwestern University offers a portfolio of family-friendly policies designed to recruit and retain talented faculty and staff. Like many of the dads at Western University, faculty at Midwestern University also spoke of their love of the local community as a safe place to raise their children. They also appreciated the family-friendly resources available on the campus, including parks and museums. Midwestern's policies echo those of Western's. The campus provides paid release from teaching duties for both mothers and fathers, a tenure-clock extension, and emergency backup childcare for sick children.

Southern University is located in a small city in the Southeastern United States that revolves around the university athletics' successes and failures. The city is also noted by many faculty as being an easy place to raise children because of its excellent schools and affordable housing. With 27,000 students and 1,400 faculty, the campus only recently implemented family-friendly policies including a teaching release for faculty of any gender as well as the opportunity to extend the tenure clock.

Finally, *Eastern University* is located in a major metropolitan area on the East Coast of the United States. Faculty tend to live within a 30-mile radius of the campus and commute to work. Their dispersal throughout the metropolitan region has many consequences for faculty life as well as the ways in which the institution can be a family-friendly campus. Despite its 37,000 students and 4,000 faculty, the campus provides few family-friendly resources. The sole provisions are a tenure-clock extension as well as a part-time tenure track option.

A SNAPSHOT OF THE FATHERS

I interviewed 70 faculty fathers across the four institutions: 16 at Western University, 19 at Midwestern University, 19 at Southern University, and 16 at Eastern University. Participants came from a variety of disciplines, including the humanities, social sciences, engineering, biological and physical sciences, as well as professional schools such as medicine, business, and veterinary medicine. Participants also represented various stages of their careers; across all four institutions, I interviewed 22 assistant professors, 28 associate professors, and 20 full professors. Participants were required to be either tenured or on the tenure track with at least one child younger than age 18 in the home. Non–tenure-track faculty were excluded because the challenges of their job differ considerably from those of their tenure-line counterparts. I opted to focus on tenure-line faculty because they are frequently the targets of institutional accommodations (such as tenure-clock extensions). Given that one of the aims of this project was to understand how campus policies might shape men's involvement with their children, it was important to focus on men who had access to those policies. However, I acknowledge that tenure-line faculty hold privileged positions in an academy that is becoming increasingly staffed by non–tenure-line positions.

Fathers from a variety of races and ethnicities were represented among the participants. Of the total 70, 46 identified as White, 5 identified as Latino or Hispanic, 5 identified as Asian, and the remainder declined to state. Additionally, 14 of the fathers identified as international faculty, although the majority had been in the United States for at least 15 years. No African American or Native American fathers opted to participate in the study. Such an absence is notable and disappointing and there is no doubt that this book would have been enriched by including their experiences. However, this study did not seek to identify ways in which racial or ethnic background or immigration status shaped fathers' parenting experiences, although literature certainly suggests that it does (Hofferth, 2003; Lansford, Bornstein, Dodge, Skinner, Putnick, & Deater-Deckard, 2011; Leavell, Tamis-LeMonda, Ruble, Zosuls, & Cabrera, 2012; Lim & Lim, 2003; Taylor & Behnke, 2005). I did not note any significant differences between the various groups based on racial identity or status as immigrants, and I leave such analysis for future studies.

All of the men whose experiences are reported here were currently or had once been married to women. I deliberately sought out single fathers

and men in same-sex couples on each campus, but failed to recruit more
than one across all four institutions. At Southern University, members
active in the campus lesbian, gay, bisexual, and transgender (LGBT) community told me that they could think of no gay fathers on the faculty. I
do not include the experiences of the sole gay father I interviewed as his
experience was an outlier in many senses. Although I would have liked
to have been able to represent nonheterosexual family structures, I am
able to provide an in-depth examination of the lives of many opposite-sex
married couples and the ways that traditional gender norms shape their
relationships and lives.

Even within this group, there was great variation in terms of family
structure. Most of the men were married to women who worked outside
of the home full time. In some families the wife stayed home at least part
time. Thirteen men were married to women who worked outside of the
home part time and another 10 had wives who stayed home full time. I
explore the differing experiences of these couples in chapter 6. The majority
of fathers in the sample had two children, although the number of children
ranged from one to five. All told, 16 fathers had one child, 41 had two, 11
had three, 2 had four, and one had five children. One assistant professor
I interviewed had just welcomed his first child into the home 5 months
earlier. I also interviewed a full professor well in his 60s who was the first
time father of a two-year-old. Another full professor I interviewed had four
children: two sons in their 30s from a previous marriage and two daughters of middle school age. Due to the biological possibilities of late-in-life
fathering, there was a greater range of children's ages for men at the full
professor level, a fact that one would probably not witness among female
full professors. Across all 70 fathers, there were 7 sets of twins. Table 1.1
contains a breakdown of the number of children for faculty at each rank.

While fathers across ranks were most likely to have two children, there
were some differences among the assistant, associate, and full professors in
terms of their children's ages. Assistant professors were more likely than
their tenured counterparts to have children younger than age 5. Of the 22
assistant professors interviewed, 18 had children younger than age 5 and 13
had children age 2 or younger. Only one assistant professor had a teenager.
In contrast, of the 28 associate professors interviewed, exactly half (or 14)
had teenagers and only 7 had children younger than age 5. The ages of
the children of the full professors mirrored those of the associate professors.
Ten of the 20 full professors had children who were teenagers while 5 had
children younger than age 5. Little is surprising about these demographics;
one might expect that assistant professors, who tend to be younger than full
professors, will have younger children. However, it is worth underscoring

Table 1.1. Number of Children by Faculty Rank

	1	2	3	4	5	Total
Assistant	8	12	2	—	—	22
Associate	4	17	6	1	—	28
Full	4	12	2	1	1	20
Total	16	41	10	2	1	70

that nearly all of the assistant professors were contending with raising very young children while simultaneously trying to produce enough scholarship to earn tenure. I return to these stresses in chapter 7.

METHODS OF DATA COLLECTION

Interviews and document analysis constituted the sole methods of data collection. All participants were interviewed once. Interviews took place either during campus site visits or via telephone for those unable to meet in person. In-person interviews typically took place in participants' offices, but sites also included cafes on and near each campus. I chatted with some dads in their offices, brimming full of books, evoking the stereotypical images of the faculty office. I spoke with other dads over coffee or lunch in loud coffee shops.

Interviews lasted approximately 45 minutes. I asked the fathers to tell me a little bit about the role they took in the home along with the ways that their department and institution facilitated or hindered achieving a work/life balance. Sample questions included, "Tell me about a time your role as professor and parent conflicted," and "How would you describe the department climate with respect to parenthood and children?"

In addition to interviewing faculty, on each campus I interviewed at least one administrator responsible for either work/family policies or faculty affairs. On some campuses, I interviewed the university's vice provost or vice chancellor while on others I was able to speak with staff who were dedicated to work/life issues. Interviews with institutional administrators typically lasted between 30 and 45 minutes and sought to clarify information gained through document analysis on campus policies and work/life climate. Sample questions included, "Describe the evolution of work/life balance policies on this campus," and "Are there any concerns about extending family-friendly benefits to fathers?" Across the faculty and administrator interviews, all but three interviews were digitally recorded and transcribed.

Additional information was collected via document analysis. Documents collected included current and past campus work/life policies and faculty senate minutes regarding institutional change efforts surrounding work/life issues. I reviewed each with an eye toward policies specifically designated for male faculty use. Taken together, the interviews and documents helped me gain an understanding of what life is like for faculty fathers on each of the four campuses.

Organization of the Book

In the remainder of the book, I continue to explore the conflict between gender norms, the ideal worker, and university culture. In chapter 2, "Conflicting Roles: The Ideal Worker or the Ideal Father?" I delve more deeply into norms of the ideal worker and explore how its two main tenets—the faculty member as one who is always working and has no responsibilities in the home—affect men's lives. In particular, I focus on how assumptions about the divisions between breadwinner and caregiver shape men's beliefs about the appropriateness of using institutional accommodations or otherwise prioritizing parenthood. In chapters 3 and 4, I conduct a cultural analysis of the experiences of faculty fathers by campus and by discipline, respectively. In chapter 3, "Family-Friendly or Father-Friendly: Institutional Culture and the Ideal Worker," I compare the organizational culture and gender norms of the two institutions nationally recognized as family-friendly campuses (Western University and Midwestern University) with the organizational culture of the two other campuses (Southern University and Eastern University). Fathers on the more progressive campuses faced less resistance and less hesitation to use policies, which point to the ways in which organizational culture shapes individuals' experiences.

Although institutional culture matters, disciplinary culture matters as well; these disciplinary differences are the focus of chapter 4, "Disciplinary Culture and the Ideal Worker." In this chapter, I compare the experiences of fathers in the professional schools (medicine, dentistry, law, and others); fathers in the sciences and engineering; and fathers in the humanities and social sciences. Each group of disciplines sends different messages about the appropriateness of men balancing work and family. Faculty in the professional schools and science and engineering noted cultures that emphasized long hours in the office and the importance of external funding, which often led faculty to feel compelled to prioritize work over family. In contrast, men in the humanities and social sciences reported being able to structure their time in ways that allowed them to balance family and career. Furthermore, men in these disciplines were more likely to report receiving messages from their colleagues that taking time off for family was valued. In this chapter, I discuss these differences and consider the role that disciplinary culture plays in reinforcing or challenging hegemonic masculinity and assumptions of the ideal worker.

In chapter 5, "How Family Life Affects Faculty Life," I consider how familial responsibilities affect the fathers' careers and focus in particular on notions of productivity and scholarly engagement. Despite their commitment to their own families, many of the men professed a belief that scholars could not be committed academics and involved parents. While a few fathers reported that their productivity had increased since becoming parents, many catalogued the ways they had pulled back from professional obligations and seen their productivity plummet. While many lamented this shift, others suggested that the trade-off was worth it.

Chapter 6, "The Ideal Worker Inside or Outside the Home?" leaves the campus to visit the home and examines the division of labor between husbands and wives. While many fathers were active coparticipants in child rearing, men tended to perform different tasks than their wives; generally men were noted for performing tasks that were more fun while their wives were solely responsible for the daily, more mundane, details of the household. While these trends were true across many couples, the employment status of the wife further shaped the provision of care. Men in couples in which the wife worked full time outside of the home adopted different behaviors in the home than their counterparts whose wives worked fewer than 40 hours a week outside the home. One particular group who was more likely to adopt different behaviors in the home was the newest crop of fathers in the academy: the assistant professors. These men are the focus of chapter 7, "Tenure versus Fatherhood: How Generation X Faculty Eschew the Ideal Worker." All were contending with fatherhood in possibly one of the more stressful times in their careers. These men also belonged to Generation X—a generation that has been defined by greater gender equality and a prioritization of work/life issues. Despite feeling the push to publish, many of these fathers expressed less interest in prioritizing their careers than their more senior colleagues, pointing to the ways in which ideal worker norms might be shifting slowly, as older cohorts retire.

In the book's concluding chapter, "Redefining the Ideal," I review the experiences of the fathers across campuses and return to the norms of the ideal worker and hegemonic masculinity to consider the role that universities play in shaping a culture that either promotes or stymies a father's involvement in the home. I conclude by offering suggestions for institutions that are interested in creating cultures in which all parents—men and women—are encouraged to be productive in the workplace and involved in the home. Universities have frequently been looked to as beacons to guide society in a number of areas, from science to social justice. By dismantling gendered structures and ideal worker norms, universities can again be leaders in promoting a more equitable society for all.

CHAPTER 2

Conflicting Roles

. ◆ ———— ◆ .

The Ideal Worker or the Ideal Father?

In chapter 1, I introduced the norms of the ideal worker, hegemonic masculinity, and gendered organizations. These three notions are inextricably tied to one another and have implications for the steps that institutions have taken to become more family-friendly. In short, gendered organizations are built on the norm of the ideal worker, which is informed by hegemonic masculinity. I review each of these concepts here as they provide the focus for the stories of the men in this chapter.

Recall that Acker (1990) suggested that organizations might be gendered in five ways, through: (1) constructions of divisions along lines of gender; (2) the use of organizational symbols that perpetuate divisions between men and women; (3) interactions; (4) the way that interactions reinforce differences in individual identity; and (5) the way that individual identities and differences shape organizational structures. Simply put, organizations are not gender neutral because they are built by (and on the backs of) men and women who have been socialized to adopt different gender roles. Men and women are expected to adopt different behaviors both inside and outside the workplace. And, because men tend to assume most leadership positions, this frequently leads organizations to value masculine traits.

Gendered organizations also depend on the notion of the ideal worker and hegemonic masculinity, which reinforce one another. The ideal worker is an employee who is always available to work and has few outside demands on his (or her) time (Acker, 1990; Ely & Meyerson, 2003; Williams, 2000). While the ideal worker may have children, he or she is not expected to engage in a substantial amount of childcare. Such an expectation depends on hegemonic masculinity, which as Connell (1995) described is the ideal masculinity to which all men are expected to aspire. Current conceptualizations of hegemonic masculinity in the United States place value on aggressiveness, competitiveness, heterosexuality, and serving as the breadwinner for the family. The most valued masculinity is one in which a man takes care of his family by earning an income, leaving the caregiving duties to his wife (Doherty et al., 1998; Emslie & Hunt, 2009; Marsiglio et al., 2000; Thompson & Walker, 1989). Recall also that while few men embody the characteristics of hegemonic masculinity, most men are complicit in trying to maintain it and profit from its existence (Connell & Messerschmidt, 2005). In fact, as scholars have suggested, while the ultimate goal of patriarchy is to enact dominance over women, men also seek to enact dominance over other men by policing the types of behaviors that are considered to be gender appropriate (Bird, 1996; Connell, 1995; Connell & Messerschmidt; Demetriou, 2001), including the ways in which they fulfill their roles as fathers.

The ideal worker and hegemonic masculinity are critical to maintaining the gendered university. The inverse is also true: disrupting the ideal worker and redefining hegemonic masculinity will have consequences for the gendered university. These three concepts are particularly important to the ways in which faculty fathers navigate their roles as professors and parents. While many indicated that they wanted to be more involved fathers, they felt that the weight of the expectations of the university and society in general impeded them from serving as caregivers for their children.

While many campuses have implemented a variety of family-friendly supports, including the four universities profiled here, they still have not succeeded in disrupting the entrenched norm of the ideal worker. And, as Kossek, Lewis, and Hammer (2009) argued, "it is unlikely that work-life initiatives can achieve systemic change without making visible and challenging basic assumptions about the ideal worker who is 'unencumbered' by family or other non-work commitments" (p. 9). In other words, work/life initiatives will not transform campus cultures until the ideal worker is no longer thought of as ideal.

This chapter focuses on the ways in which the norms of the academy and society at large have impeded men's involvement in the home. In particular, I argue that norms of the ideal worker maintain a stronghold on academic culture by expecting faculty to work long hours while relying on others to perform care in the home. Although institutional policies and programs might exist to help parents balance their home and work demands, the underlying expectation is that such policies are meant to be used by women. The fathers profiled here worked for four institutions that to varying degrees have adopted policies designed to help faculty balance their work and home responsibilities. Despite the policies' existence, not all fathers felt able to use them. While some men outwardly received praise for being involved fathers, the majority reported that the message was that being involved was acceptable, but only to an extent. Instead, the expectation was that the majority of care should be left to their wives. Although policies existed for major life events, many campus practices continue to ignore men's nonwork responsibilities. I discuss the negative feedback many of the men received about fathers who devoted too much attention to their children at the expense of their careers. Being an overly involved father raised questions about the degree to which a man fulfilled the demands of the ideal worker and hegemonic definitions of masculinity. Although the academic career places numerous demands on faculty fathers, it also affords tremendous opportunities for those who wish to be involved. I begin with a brief discussion of one particular benefit.

The Faculty Career Is Ideal for Parenting?

Faculty are part of an elite group of white-collar workers who have tremendous control over shaping their own schedules; those in other professions—particularly those in blue-collar jobs—do not have the same freedom. As Williams (2010) pointed out, many blue-collar workers are required to perform their work duties from a fixed location and are closely supervised. Many do not even have sick or vacation leave to use in the case of family emergency. Although numerous burdens are associated with the faculty career, significant freedom comes with having a white-collar job, particularly one that brings with it so much autonomy. Many of the fathers in this study recognized this privilege; 34 of 70 fathers argued that the flexibility that accompanies the faculty career was a huge benefit, allowing them to take a greater role with their children than their counterparts in nonacademic settings. Some participants appreciated that the faculty career allowed them the freedom to spend time with their children during standard work hours. Many fathers commented that they could do more than "normal fathers" because they had the flexibility to work when they wanted to do so. The amount of time participants spent with their children varied; some occasionally drove their children to after-school activities while others regularly left the office midafternoon to engage in care.

Other fathers commented on the benefit of being able to volunteer at their children's schools or attend school plays. One father described his experiences:

> When my children were in grade school, they had little plays and so on at three in the afternoon a lot and I'd go to almost all of them. . . . So I'd go to their school, watch them perform for

20 minutes, come back [to the office],—gone for two hours for a 20-minute performance.

While that father appreciated being able to step out to attend occasional school performances, another father was regularly involved with youth baseball. He discussed the flexibility that allowed him to determine his own schedule. "When I take off at 4 o'clock to go umpire my kid's baseball game or something, that's . . . I mean, it's never a problem. Nobody's tracking your hours or anything like that." This father recognized the freedom that he had by not having to account for his time to a supervisor. Several fathers shared how they regularly volunteered at their children's schools, such as this participant:

> Another decision I made is to be very involved in their . . . preschool, especially. We were part of the coparenting school, and we had to work one day a week, and it was always a little bit of a drag having to go. But then once we were there, it was a very good experience to see the kids with other friends, and with other parents, and to see them growing in this preschool. So . . . and again, thanks to my job, I was able to do that, and other types of jobs wouldn't have allowed me to do this.

Many of the fathers expressed gratitude for the flexibility built in to the faculty career that allowed them to participate in their children's activities and lives during standard work hours. Of course, as many noted, there were trade-offs to attending events during the day.

While they could be involved with their children in ways that fathers in more restrictive jobs could not, they often spent many nights and weekends working to compensate for this flexibility. However, as one participant shared, "I still believe that being a father . . . while [a] faculty member, I think that's an unbeatable combination. I think the flexibility that we have is very, very important."

For some fathers, this flexibility also led to feelings of increased responsibility toward managing their multiple roles. Many fathers underscored the autonomy and individual responsibility that accompanied faculty work. As one professor explained: "This is a great career . . . it gives you tremendous freedom. You are free to fail. So you have to work really hard and you have to be very competitive." For this professor, the faculty career rests on individual effort and action. This same sentiment extended to other participants' conceptions of flexibility, including this scientist: "It's very flexible. You can take off during the day if you want or I can go—because it's really my decision to know whether I'm working or when I'm here. It's my decision, not the university's decision." This father pointed to one of the key facets of faculty life: professors set their own schedules and rarely can other faculty or the administration dictate when faculty need to be on campus. As a result of this autonomy, many men felt that the faculty career provided opportunities for them to engage with their children more than they might in other jobs. For all the benefits of flexibility, the demands of faculty work and the assumptions of the ideal worker placed several strains on men with significant familial demands.

The Ideal Faculty Member Is the Ideal Worker

While institutions might provide policies for major life events and fathers might feel free to occasionally leave work early to take care of a sick child, the general tenor of institutional life suggested that standard operating procedures remained intact. The other structures of faculty life—hours worked, and scheduling of meetings and teaching obligations—remain unchanged and continue to expect men and women to prioritize work obligations at the expense of family. As I discuss in chapter 4, while some disciplines are more impacted than others with their shifting teaching schedules, many fathers across disciplines and campuses report that the expectations of the always-working ideal worker remain intact.

Faculty shared that while they might have great flexibility in when and where they perform their work, they felt as if the institution expected them to put in workweeks that far exceeded the standard 40 hours. Thirty-eight of the 70 participants discussed regularly working early in the morning or late at night. Some participants spoke fondly of using time in the early mornings to get work done before the rest of the family woke. One participant explained, "I get up around 5 in the morning every day (a) because I'm a morning person and (b) because that's when I get the work done that I have to do for my own research and stuff like that." Said another father, "I usually wake up around 4:30 or 5:00. I will check my e-mail, write or prep for class before my kids wake up, which is at 7:00." These fathers found that mornings were their best time for getting work in. Other fathers squeezed work in at the end of the day, like this father: "Usually I do some reading in the evening. Students' reports, manuscripts, all those kind of things. So, usually, maybe until midnight or so. Maybe between 10:00 and 12:00, I get another two hours of work done." Another father reported that his "best hours for the hard stuff" was 7:00 or 8:00 P.M. until about 11:00 P.M. Many fathers felt that they needed these extra hours at the beginning or the end of each day simply to keep on top of the tasks required of them as faculty members.

While about half of the fathers reported working regularly in the mornings or evenings, a slightly greater number—44—said that they regularly worked on weekends, with an additional group reporting that they worked on the weekend when work demands necessitated that they do so. Of those who did work on weekends, the typical professor worked for several hours each day. One father reported working from 5:00 A.M. to 10:00 A.M. while he waited for the rest of his family to wake up. Another reported working anywhere between 4 and 16 hours on the weekends. And as the numbers suggest, these extra hours worked are not that unusual. Given that national statistics suggest that faculty work on average 49 hours per week (National Center for Education Statistics, 2005), the faculty fathers in this sample seem to be the norm.

And, as some suggested, faculty sensed an expectation that they were supposed to work outside of standard work hours. When asked whether he worked on the weekends, one father responded, "Oh yeah. I think every-body in academia does, everybody who does research. . . . If you're doing research . . . it's something that we're passionate about. It's work, but at the same time, it's a hobby." His remarks are notable for two reasons. First, he assumes that all faculty work on weekends. Judging by other fathers' responses, he was not far from the truth. Second, he noted that many faculty are passionate about their work and want to engage in research or other duties related to their jobs. Many institutions might count on this passion to drive their faculty to work more hours in order to be successful.

As one professor concluded, the expectations of work necessitate that faculty spend as many hours as possible working. He explained:

> This job here is not done 40 hours a week. Period. And you can always spend more than 40 hours. . . . But that's something you have to get used to. You're never really finished, and there is always something . . . at least these piles of papers that I should be reading and I never really get to because there are too many other things. . . . Yeah, I always have some work in my backpack when I get home.

This professor underscored how he and others always had work that they could be doing—whether it be research to conduct, articles to write, grants to submit, or papers to grade. And while many faculty indicated that they simply had to make the choice to be done for the evening, they always felt the pressure of work, even when spending time with their children.

In addition to performing research and other work obligations on a demanding, though flexible, schedule, institutional structures relied on the notion of the ideal worker in still other ways. Eighteen of the fathers dis-cussed more scheduled events, such as frequent after-hours meetings, teaching schedules, and other university obligations and the strain that accompanied these extra demands. One father, who taught in a professional school, noted that he now frequently teaches on the weekends, which took him away from time with his children. He explained how his weekend absence was noted in his home:

> So [my wife] would say things like, "We could go on Saturday but your daddy is teaching on Saturday so we can't do this." So those kinds of things happened and I think that my kids are kind of accustomed to it. So they kind of take it in stride and they all know on certain weekends, Dad will not be around. . . . From my viewpoint, I would like to be there for those things but the schedule is such that I have been asked to do things on some of the weekends. One of the things about being a faculty [member]—at least now—is you need to do more weekend . . . teaching.

Although weekend teaching was certainly not the case across all fields, faculty in certain disciplines noted that shifting markets and student demands necessitated that they teach outside the traditional workday. Although universities might be responding to market demands by offering courses at night and on weekends, they do so at a cost to faculty with significant familial obligations. Such practices indicate an adherence to ideal worker norms and hegemonic masculinity that assume that faculty are not their children's primary caregiver and instead have a wife available to care for children.

In addition to shifting teaching schedules, several disciplines were noted for holding meetings early in the morning or in the late afternoon and evening, which similarly illustrates a disregard for those with familial responsibilities. Six of the fathers expressed concern about their departments' tendencies to schedule meetings early in the morning. One Eastern University faculty member reported that he did not attend an 8:00 A.M. meeting because it conflicted with his responsibilities to his children.

> PROFESSOR: . . . The other day we had a meeting at 8:00. They know that I'm in charge of my kids in the morning, and we have the whole day for that, and they set the appointment a few days in advance. You're expected to get a nanny to come for one hour. I don't want somebody to drive my kids to school if there's anything I can do to avoid it. I said to them, "I can't go—the earliest I can be here is 9:00. I think other parents with children would appreciate [it] if you gave the courtesy of not setting appointment before [then]."

> MARGARET: So was it okay that you didn't come to the meeting?

PROFESSOR: I don't know if it was okay. I didn't go. I stepped up
and told them why.

Although administrators scheduled 8:00 A.M. meetings, these times were not
conducive to faculty, used to flexible schedules, who took their children to
school in the mornings. This professor, like the one I discuss next, was able
to skip the meeting without consequence. Another senior faculty member,
a professor at Midwestern University, described his experience trying to
challenge the system:

> I was asked to be on a committee so—a schoolwide committee at
> 7:30 in the morning. I went to the first one and I said I really can't
> do this at 7:30 in the morning. . . . I asked, "Why do you meet
> at 7:30 in the morning?" and it was like, "What are you talking
> about? We've always met at 7:30 in the morning." And I go, "Well
> you know that's kind of inconvenient for me. I've got to help get
> my kids off to school," and they look at me like I'm bonkers. They
> go, "Don't you have a wife?" I go, "Well, yes, I do, and she's got
> to be at work too, by God. . . . I have no problem with this com-
> mittee and I have no problem doing the work, but let's just move
> the time." And they said, "Well, we've always met at this time."

As this father recounts, he encountered intense opposition from his colleagues when he tried to get them to change the meeting time. He proposed
changing the meeting time from 7:30 to 8:00 A.M. and still was unable to
get any support. As a result of the time conflict, this faculty member had to
bow out of this prestigious committee opportunity. There was no room for
this man to be both a committee member and involved father; others on the
committee assumed that his wife could take care of their children. Again,
such assumptions point out the degree to which traditional gender norms
continue to operate within the university. This situation further underscores
the gradual creep of work responsibilities into family time accompanied by
the assumption that work responsibilities should supersede familial responsibilities regardless of the time. This father was lucky to be a full professor
and able to make the decision to step off the committee.

Other men—particularly those who were assistant professors—did
not always have the freedom to make the same choices. For example, one
assistant professor from the same institution reported feeling obligated to
go to recruiting and departmental events at night and on weekends. "If it's
something where one of those senior people or the department chair asks
me to go to, there's definitely that feeling of obligation to be there and say
yes." He and his wife made arrangements to negotiate childcare or, if both

were required to be at the event, find a babysitter. Unlike the full professor, the assistant professor did not have the same privilege to be able to turn down requests without fear of hurting his career. Many other participants also noted the demands that attending required campus social events as well as recruiting graduate students and prospective faculty placed on them. Several described negotiating with occasionally resentful spouses to care for their children while the professors enjoyed a nice dinner as part of the work evening. Others, like this father, discussed the struggle and the cost of finding a babysitter for after-hours events.

> Anytime you want to work on the weekends or work late in the evening or support a lecture or meeting on campus or some event that's happening in the evening or on the weekend, you have to have thought of it a few days in advance and plan for it and clear it, you know. I have to clear it with my wife. Or if we both want to go, we have to get a babysitter. Or if I want to go and she also has something else, we have to get babysitting and that kind of thing.

For this father and others, negotiation occurs around attending events after hours. Sometimes these events are voluntary, such as the desire to attend an evening lecture, while other times, they are a required part of faculty work, such as early morning meetings or weekend teaching. In all cases, these events are founded on the assumption that the faculty member has no responsibilities in the home, or at the very least, a wife who can take care of their children. It is this second part of the ideal worker norm—the split between caregiving and breadwinning—that I turn to next.

The Ideal Worker as Breadwinner, not Caregiver

As the stories of the fathers suggest, the trope of the always-working ideal faculty member remains intact. In addition, faculty members reported that the other expectation of the ideal worker—lack of caregiving responsibilities in the home—remained at the foundation of faculty work, despite the provision of some family-friendly accommodations by universities. Men received messages that being a male faculty member should be equated with working long hours, not with providing care for children. Despite the fact that only 10 of the men were in marriages in which they were the breadwinners and their wives were the full-time caregivers, typical gender norms continued to influence the ways that some in the university approached the idea of fathers using leave. In this section, I discuss men's reflections on appropriate gender roles and consider how they shaped their willingness to access leave policies.

MOTHERS VERSUS FATHERS: BIOLOGICAL AND
SOCIALLY-CONSTRUCTED DIFFERENCES

Although many fathers challenged the breadwinner/caregiver dichotomy, some acknowledged that the demands of motherhood were much greater than the demands of fatherhood. Some tied this explicitly to the physical demands of pregnancy and breastfeeding. For example, one participant said, "I wasn't a woman dealing with breastfeeding. It's harder [for them]." Another discussed watching his wife having to breastfeed their twins:

> Yeah, I can't imagine having breastfed the twins. You know? . . . Because I watched my wife do it. They were on demand, and we sort of filled out a little chart for a day. And you know, the amount of time that she was spending nursing the kids was enormous.

Another father, whose wife was also a faculty member, similarly remarked not just on the amount of time his wife spent breastfeeding, but on the other demands it placed on her:

> Well, I think the most important thing is just physically; psychologically it's just not the same thing for me to have a kid as it is for my wife to have a kid. I mean, to be pregnant, to have her body change, to be breastfeeding, to need to leave a one-month-old baby who she's breastfeeding, to get dressed up and feel professional and look professional and leave the house and stand and go to a faculty meeting or talk to students. I just think it's a bigger, bigger challenge.

These fathers all were cognizant of the demands that pregnancy placed on a woman's body and the ways in which becoming a parent had different consequences for women than for men.

Some suggested that the differences between mothers and fathers did not end after the breastfeeding period, but rather that women maintained increased responsibility for their children throughout their lives. While some participants did not espouse this viewpoint themselves, they shared their perceptions of their colleagues' points of view, as this father did:

> There's no doubt in my mind that women have a lot harder than men. . . . But I think a lot of men . . . they are a little bit detached from their kids, like they expect that the wife is going to take care of the kids, you know. I think. I may be wrong. But, so for the most part, I would suspect women have it, you know, harder.

While this father assumed a more active role with his children, he felt that some of his colleagues anticipated that women would bear the brunt of the child-rearing responsibilities. Another father confirmed this:

> I don't know how women do it. I really don't . . . because it seems like women have a lot more responsibilities at home and at work. Well, they have the same ones at work, but . . . they tend to—just with younger kids—they just have to have more contact with their kids. And, most of the faculty here have really young kids. . . . I don't know how they do it.

This father suggested that women worked a "second shift" (Hochschild, 1989), with additional responsibilities for their children, in ways that men did not. Another man suggested that being a father led to different feelings of psychological burden and responsibilities.

> You know, guys have different reactions to being parents. You know guys. It's much easier for me to somehow switch into work mode and then switch back into parent mode. My wife has a more difficult time doing that. And she has a lot more guilt if she feels like she's neglecting her role as parent.

For this father and others, being a parent had different consequences for men than it did for women. Whether it was the demands of pregnancy and breastfeeding, assuming more responsibility in the home, or simply a different sense of psychological responsibility, many suggested that there were perceptible differences between what parents of each gender experience.

In addition to pointing to biological notions of difference, some fathers discussed the different characteristics that society expected men and women to have. Several fathers, for example, discussed what they perceived as expectations for the types of family-related work men and women are supposed to perform. One father discussed how the role of the father contrasts with that of the mother:

> There is a way in which . . . the relationship between the mom and the child . . . is always kind of prioritized over . . . the father. . . . Whatever the father brings into the [home] . . . you know, it's kind of like a sternness or protectiveness, but not a kind of . . . nurturing . . . whatever it is, like how the gender roles are split.

As this father pointed out, men are expected to be stern and protective while women are generally assumed to be more nurturing. He was not the only father to discuss the fact that mother-child relationships are often held in higher esteem than father-child relationships. Said one father, "It seems like there is an extent to which you probably get more play as a mother than as a father." Another father stated:

> There's definitely a greater expectation of me not doing the kid thing. You know, if a female faculty member has a baby and basically doesn't show up for a year, that's pretty expected. If I were to do that, I think there would be trouble.

This father and others pointed out that gendered assumptions are associated with acceptable behaviors for men and women. Of most relevance here, women are allowed to prioritize caregiving whereas men are not; these differences are rooted in definitions of hegemonic masculinity. Such a stereotypical division of labor has implications for the ways in which men thought about the appropriateness of fathers accessing institutional accommodations.

CONTRASTING OPINIONS OVER POLICY USE

Although each of the institutions provides policies for faculty use, there was no consistent response as to whether fathers should use such resources. Rather, the conflicting approaches to masculinity and fathering (involved fathers as individuals to be praised or punished) led to a range of positions that men took about who should use family-friendly policies. Some suggested that institutions need not provide policies to anyone; others suggested that policies were only for use by women; still others came from departments with a rich history of men accessing leave. Participants' positions mirrored national rates of policy usage, which point to differences in rates of use by men and women.

Although the tenure-clock extension is one of the most oft-cited and oft-used policies, not all eligible faculty use the benefit (Mason, Goulden, & Wolfinger, 2006; Pribbenow et al., 2010; Quinn, 2010; Waltman & August, 2005). Across several studies and campuses, rates of usage typically hover between one fourth and one third of eligible faculty. For example, in their survey of 4,459 tenure-line faculty in the University of California system, Mason and colleagues (2006) found that 30% of those eligible to use the tenure-clock extension did. On other campuses, the percentages were even lower; Quinn found that 24% of faculty at one research university used tenure-clock extensions, while Pribbenow and colleagues found that 23% of faculty at the University of Wisconsin–Madison used the same policy.

Disaggregating by gender reveals differences among rates of usage between men and women. Across studies, women report using tenure-clock extensions as well as other family-friendly policies at higher rates than men (Manchester et al., 2010; Mason et al., 2006; Pribbenow et al., 2010; Quinn, 2010). In Quinn's study of faculty at one research university, 32% of women but only 18% of men received tenure-clock extensions. In the University of California faculty sample, 30% of female assistant professors used the tenure-clock extension compared with just 8% of men. These disparities are striking and all underscore that women are far more likely to use family-friendly policies. What these studies do not reveal is why fathers access policies at lower rates than mothers. The experiences of the fathers in this study suggest similar variation in terms of willingness to take advantage of institutional accommodations. Some described institutional cultures and norms that did not encourage men to use policies and, in some cases, penalized those who did. I have placed men's characterizations of the role of the institution in aiding faculty on a continuum, ranging from institutions providing no family-friendly accommodations for any faculty, to institutions providing policies for women, to institutions providing policies for men and women. I discuss each of these positions here.

No institutional assistance for anyone. A small group of fathers suggested that parents should change their behavior to fit in to the norms of academia; these individuals were less concerned with institutions providing work/life support and instead suggested that individuals needed to come up with strategies on their own to balance home and work responsibilities. One professor stated, "I personally don't believe that [parents] should be treated differently. . . . I chose to be a parent. It's not anybody's fault, and nobody should pay for it but me." Although his language suggested that consequences arise from parenthood, this professor bluntly stated that he did not expect the institution to treat him differently than his childless peers. Other participants echoed this sentiment:

> I come from a very sort of blue-collar background, . . . and I don't think about there being some kind of expectation that an institution like this would want to do something for me. So, I like made a choice on my own to have a baby, and like that means taking responsibility for it. Right?

Although this father later explained that he utilized institutional accommodations for new parents, he believed that each individual should find a way to balance work and family. Another participant shared similar beliefs when asked about whether the department or university should support him and other faculty with children:

> The department doesn't really do very much to . . . you know, to support that. . . . One could possibly ask the question whether work expectations would be different for someone who has a family and someone who doesn't have a family: (a) I don't think that should be the case, and (b) I don't think it is the case. So, yeah, . . . it's not necessary.

Like some of his peers, this faculty member underscored the importance of equal treatment for faculty with and without children. In some ways, this group of fathers placed the obligation on the individual to identify ways to navigate parenting demands. Rather than expecting university structures and cultures to change to accommodate parenting demands, faculty were expected to work within the constraints of the system to meet their obligations. These fathers' descriptions of the role of the university suggest that it is gendered indeed, creating space for neither men nor women to adopt behavior that differs from the norm. Similarly, participants in the next group also valorized gendered university structures, though to women's benefit.

Policies exist to support mothers. Although policies might have been gender neutral, administrators on several of the campuses suggested that balancing work and family was a greater concern for women than men. At Southern University, a vice provost suggested that work/life issues are more a concern for women, despite increasing numbers of men assuming caregiving responsibilities for children. Western University was motivated to begin offering more comprehensive family-friendly policies after recognizing, in the late 1990s, that their recruitment and retention of female faculty lagged behind their peers. Both campuses offer family-friendly policies on a gender- neutral basis, but these comments suggest that balancing work and family might be more of a challenge for women than men.

This focus on providing assistance to mothers extended to the department level as well. One father stated that his colleagues saw parenting as a woman's job and, to their credit, were supportive of women. He further shared that when candidates interviewed for faculty positions, search committees emphasized the family-friendly policies to women, but did not have the same conversation with men. Despite this professor's objections, this practice continued in the department. Such a pattern illustrates the gendered assumptions that permeate organizational life. By supporting only women with children, this department creates an environment that suggests that parenting is not a man's concern. Faculty across the study reported similar instances of others who framed parenthood as a feminine construct. A faculty member at Western University reported that administrative staff in his department and in the dean's office told him that he was ineligible to apply for accommodations from the university because he was a man.

> I was asking [the administrative staff] about, you know, I had a couple kids here, is there anything I can do to defer a [review] . . . can I put off one of those a year 'cause I knew I was behind. . . . She [said], "I think they might do that for women, but I don't know, you'll have to ask the dean's office." So, the woman in the dean's office said . . . and she still works there . . . lovely person, she said, "Oh, it'd be very unusual for them to give that kind of allowance to men. . . ." She says, "But they do do it for women sometimes."

This misinformation is particularly of note in that Western University has made a concerted effort to promote its family-friendly policies across campus. However, administrative support staff, who are often the conduits of campus policies to faculty, were misinformed and shared incorrect information with this professor. This misinformation links back to notions of appropriate gender roles; women need extra accommodations because they are the ones who are expected to assume the bulk of caregiving duties.

A handful of fathers (incorrectly) reported that tenure-clock extension policies were only available for women. One father at Eastern University said that "women get a year off their tenure clock." A counterpart at Western University, a campus with even more progressive policies, also thought that the tenure-clock extension was solely for female faculty. He described the ways in which taking advantage of a tenure-clock extension had significant consequences for women's academic careers:

> It's supposed to stop for female faculty. But, the experience of some of my female colleagues and friends, is that yes, it's true, but then when it comes . . . time to go up for evaluation, there is a gap of one, perhaps two, years. And then that is hard to justify, and even if it wasn't hard to justify, it's not easy to disconnect from your research for a year, year and a half, two years, and then come back and pretend that nothing has happened. It's hard to reengage with graduate students. It's hard to reengage with data collection and with analysis, with conferences. So, I think for them, it's a little bit harder, I would say.

For this participant, using the tenure-clock extension or taking leave was a problem that could have consequences for the careers of female faculty. Many fathers pointed to the challenges that women face balancing work and family and spoke of their institution's efforts to aid in this balance for women.

Policies are gender neutral, but men do not use them. While the majority of faculty members knew that policies were available for both men and women to use, many reported that no male faculty had ever used the policies in their department. Such approaches suggest that institutional change is not yet complete and that gendered norms retain their stronghold on the organization. As one professor at Midwestern University stated, "On the books, there are, without question, legalistic, the same potential possibilities for men [to use family-friendly policies]. . . . But in practice, it has never been used for men. Ever." Several fathers in the sample opted not to use any institutional accommodations. Some men suggested that they simply did not think that they would need the extra year of time, like this father: "I didn't think it was necessary [because] I continued to work pretty much the same amount." Another professor shared similar sentiments: "[My department chair] advised me that I could. . . . But, I never looked into it. I just decided to forge on. Part of the reason was that my wife wasn't working." Despite being encouraged by his department chair to access institutional accommodations, this father felt that because his wife was able to fulfill the majority of child-rearing functions, he could devote his time to being productive and keep pace toward tenure.

These two were not the only fathers who opted not to use policies. Said another:

> I didn't [use accommodations] because I kind of had everything I needed. I wasn't at the point where I needed to stop the clock here at this time. And we had a baby in the beginning of summer so the hard part was in summertime and I had flexibility.

This father suggested that he was able to find ways to balance work and family without needing institutional assistance. Because his child was born in the summer, he felt that he had the flexibility to structure his time without asking for help. Another father shared that he simply did not want to take leave. "I didn't really want to . . . you know, I stayed home a fair bit, and took some time off informally, but I didn't really want to put my job here on hold." This father felt a commitment to the workplace and did not want his colleagues to be impacted by his absence.

Even fathers who took hands-on roles with their children noted their reticence to use institutional policy. One father whom I interviewed was notable for not working at night or on weekends, unlike most faculty. Yet, he opted not to use any release time that his university provided. He discussed the informal arrangements he was making in preparation for the impending arrival of his third child:

> We're going to have the baby in [the spring] and I've already arranged with my department head that someone's going to take over the class I'm teaching for two-plus weeks. But I need to make a lot of the lecture notes in advance. So, I'm working on the lecture notes now, so that I can hand them off. And then there's summer, so I get some time and I'm probably not going to get the buy-out teaching, other than this guy taking over for me.

This father did not elaborate on his decision not to use institutional accommodations, but instead opted to piece together a few weeks of help so that he could be home with his wife. These men's decisions not to use accommodations suggested that they did not necessarily feel that accommodations were for them to use.

The norms of the ideal worker were evident in many men's reticence in using institutional policies. One faculty member at Eastern University reported hesitation to extend his tenure clock after his senior colleagues told him that they would expect extra productivity from him during the additional year. "If I do take an extra year," he said, "there may be a burden of having additional productivity for that extra year." Such expectations are contrary to the intentions of the tenure-clock extension because faculty are not supposed to have demands of extra publication along with that extra year. In this case, the senior faculty's expectations reinforce those of the ideal worker; while the assistant professor could use a tenure-clock extension, he would need to produce more in exchange for its use.

A few fathers suggested that they might have considered extending their tenure clocks, but were discouraged by institutional procedures. One father explained:

> It was unclear whose priority it was to use it. I remember—actually that was sort of a strange thing because when I called Human Resources to see whether I could have it extended by my choice, they said that the dean had to request it. So that felt funny. So it doesn't look like it is a right.

Having to seek additional approval discouraged this father from investigating the policy further as he understood the policy not to be intended for everyone's use.

Policies are for men's use. While some men opted not to use policies, a few fathers reported that they had used or were planning to use the tenure-clock extension or other leave policies. The fathers who reported using the tenure-clock extension suggested that its use had been crucial to their careers and well-being. Said one father:

> I've had them push back the tenure clock for me by a year, which is . . . that's key . . . I don't know if I would have had tenure, but definitely my chance of having tenure would have been have been a long one if I didn't have that extra year.

This dad, who had contended with significant life events during his pre-tenure period, readily attributed his professional success to using the institutional policy. Another father, who was similarly successful, also reported the great relief he felt using the tenure-clock extension at his university:

> I probably won't need that extra year but it sure gave me a lot of peace of mind the last couple of years because I figured that it approximately . . . gives me about an extra hour a day, . . . so that's made my life a lot less stressful.

While this father certainly spent more than an hour a day with his kids, he felt that this extra assistance was crucial to his success. For these fathers, using the tenure-clock extension provided a small bit of assistance to allow them to be successful.

Some faculty members at Southern University reported that they were the first men in their department to take advantage of leave policies. One dad said:

> I think in our department I may be the first man, father who has asked for something like this. I don't know that for certain. It's become standard for our colleagues who are women and have children to get a zero teaching semester but less standard for dads to ask for some kind of benefit or teaching release or something like that.

While this dad was the first in his department to take advantage of a reduction in teaching duties, a few other men reported that their departments had a considerable history of fathers using family-friendly accommodations. A Midwestern University professor who had recently become the father of twins described his department's history of encouraging male faculty to take leave:

> In the past seven years, it has become the norm that men who apply for paternity leave get it. . . . It means no teaching, but you still have all this committee work and as I said, I've been on tons of committees so I've still been going to work every day but I did have a whole year when I didn't teach and that was amazing. That was great. That made it possible because they were infants—that was very difficult.

Many of these men pointed to the fact that department culture encouraged men to take advantage of existing policies: the extension of the tenure clock on all campuses and the reduction in teaching duties on three of the four. I asked one senior faculty at Midwestern University if it was standard for male and female faculty to take advantage of a release from teaching duties. He responded:

> Absolutely. . . . Occasionally we had to fight for people over at the college. . . . I had to tell one of my colleagues that he could apply for this, . . . and he said, "Is there going to be any repercussion on my career?" I said, "No, absolutely not. No." No there has been none. Yes people have taken advantage of them and no, there have been no repercussions.

In several cases, men felt able to access institutional policies, although, as this father suggests, were worried about potential negative repercussions. This senior faculty member served as an advocate for his junior colleagues, reassuring them that taking a release from teaching duties was not negatively viewed in the department. The experiences of these men reflect findings from past studies that suggest that having the support of supervisors and colleagues who have themselves taken leave helps to create a culture that encourages all men to use institutional accommodations (Haas & Hwang, 1995, 2009). In other words, seeing a more senior faculty member use institutional policies might encourage an assistant professor to do the same; in turn, his use of an institutional accommodation might then encourage his colleague to access policy. In time, policy use might become institutionalized in department culture, thereby creating an environment in which both men and women feel free to use the policies and, in the process, making progress toward challenging the gendered university. However, not all men found themselves in situations that promoted male policy use. Some departments encouraged women to use institutional accommodations, but not men. Others suggested that faculty who used accommodations would find themselves punished in several ways.

CAREER AND IDENTITY CONSEQUENCES FOR POLICY USE

Some fathers in this study hesitated to use policies because they feared doing so would have negative repercussions on their identities and their careers. They join a long line of faculty before them who revealed the same hesitation, as previous studies have found. Pribbenow and colleagues (2010) found that 19% of female faculty and 8% of male faculty wanted to take a tenure-clock extension, but did not. In their study, along with many others (Hollenshead et al., 2005; Mason & Goulden, 2004; Mason et al., 2006; Waltman & August, 2005), faculty pointed to a fear of career repercussions due to taking leave or using other family-friendly accommodations. For example, in their study of tenure-line female faculty at the University of Michigan, Waltman and August found that nearly two thirds of women who opted not to use the tenure-clock extension did so out of fear of negative career repercussions. Twenty percent of respondents in Pribbenow and colleagues' study reported fear of career repercussions for accessing policies. This hesitation to use policies extends beyond just the tenure-clock extension. For example, Mason and colleagues found that 51% of female faculty and 26% of male faculty opted not to use the modified-duties policy, worrying that doing so would hurt their careers.

The men in this study reported similar concerns. Unlike the national studies that pointed to career repercussions, many fathers worried that career repercussions would be accompanied by challenges to their identities as men. One father mentioned that he knew about family-friendly policies at his institution, but worried that he would be judged for seeking to use some of them.

> I'm pretty sure that the new family leave policy at [this university] encompasses fathers. And there's a part of me that feels like I'm going to be laughed at if I go in and ask for compensation or for whatever.

Perhaps this father's concern that he might be "laughed at" for seeking to use the policy was related to the concerns that other men expressed about seeking to use leave. A Western University faculty member who had recently become a first-time father discussed this double standard for parental involvement and pointed to the ways it might discriminate against fathers.

> One thing I think is really different is just the societal expectations about fathers versus mothers and their roles, and kind of how that plays out in work as well. . . . There are certain expectations about

how a mother's going to be involved, and you know, for fathers, if they're more involved that's maybe seen as kind of noble or progressive or something like that, whereas it's just expected for women. I'm not exactly sure. But on the other hand, I think that in some places it can be hard for men to take time off for their family in the way that I'm doing, because it's seen as somehow like . . . maybe it's seen as being not as serious about work or something like that.

This professor was fortunate to work in a department where he felt comfortable taking time off following the birth of his child, although he simultaneously acknowledged that his colleagues might assume that he was not "as serious about work" for prioritizing his family over his job. A faculty member on another campus explained that no one in his department had ever used the tenure-clock extension; "it seems like there is a bad image for some people that use it—that they are not serious about their work or whatever." Two men used the exact same language—"not serious about work"—to explain the hesitation fathers might feel at accessing leave policies. This points to the heart of the problem for many fathers, particularly those who want to take a greater role in their children's lives. Given that hegemonic masculinity suggests that men are to provide for their children financially and leave caregiving to their wives, those who engage in more care may be accused of failing to live up to expectations not just in the workplace, but as men. Although universities might provide leave policies for faculty use, many fathers expressed hesitation using them because doing so challenged their identities inside and outside the workplace.

As one Southern University professor who took minimal time off following the birth of a child explained, taking time off is not aligned with images of masculinity:

If you're an untenured faculty, you want to be seen as sort of the tough guy. "I don't need time off," and uh . . . you don't want to be seen as like, "Well, you know, you took all this time off. You should be worried about your tenure. You need to get in here." . . . Yeah, I guess that figures into your decisions for doing different things.

It seems particularly appropriate that this father used the language "tough guy" to describe the expected behavior of academics. His response suggests that setting aside time for one's child and being an academic are not compatible goals, at least not for men.

Like the previous father, another Southern University faculty member who took minimal time off following the birth of a child suggested that men who were too involved with their children faced prejudice. "[There is] a gender bias against males taking time off to be with their newborn. Whereas, you know, if a woman did that, they'd be like 'Oh yeah, of course, you know that's what's expected.'" Despite the fact that policies exist on this campus to allow men to take time off following the birth of a child, the general expectation is that men will not use them. Both fathers were concerned with what their colleagues might think of their actions and, implicitly, of their identities as men. Such statements underscore the fact that gender—and definitions of hegemonic masculinity—are created and policed through interactions with colleagues. Concerns about colleague perception of their identities as faculty and as men were sufficiently strong enough to convince these men not to take full advantage of institutional policies. A Midwestern University professor mused about the ways that his colleagues might view his desire to take an extended leave of absence to spend time with his children:

> I can say, "I'm not coming in. My child is sick"—the lab accepts that for sure and that happens occasionally. But if I was to say, "Well, I'm going to take a few months off just to watch my son grow up," I don't think that would go over very well whereas a woman could probably get away with that fairly easily. In theory I could, but in actual practice there's a lot of societal pressures that would say no, no, no, you're the breadwinner here, you're the man, you can't spend that much time with your kids.

Setting aside the question of whether a woman could frame her leave of absence as taking "a few months off just to watch [a child] grow up," this professor points to the double standard present for most fathers. While being an involved father is generally praised and indeed institutions provide accommodations to allow men to balance their competing responsibilities, they felt discouraged from taking advantage of them. Rather, being an involved father seems to be contrary to the norms of fathers as breadwinners and academics as the ideal and always-available workers.

Perhaps related to violating gender roles, 18 fathers discussed the ways that parents who had used institutional accommodations had experienced some significant career repercussions. Some participants suggested that faculty (of either gender) who took leave were less serious academics. One professor described a female professor who did not get tenure:

> She basically said, "Oh great I can take this time to build a large family and keep putting off my tenure decision." The problem is she didn't focus on her professional development so when it finally did come time for tenure, she hadn't accomplished anything.

This professor's response suggests that his former colleague was not serious about academia and instead used institutional accommodations to allow her to have children. He did not consider that she may have been overwhelmed by the demands of balancing work and family and was not able to meet the criteria necessary for tenure and promotion. Such opinions emerged in other responses as well. For example, an administrator at Eastern University suggested that tenure-clock extensions had done little to assist in meeting the demands that having children brings to faculty members' lives. She suggested that those who took the tenure-clock extension were less likely to be promoted, but that this data did not account for the "kinds of people" who opted to use family-friendly policies. Although neither the professor nor the administrator's comments were geared specifically toward men, they both underscore how the ideal worker norm applies to all faculty in the academy. The suggestion is that raising children can distract from the tasks required to earn tenure. The comments similarly point to the ways that the gendered university continues to exist—to the detriment of both men and women.

Across all four campuses, stories emerged of faculty members with children experiencing other consequences as a result of accessing family-friendly policies. Another faculty member at Eastern University explained how a former colleague had used a tenure-clock extension twice and was ultimately denied tenure. When I asked whether there were any stigma in the department about stopping the tenure clock, he answered, "I don't know, but I imagine there very well might be. . . . I certainly think there's value attached to people trying to move toward promotion and tenure, frankly." The message was clear: policies are there, but use them at your own risk.

Some suggested that accessing policies was a privilege to be earned and not a right. One professor at Southern University described an assistant professor who had recently taken leave to care for a newborn, much to the chagrin of his colleagues. As his colleague described:

> He's a young faculty member and, yeah, I mean, there has been backlash. But I don't think it's because of paternity leave. I think people would really have been supportive if he had been . . . meeting the expectations of the other faculty.

This response is characteristic of many other responses. If the faculty member were more productive, he would earn the right to parental leave. A full professor at Western University explained how his academic success brought him the privilege to allow his family life to intrude occasionally on his professional life:

> I have a great level of confidence in my own status. . . . So, that's
> relevant to all this. I'm not insecure about my position [in the school]
> in any way. And so, that gives me a greater latitude to run home.

Because this faculty member had already proved himself in the academic
arena, he had garnered some goodwill, which allowed him to attend to personal needs in contrast to the assistant professor described earlier. It appears
that, for men, using both formal and informal family-friendly accommodations is not an entitlement, but a privilege that one must earn.

Although faculty work brings flexibility that might allow fathers to
spend more time with their children, the norms of the ideal worker remain
ever-present in the academy. Faculty work demands near total devotion of
its employees. It also demands that faculty have few demands in the home.
Many of the fathers described ways that parenthood was associated solely
with demands on mothers. Others discussed their reticence at using institutional policies because doing so might lead to serious consequences both
for their careers and for their identities as men.

Conclusion

As the experiences of the faculty fathers suggest, gendered organizations,
ideal worker norms, and hegemonic masculinity play a critical role in shaping the ability of men to balance work and family. Several notable scholars
(Acker, 1990; Ely & Meyerson, 2000; Kossek et al., 2009) have outlined the
ways in which organizations might be gendered. As Ely and Meyerson suggested, the structures of organizations and the interactions of people within
them replicate gender. As the experiences of these fathers suggest, such a
statement applies to the academy as well. Many of the fathers reported
receiving negative feedback about their desire to take an extended leave
following the birth of a child, though reported that women making such a
choice would be expected and accepted. I conclude by discussing how the
practices of the gendered university continue to favor and indeed perpetuate
ideal worker norms and hegemonic masculinity.

With its emphasis on constantly working and a separation of gender
roles, the ideal worker norm remains intact. Faculty on all four campuses spoke of the strain that the intensive time demands of their jobs and
after-hours obligations placed on them. Many fathers felt that the demands
of their jobs were so intense that they regularly had to work nights and
weekends, putting in well in excess of the standard 40-hour workweek. Some
found that other fixed obligations encroached on time with their families.
One father had to drop out of a committee that met so early in the morning
that it conflicted with his responsibilities to his family. Other fathers talked

about the occasional challenges of having to find a babysitter in order to attend graduate student recruitment events or dinners out with prospective faculty. While the institution might provide policies for major life events, faculty were left to negotiate the daily challenges on their own. For many participants, this meant that work obligations impinged on family time.

The ideal worker is also based on a separation of gender roles; men are breadwinners while their wives are caregivers. And, for their part, many of the fathers pointed to ways in which gendered divisions of labor continued to inform their actions. Many suggested that parenthood was more difficult for women than for men, not simply because of the physical demands that pregnancy and breastfeeding places on a woman's body, but because women maintained greater responsibility for their children. These beliefs informed many fathers' conceptions about whether universities should provide family-friendly policies and whether faculty should use them. Some fathers suggested that institutions should bear no responsibility for helping any parent balance work and family; others were more likely to suggest that policies should be used by women. Both sets of beliefs illustrate the rigid separation of work from family and support ideal worker norms, hegemonic masculinity, and the gendered university. Some men also suggested that fathers could make time for family. However, many of these men also recounted ways that their male colleagues were penalized for availing themselves of institutional resources. Some failed to earn tenure while others had their masculinity questioned. Both penalties were significant.

While ideal worker norms were evident in the ways that fathers navigated personal and professional concerns, their actions were simultaneously informed by and reflected norms of hegemonic masculinity and appropriate gender roles. Some men suggested that men should not access institutional accommodations because such policies were really only intended for women. Others discussed wanting to use these policies themselves but worried that their masculinity would be challenged. Recall one father who discussed wanting to be seen as the "tough guy" and another who suggested that society saw men only as breadwinners. Both of these men policed their own behaviors based on interactions (both real and imagined) with other men, which underscores the important role that others play in shaping gender-appropriate behavior (Bird, 1996; Connell & Messerschmidt, 2005). Faculty did not always make decisions that made the most sense for their families, but instead made decisions that made the most sense for their identities and careers.

Reinforcing behavior through interactions is one of the hallmarks of Acker's (1990) theory of gendered organizations, which suggests that organizations are gendered in five ways, including that divisions are constructed based on the assumption of a division of labor between the genders. One should not assume that such a division only applies on campus. Rather, as I suggested, the academy still operates under the assumption that the ideal worker is one who has a stay-at-home wife to attend to the domestic domain. Men can be productive academics because they are not expected to be responsible in the home. Although many men are now married to women with careers outside of the home, traditional gender roles have not changed significantly. Studies suggest that many men perform significantly less childcare than their wives, both in society at large (Gerstel & Gallagher, 2001; Lamb, Pleck, Charnov, & Levine, 1985) and in the academy (Mason & Goulden, 2004). Others have found that men are less likely to engage in activities that are typically labeled feminine, such as housework and cooking (Bianchi, Milkie, Sayer, & Robinson, 2000; Brandth & Kvande, 1998). One might wonder whether these roles remain intact because organizational structures do not create the conditions for men to be both good fathers and committed academics. Men are expected to choose one role at which to excel; those who choose fatherhood over academia may be penalized.

In part, as Acker (1990) argued, these divisions of labor are perpetuated by organizational symbols and images. The productive academic is not one who is dividing his or her time between scholarly work and childcare. Rather, the productive academic is one who prioritizes scholarship over family, thus reinforcing the norms of the ideal worker. The productive academic is also, by default, the masculine academic who eschews caregiving and embraces a separation of gender roles. In this way the ideal worker depends on and is informed by hegemonic masculinity; both concepts are implicit in—and integral to—the success of the gendered university. Even when institutions promote work/life policies for faculty use, the underlying rhetoric suggested that men were not to use such policies.

Organizational symbols are further reinforced through gendered interactions with department staff and others on campus (Acker, 1990). Many men worried that being an involved father indicated that they were not serious academics, or worse, were not fulfilling their roles as breadwinners. One professor noted that taking leave after the birth of a child would be suspect for male faculty while another noted that a man taking an extended leave of absence would challenge assumptions about appropriate male roles. These considerations were tied to notions of hegemonic masculinity and, in particular, the assumption that the appropriate male role model was one who financially provided for his family and did not engage in substantial caregiving. While many of the participants knew that their institutions provided some accommodations for new parents, fewer opted to use them. More than one fourth of participants shared stories about ways in which they or other male colleagues had been penalized for using institutional policies.

As the literature from outside academia suggests, several factors determine the likelihood that a father will take time off to spend time with his children, including whether the organization has a history of men using leave (Bygren & Duvander, 2006; Haas & Hwang, 1995) and managerial support for paternal involvement (Russell & Hwang, 2004). Both factors played a role for these faculty fathers. Some participants came from departments where men had never taken parental leave despite the fact that an institutional policy existed. Others pointed to a relatively well-established history of men taking leave over the previous decade. These contrasting environments paint differing pictures for faculty about the valued characteristics of a male academic—one who prioritizes work over family or one who creates space for both.

Furthermore, some participants suggested that their more senior colleagues deterred them from taking leave or placed additional demands on their time. If an assistant professor hears from a significant number of tenured colleagues that prioritizing family over work is not valued or that taking advantage of institutional accommodation will be problematic, he will likely be hesitant to use the policy himself. These stories suggest that these gendered interactions reinforce the symbol of the productive academic. The next two chapters will look closely at the role that interactions with colleagues, department chairs, and other administrators play in shaping men's willingness to use leave and other family-friendly accommodations.

Acker (1990) also suggested that organizational processes reinforce individual identities. Policies existed for both male and female faculty use. However, many participants suggested that men might be looked down on for using them, whereas women were expected to take advantage of these policies. Such differences in expectations reinforce differences between the genders: women are allowed to make space for child rearing in ways that men are not. Together, all of these processes—divisions of labor, gendered interactions with colleagues, and differences in individual identity—reinforce organizational structures, ideal worker norms, and hegemonic masculinity. The academy continues to operate under the assumption that the ideal worker has unlimited time to give to work. For men, such a notion suggests that to excel requires prioritizing career over family. For men or women with significant domestic responsibilities, this notion creates a role that few will be able to fulfill.

While scholars have typically pointed to the ways that gendering of organizations discriminates against women in the workplace, the inverse is also true. Traditional gender roles and the norms of the ideal worker discriminate against fathers who wish to be involved parents. While many fathers worked to share parenting responsibilities with their wives, they reported messages from colleagues that parenting should never supersede academic responsibilities. Not all fathers had a problem with this system. Many, in fact, suggested that academic work should come first. Whether participants were committed parents or committed academics, some institutional practices and much of the institutional culture prevented fathers from being able to excel at both without penalty.

CHAPTER 3

Family-Friendly or Father-Friendly

.◆———◆.

Institutional Culture and the Ideal Worker

Considerable scholarship has focused on the experiences of faculty parents at a variety of institutional types. For example, Ward and Wolf-Wendel (2004, 2012; Wolf-Wendel & Ward, 2006a, 2006b; Wolf-Wendel, et al., 2007) have described how work/family issues differ for faculty at research universities, comprehensive colleges, liberal arts colleges, and community colleges. Other scholars have focused particularly on the challenges that research university faculty face (Lundquist, Misra, & O'Meara, 2012; Mason & Goulden, 2002, 2004; Mason, Wolfinger, & Goulden, 2013; O'Meara & Campbell, 2011; Quinn, 2010). Rarely have studies focused on differences between similar types of institutions. One might expect, for example, that being a faculty member at Harvard would be different than being a faculty member at Cal Tech, yet both are elite research universities. Each university's history, location, leadership, and faculty, to name but a few factors, lead to differences in the culture of each institution. Similarly, universities develop different norms related to work/family issues.

While most institutions offer family-friendly policies with gender-neutral language, campus cultures do not always encourage faculty to access these policies. Some campuses have adopted family-friendly policies, not due to a genuine interest in helping faculty balance work and family, but in an effort to compete with their peers. Referred to as mimetic conformity (DiMaggio & Powell, 1983), such actions are not focused on organizational and cultural change, but rather on maintaining an advantage in the marketplace. For example, if nearly all AAU institutions offer comprehensive family-friendly policies for faculty, the remaining institutions may adopt similar policies to be able to recruit from the same pool of faculty.

57

In contrast, change agents on some campuses are interested in introducing policies designed to help women and men balance the demands of work and family. Initially, most campuses provided policies directed toward women, in recognition of their role in child rearing. Thus, these campuses were not aiming to be family-friendly as much as mommy-friendly. However, as will become clear in this chapter, even campuses that have enacted policies for women to use do not always succeed in creating a culture in which they feel free to do so. Other campuses have incorporated attention to fathers into their definitions of family-friendly; simply stated, the campuses are father-friendly. They have created cultures in which fathers are actively supported in using institutional accommodations and otherwise balancing their personal and professional responsibilities.

In this chapter and chapter 4, I consider the role of organizational culture in shaping men's experiences on campus. While many in higher education have considered the importance of organizational culture (Kezar, 2001; Kezar & Eckel, 2002; Tierney, 1988), I draw on Kuh and Whitt's (1988) definition of culture, which they explain to be "the collective, mutually shaping patterns of norms, values, practices, beliefs, and assumptions that guide the behavior of individuals and groups . . . and provide a frame of reference within which to interpret the meaning of events and actions" (pp. 12–13). Two points emerge from their definition. First, values and practices are created and reinforced by an intact group of individuals. Culture is not a static entity, but is created through interaction. Just as individuals are shaped by culture, so too do individuals shape a culture. Second, culture provides a frame of reference for interpreting daily life. The same behaviors performed on different campuses—such as a professor leaving work early—are likely to be interpreted differently. Why? Different campuses give rise to different cultures.

To frame my analysis, I incorporate the spirit of Acker's (1990) theory of gendered organizations into Schein's (2004) theory of organizational culture, which suggests that culture might be analyzed at three levels, via artifacts, values, and assumptions. *Artifacts* consist of objects and practices that can be observed. All artifacts can be analyzed and inferences can be made about the *values* that group members hold. Finally, *assumptions* are often unconscious and deeply embedded in organizational structures and practices; these assumptions are based on the values of group members. As I discussed in chapter 1, Schein's framework provides a comprehensive approach to analyze culture while Acker's theory focuses particularly on the ways in which gender is produced and reinforced through organizational culture. I consider how Schein's framework might be used to better understand how gender operates on the four campuses and the roles that ideal worker norms and hegemonic masculinity play in perpetuating a gendered organizational culture.

Artifacts consist of several items, including the physical environment, social environment, technology, written and spoken language, overt behavior, and symbols (Schein, 2004). *Physical environment* often refers specifically to architecture. What does the allocation of space reveal about a university? Which departments have state-of-the-art buildings and which departments are housed in old buildings with sagging ceilings? *Social environments* focus on the ways in which individuals within an environment interact with each other. Are relationships collegial or hostile? Despite modern connotations associated with the word, Schein used *technology* to refer to the ways in which in which inputs are transformed into outputs. For example, what resources are necessary for a faculty member to conduct research and how might those resources differ by discipline? *Written and spoken language* also conveys an institution's values. With respect to work/family issues, what types of policies might a campus provide? Do policies carefully spell out who is eligible to use them? *Overt behaviors* also reveal the values of an organization. Do faculty work in their offices from 8:00 A.M. to 5:00 P.M. or do they vary when and where they perform their work? Finally, *symbols* represent ideas that organizational members view as important and can take the form of institutional heroes, rituals, or myths. For example, a campus that has multiple Nobel laureates may point to them as symbols of the value the campus places on innovative research. In this chapter, I focus in particular on the physical and social environments, written and spoken language, and overt behaviors to examine differences by campus.

While artifacts are observable, values and assumptions are not. For example, if an institution's work/family policies provide assistance only to mothers and not to fathers, one might infer that the campus values traditional gender roles. As I will explore throughout this chapter, differing beliefs about gender roles are evident when analyzing the artifacts on different campuses. Additional explanation about gender norms is warranted because research has suggested that adherence to traditional gender norms influences the degree to which faculty feel able to balance work and family. As Haas and Hwang (2007, 2009) suggested, organizations that are more supportive of women's equality and gender-neutral norms are more likely to be those in which fathers access family-friendly resources. The authors found that corporations that had a strong interest in improving women's pay were also more father-friendly. In addition, companies that adopted less traditionally masculine values were those that offered more informal flexibility to fathers, such as making it easier for fathers to stay home to care for sick children. Interpreting these findings using Schein's (2004) framework as a lens, the fact that corporations offered informal flexibility to fathers (an artifact) signals less adherence to traditionally masculine values. The types of values adopted by the employees and managers of a company both determine and reflect the degree to which men feel able to use work/family policies.

In this chapter, I explore the role that institutional culture plays in shaping the degree to which fathers feel supported in attending to both their work and family responsibilities. I examine four campuses to understand what the artifacts reveal about institutional values and assumptions. The artifacts on each campus point to different values about gender roles and the importance of work/family issues that signal the degree to which each campus either accepts or challenges assumptions about the ideal worker model, hegemonic masculinity, and, by extension, the gendered university as appropriate organizing structures for life on and off campus. I begin the chapter by reviewing the literature on characteristics of father-friendly work-places. I then turn to profiles of the four institutions to consider the ways in which their location, policies and programs, administration, and faculty shape the degree to which men feel able to navigate their roles as fathers and faculty. I conclude the chapter by returning to the elements of culture that Schein (2004) identified and consider how the artifacts on each campus illustrate different values and assumptions regarding hegemonic masculinity and the ideal worker.

Elements of Organizations that Shape Men's Ability to Balance Work and Family

A robust body of literature suggests that the workplace and organizational norms play a significant role in shaping men's experiences as fathers (Haas & Hwang, 1995; Lamb et al., 1985; Russell & Hwang, 2004; Waters & Bardoel, 2006). In fact, Haas and Hwang suggested that the workplace might be the largest barrier to men's usage of family-leave policies. While societal norms, particularly related to gender, influence a man's decision to take leave, the conditions on the ground in the workplace may be even more important. What makes a workplace supportive of fathers? The father-friend-ly organization is one in which men are encouraged and expected to access family-friendly policies and resources. Such organizations provide several formal and informal policies targeted toward and used by men. They also are characterized by formal support from managers and colleagues for those with responsibilities in the home. As there have been few studies conducted on the characteristics of father-friendly universities, I draw primarily on the literature on father-friendly corporations.

EXISTENCE OF FORMAL POLICIES

At the bare minimum, a father-friendly organization is one that provides formal work/family policies for male employees to use. Such policies might include paid paternity leave, dependent sick leave, and flextime policies. Haas and Hwang (1995, 2007, 2009) found that the most father-friendly corporations were those that provided formal policies for fathers to use. For many universities, providing formal policies for faculty fathers is a way to signal their status as family-friendly. Yet, even if policies are available, fathers do not always feel able to use them, as discussed in chapter 2. As Haas and Hwang's (1995) research suggests, father-friendly organizations are those that both provide policies and have created a culture that enables men to access the policies.

HISTORY OF POLICY USE

A father-friendly organization is one in which men have a history of using family-friendly policies and resources. Research in higher education settings indicates that men are less likely to use family-friendly policies than women (Lundquist et al., 2012; Mason, Goulden, & Wolfinger, 2006; Quinn, 2010). However, a father is much more likely to use work/family resources if he knows that other men have done so (Bygren & Duvander, 2006; Haas & Hwang, 1995, 2009). In their study of 3,755 Swedish men, Bygren and Duvander found a modest increase in the average number of parental leave days used by men in companies where male employees had already accessed leave policies. As the authors noted, "for a 10–day increase in the average number of parental leave days previously used by fathers in the workplace, the expected number of fathers' parental leave increase by 1.7 days" (p. 369). While the increase is small, it suggests that having male coworkers previously access the policies leads to increased use.

MANAGERIAL SUPPORT

While many features influence the father-friendliness of an organization, several studies point to the critical role that immediate supervisors and company managers play in determining whether men access work/family policies (Blair-Loy & Wharton, 2002; Haas & Hwang, 2009; Russell & Hwang, 2004; Thompson, Beauvais, & Lyness, 1999; Waters & Bardoel, 2006). In their study of 276 male and female MBA recipients, Thompson et al. found that companies with supportive managers were more likely to have employees use work/family benefits. Other studies echo the important role that supervisors play in determining norms around taking leave. While managers who support their employees' right to take parental leave is important, those who actually take leave sends an even more powerful message that balancing work and family is valued. One third of corporations in one study reported that senior managers had taken leave or used a reduced workweek themselves (Haas & Hwang, 1995). One might then surmise that such managers would be even more likely to support their employees who aim to do the same. Few studies in higher education environments have explicitly examined the role of central administration or department chairs in helping faculty navigate work/family issues. Given the important role that department chairs play in shaping departmental culture (Hecht, Higgerson, Gmelch, & Tucker, 1999; Seagren, Creswell, & Wheeler, 1993) and the literature from the corporate sector on the role of managers in shaping the father-friendliness of an organization, leadership clearly makes a difference.

COWORKER SUPPORT

In addition to the importance of supervisor support, coworker attitudes also shape men's willingness to access work/family policies (Blair-Loy & Wharton, 2002; Haas & Hwang, 2009; Russell & Hwang, 2004; Waters & Bardoel, 2006). Blair-Loy and Wharton found that employees whose coworkers had been with the organization longer were more likely to access work/family policies. The authors hypothesized that more senior employees might provide a buffer to help the individual navigate challenges taking leave. The important role that colleagues play translates to universities. As I discussed in the previous chapter, some have reported that faculty were hesitant to take leave or use institutional accommodations out of fear of negative career repercussions; faculty worried that their colleagues would think less of them (Finkel et al., 1994). In their study of Australian faculty and staff, Waters and Bardoel (2006) found that employees were reluctant to take leave because they worried that doing so would inflict extra work on their coworkers and lead to resentment. The literature suggests that in academic environments, faculty are particularly nervous about the reactions they might receive from coworkers about using work/family accommodations.

In sum, several features determine the family-friendliness and father-friendliness of an organization, including the types of policies available and the degree of support from managers and colleagues about accessing those policies. Some organizations might have policies available, but expect employees not to use them. Still others might expect that women will use the policies, but not men. Using Schein's (2004) typology, each of these factors are types of artifacts that elucidate the values and assumptions related to the importance of fathers navigating work and family and the role of the institution in helping them do so.

In the remainder of the chapter, I provide profiles of the four institutions and consider the ways that campus cultures either encourage or discourage fathers from accessing policies. Each profile considers the availability of campus policies and programs, the actions and messages of central administration, and the support of those within the department, including both department chairs and other colleagues. Additionally, geographical location makes a difference on some of these campuses in shaping the ways in which fathers are able to balance work and family, and so I begin each section by including more detail about location. I begin by discussing Eastern University and Southern University, institutions that, as the portraits will suggest, are not father-friendly campuses, but for decidedly different reasons. I then discuss how Western University is enacting a father-friendly culture and the challenges it still faces. The final profile of Midwestern University illustrates the ways in which campus culture is rarely uniform as faculty fathers in some departments reported great support for their lives outside the workplace while others noted that support was absent for men and women.

Eastern University: Neither Father-Friendly nor Mother-Friendly

Of the four institutions, Eastern University seems the least invested in helping faculty balance work and family. While some campuses offer numerous family-friendly policies, the offerings at Eastern University remain noticeably slim. Eastern University seems to approach work/family issues as an individual responsibility and does not play a significant role in helping faculty bridge that divide. Many faculty attributed the lack of attention to employees' lives to the institution's location.

LOCATION

Eastern University is located in a major metropolitan area on the East Coast of the United States. Of the four campuses profiled, Eastern University is in the most urban environment with the highest cost of living. Nearly three fourths of the fathers interviewed lived at least 30 minutes from campus and planned their days around their commutes and traffic patterns. In part, this distribution across the area was due to high real estate costs. Younger faculty, in particular, could not afford to buy homes near campus. One assistant professor described why he and his wife chose the house that they did:

> It was also probably dictated by cost. So we were here and we moved here and it was kind of like the housing market was still ridiculous. And so we kind of lived as close as we could [to] the city center that we could afford to.

While some faculty might have preferred living closer to campus, their income and housing costs precluded such a choice. And, as many told me, traffic was so bad in the metro area that they opted not to come to campus five days a week. One father reported that his commute took an hour each way. Another dad shared that he lived 15 miles away, which translated to a 30- to 40-minute commute. Another father said that he and his wife lived 30 miles away from Eastern University. "It's mostly freeway driving, so if I leave [home] before 7, it takes me 25 minutes—that's not bad. But if I get stuck in traffic or I leave in traffic, it could be an hour and a half." Given these substantial commute times, many faculty reported that they had home offices where they worked at least a couple of days a week.

Many fathers suggested that both traffic patterns and institutional location hindered the development of any sense of collegiality and support of family-friendly initiatives. A couple of fathers suggested that because they lived in such an interesting city, they did not look to the university to serve as a center of social activity as they might have if they lived in a smaller town. Said one father, "There's just so much other stuff to do. For example we have a great performing arts center. We never get there, just because there's other [stuff] to do." He went on to suggest that if he were at Ohio State or the University of Michigan, he and his family would turn to the university more as a center of social life.

In addition to not looking to the university to provide cultural entertainment, many fathers also suggested that its urban location meant that they did not look to their colleagues as forms of social support. Many fathers suggested that their colleagues "come in, do their work, . . . and leave." Another father explained that this mentality was due to its location:

> It's an urban campus in a very, very big urban center and there isn't a lot of social interactivity among the faculty that you'll see at a more rural campus like, say, Bloomington or things like that. The truth is that faculty doesn't meet a lot together socially—hardly at all.

Another father reflected fondly on his days as a graduate student in a small town when his wife would regularly bring their kids to campus in the afternoons and evenings to watch him play on a department sports team. Because of traffic, such a trip would be unthinkable at Eastern University.

Finally, the majority of the fathers whom I interviewed at Eastern University were in dual-career couples. Of the 16 men, 13 were married to women who worked outside of the home at least 75% time. In part, these employment patterns were due to cost of living in the area; faculty simply could not afford to be in single-earner families. Unlike at other campuses where many faculty spouses had part-time jobs, these men reported that their wives worked in a range of full-time positions, including as teachers, government officials, medical professionals, and lawyers. Of note, few were married to other academics. The Eastern University metropolitan area offered many opportunities to professionals in a variety of fields, which was not always true of the other towns and cities where the three other institutions were located. In many of these marriages, both spouses were juggling full-time careers, which had implications for the ways in which faculty lives played out. These employment patterns contrast significantly with those of faculty at other institutions who were more frequently in dual-career academic couples or families that adhered to more traditional gender roles.

In many ways, the campus location shaped the family-friendliness of the institution. Because faculty lived throughout the metropolitan area, many were not on campus several days a week. By reducing the time they spent on campus, many faculty did not build the same types of connections with their colleagues, and the same interests in each other's families, as faculty reported on other campuses. In essence, faculty's professional lives were regarded as paramount to their personal lives. In addition, as I will soon discuss, the fact that faculty were so dispersed throughout the area made department parties that were inclusive of families difficult to plan. While traffic patterns and a high cost of living help to explain some of the reasons for a less-than-collegial environment, they do not explain the institution's decision not to provide standard work/family policies.

POLICIES AND PROGRAMS

Eastern University offers few policies to help faculty balance work and life. As I outlined in chapter 1, the campus offers an automatic extension of the tenure clock for one year for a major life event, such as the birth of a child or in case of any work-related setbacks, such as a fire in a lab. The campus also offers a part-time tenure-track option, with part-time pay, which faculty may use for a period of up to two years. Both policies are available to men and women. I also learned through interviews with an administrator that the campus offers an unofficial spousal hiring program, although programs were neither publicized on the website nor did I learn of any faculty using the policy. The campus has a lab school/childcare center, which, while a great resource for faculty and staff, has approximately 100 spaces, thereby failing to meet the needs of the majority of the campus population. Since some faculty lived a considerable distance from campus, they opted not to put their children in the campus childcare center, preferring locations closer to their homes. Unlike some other campuses, the institution employed no staff members specifically charged with administering work/life programs.

CENTRAL ADMINISTRATION

This lack of policy attention to work/family issues translated to lack of attention from administrators as well. Faculty receive few messages from the central administration about the importance of balancing work and life. As one faculty member said, "it's sort of my sense that it's my responsibility to balance work and family. . . . I don't consider the institution as acknowledging parenthood in any of the ways we go about doing our job." Another faculty member echoed this sentiment: "I don't see signs across the university that we're a family-friendly environment. In fact I never even thought about it." Both men pointed to the fact that the institution does not send any consistent messages about the importance of balancing work and family. The first even suggested that by the absence of rhetoric, the institution sends a message that work/life balance remains an individual responsibility.

Conversations with a senior administrator both echo and contradict these statements. The senior administrator suggested that she thought the campus was family-friendly, although she agreed the policies were certainly lacking when compared to campuses such as the University of California–Berkeley or University of Michigan. She emphasized the institution's commitment to providing policies that were available to all without discriminating based on gender, race, or job status. In other words, Eastern University does not provide either leave or a reduction in teaching duties following the birth of a child to faculty because such a policy cannot be made available to staff as well. As the administrator shared, we "can't in a university community have one constituency get privileges that another doesn't get." In this way, Eastern University differs dramatically from other institutions in the sample as it embodies a commitment to equality in opportunity, although not necessarily equity in outcomes.

While the campus provides the opportunity to extend the tenure clock, the administrator framed the policy as not particularly successful; she suggested that the individuals who use the tenure-clock extension are less likely to be promoted than those who do not. However, as I reported in the previous chapter, she explained that this discrepancy does not account for the "kinds of people" who use tenure-clock extensions. Such rhetoric suggests that there is a type of faculty member who is likely to succeed at Eastern University—the ideal worker and not the involved father.

DEPARTMENT-LEVEL SUPPORT

While institutional culture is important, family-friendly culture and policies are enacted at the department level. This was particularly true at Eastern University where the enforcement and perceived availability of policies differed across departments. As one faculty member explained:

I don't think that there's one culture that runs across the campus. I'm sure it's different [from] department to department. It has been a very eye-opening experience to me though to realize that for as supportive as the department is, the institution really leaves a lot to be desired beyond. I feel very fortunate to be in this department because I know that other departments aren't as supportive.

To be sure, there were departments in which faculty reported feeling supported by their department chairs. One faculty member in the social sciences recounted that his department chair brought him the necessary paperwork to request a tenure-clock extension, saying, "Why wouldn't you do it? They are offering this. This is university policy." However, these stories seemed to be the exception to the rule. A faculty member in the sciences discussed the challenges he faced when trying to request the very same tenure-clock extension:

My understanding of the policy was that it was sort of automatic. . . . You have got to [request] it when the child is born so that's what I did. Now this was a policy that started right when I started. My chair didn't know anything about this policy so that conversation with him went just about as badly as you can imagine. "Why are you asking for a one-year tenure delay—you don't need this. It's too early; what are you doing?" I was like, "Well from what I understand this is an automatic policy and this is just a formality. . . ." So he discouraged me from doing it.

The department chair discouraged his faculty from using the policy in part because central administration had imparted no strong messages that the institution valued work/life balance.

As I soon discuss, faculty on other campuses reported that children were frequently invited to department events or made occasional appearances in the department; Eastern University faculty were far less likely to report the same. Many pointed to the institution's location as enforcing a rigid separation between work and family. When I asked one professor if children ever appeared at department events, he succinctly replied: "Nah. It's just not the culture of a large metropolitan area." Another father echoed this reply to the same question:

Almost never. Part of it again is I think people live too far away. That is something I do miss [about my previous institution]. And I think that's something actually really helps build interpersonal relationships, which then leads to better working relationships.

This father confirmed that people's living situation prevents them from bringing their children in, but also went on to elaborate that because members of the department live so far from one another, the development of a more collegial environment and relationships has been stymied. One faculty member who was a graduate program director in the social sciences reported that he was trying to create more events that families could attend:

> I went into the position trying to do and have tried to do . . . more family-friendly sort of stuff in our department. . . . We have an annual picnic but it's in the middle of a workday out on the side of the building. So it's not realistic that anybody would bring a spouse or a partner or kids to that, and we just don't do things that people would bring their kids to. And so last year we had a picnic at a park on a Saturday, and we're doing it again this year.

This professor made a concerted effort to create an event for faculty and their families, organizing it on a weekend and at a location that would be conducive to family schedules. It should also be noted that this father was in the social sciences, which as I discuss in the next chapter, is the discipline that reported the most attention to work/family issues across institutions. The majority of Eastern University faculty simply pointed to the campus's location as a reason why work and family were so separated.

Overall, Eastern University's environment does not encourage either men or women to balance work and family. The campus' policies fall far behind its peers. There is no concerted push from the administration to support a family-friendly culture, which means that departments differ in the degree to which they encourage faculty to use the few policies that exist. Many faculty pointed to institutional location as an excuse for why the campus does not cultivate a more family-friendly environment, or at least, why they do not expect support from the institution. However, faculty on other campuses were more likely to report slightly more support for family-friendly issues.

Southern University: Family-Friendly or Mommy-Friendly?

Whereas Eastern University did not incorporate any attention to gender into discussions of work/family issues, Southern University's culture has defined the family-friendly campus as a woman's issue. Until recently, Southern University's work/family policies were not actively publicized. In the past few years, new administrators have touted existing policies and implemented new ones, which brings the campus in line with its national peers. Despite support from central administration, the campus culture has yet to become one that encourages all faculty to use these policies. While men report that women are encouraged to use the policies, they explained that they would be looked at askance if they were to access family-friendly resources. The campus culture seems to suggest that work/family issues are not a concern for men.

LOCATION

Southern University's location in a small city in the South shapes a variety of facets of faculty and family life. Of the four universities profiled, the region has the lowest cost of living and more families reporting traditional divisions with man as breadwinner and woman as caregiver. While Eastern University faculty lived throughout the greater metropolitan region, most Southern faculty live within an easy 20-minute drive to campus. Several of the fathers discussed the benefits that the city brought to faculty with families. One father remarked that "it's a good place to have a family." Another father remarked how the institution's location is often highlighted when bringing in prospective hires:

> Anytime we have job candidates, people will talk explicitly about what an easy town [this] is for people who want to settle and have kids, and the cost of living is low and the schools are relatively good, and there are different neighborhoods to choose from. And I think people do think that that quality of life is one of the things that could attract people to [this city].

While faculty at Eastern University were able to tout the cultural benefits of living in a major metropolitan area, those at Southern University were proud of the affordability of the region and the opportunities that the area provides to families and children.

Across all four universities, faculty at Southern University were most likely to have stay-at-home wives. Of the 19 married faculty at Southern University, six had wives who currently stayed at home with their kids. An additional three had wives who had stayed at home until recently. Nearly half of the men interviewed had marriages that conformed to traditional gender norms in which the man was the breadwinner and the woman was the caregiver. One tenured professor commented that the fact that his wife had stayed home as the full-time "house manager" while he was an assistant professor had freed him up to focus on work responsibilities. "That's one of the reasons that I was able to do what I was able to do during that time. Because all that work she did, it . . . let me focus energy elsewhere." This father was not the only to attribute his success to the fact that his wife was able to perform the majority of the work at home.

Of the wives who worked outside the home, two were full-time academics (one at Southern University and one at a nearby college), and others were in fields such as teaching and law enforcement. However, the city did not offer the same types of career opportunities as those available to the spouses of Eastern University faculty. One faculty member's wife moved out of state to take a job because of the few opportunities in her line of work, thus committing the couple to a long-distance marriage. Although Southern University was located in a city with a low cost of living, which served as an attractive feature for more junior faculty, its size meant that the spouses of faculty had a more difficult time finding employment. Many faculty at Southern University found themselves in marriages with more conventional gender roles in which caregiving was assumed to be the woman's responsibility. Such an assumption translated to assumptions around accessing work/family policies on campus as well.

POLICIES AND PROGRAMS

Southern University first implemented leave following the birth of a child for new faculty more than 15 years ago. However, the policies were not publicized due to concerns over objections from the Board of Trustees. Five years ago, the policies were finally codified in the faculty handbook and are now actively promoted on the institution's website. The campus offers tenure-line faculty several policies to use following the birth of a child. Faculty of either gender are eligible for a total release from teaching duties for one semester following the birth of a child. Faculty can also extend their tenure clock for a year for the birth of a child. The campus also offers formalized dual-career hiring programs, which are publicized on its website. The campus provides on-site childcare, which has recently expanded to accommodate more children. While there are no designated work/life staff members on this campus, one senior administrator reported spending a significant amount of her time on work/family issues, including facilitating dual-career hires. While policies are gender neutral, many fathers suggested that mothers are encouraged to access them more than fathers are.

CENTRAL ADMINISTRATION

Unlike their counterparts at Eastern University, faculty at Southern University were a bit more knowledgeable of existing family-friendly resources on campus. Some referenced emails they had received from the administration about policies. Others, however, thought that the campus did not take a stance regarding work/family issues at all, as this professor shared:

It doesn't seem like it's going one way or the other. I don't know that it's negative but there is certainly nothing that leads me to believe that it is positive either in the sense that I really don't see a lot of encouragement one way or the other.

This participant did not find the campus to be either hostile or encouraging. However, other participants were able to point to existing resources, as one father excitedly explained:

In the last few years, there have [sic] been the institution of the family leave and I think it's wonderful that it applies to both men and women. So, it's not just like maternity leave, a woman has a baby and is allowed to take a semester off, or a few months off. It applies equally to males and females. So, my impression is that it is a good climate.

This faculty member was not the only one to point to policies and ways that the campus helped faculty after the birth of a child. Throughout interviews, several faculty discussed the role that senior administrators played in establishing and promoting family-friendly policies. One father said that both his dean and staff in the provost's office were supportive of him extending the tenure clock. Another faculty member suggested that one senior administrator in particular was responsible for promoting family-friendly policies and making them accessible to men and women.

These administrators do indeed deserve a significant amount of recognition. Since assuming her role fewer than five years ago, one of the vice provosts mentioned that she has worked actively to highlight existing policies. She spoke of her actions as trying to bring about a "cultural change," although she pointed out that, with the constant influx of new faculty and a frequent shift in department heads, efforts to promote family-friendly policies are not always successful. The vice provost said she was motivated to act after hearing stories about multiple faculty in the same department getting different treatment after similar life events; one faculty member might have been given a release from teaching after the birth of a child while another received no accommodations. Campus policies were needed to address these disparities.

Despite the gender neutrality of campus policies, senior administrators suggested that work/life issues remain a greater concern for women than for men. The data related to these policies bears this out: more women than men have used a release from teaching duties following the birth of a child. Furthermore, in focus groups conducted with early-career faculty,

more women than men mentioned that they were concerned about work/
family issues. The administrators reported that there was also initial concern
from some of the deans that men might unfairly access the tenure-clock
extension in order to get more time to produce scholarship. Unwilling to
regulate the policy usage at the university level, central administrators gave
the departments discretion. Although the policies are gender neutral, central
administrators suggested that these policies are more critical for women than
for men, and indeed, many suspect that men might deceitfully access such
policies. These concerns remain evident at the department level.

DEPARTMENT-LEVEL SUPPORT

Many participants spoke about the roles that their department heads played
in supporting faculty trying to balance their home and work lives. A faculty
member in the social sciences explained the instrumental role that department heads played in shaping the acceptability of using leave. The last
three department heads:

> stood up for parents to apply for leave, zero teaching semesters dur-
> ing the semester if they're having kids and that now has become
> fairly standard. People don't ask questions about it; they just see it
> as a standard way [for] the university.

In this department, a reduction in teaching duties had become standard
for men and women. Other participants suggested that their chairs were
supportive, asking about their children and encouraging them to access
family-friendly resources. A handful of participants commented that their
department heads and even the university administrators understood the
issues because they were mothers themselves. Described one father, "I have
a department head who is also a mother. . . . So she knows the deal." While
other fathers discussed that their male department chairs were supportive
of work/family issues, none of that support ever was linked to the fact that
they were fathers themselves. Some of the faculty operated on the principle
that being mothers gave chairs a special kind of empathy while fatherhood
did not bring the same benefits to men, thus reinforcing the stereotype that
parenthood resides in women's domain.

  While men noted that their department chairs were supportive, there
was an undercurrent in faculty responses that the campus continued to operate from a traditionally gendered perspective by expecting only women to
access leave policies because men presumably had a wife at home to take
care of their children. One professor pointed to the disparity in maternity
leave versus paternity leave:

It seems like there is an extent to which you probably get more play as a mother than as a father when you are a parent, in the sense that . . . people always talk about maternity leave but [act as if] there is no paternity leave.

Although many participants knew that leave was available for faculty parents of any gender, the dominant rhetoric suggested that such leave was best reserved for women. Another participant explained, "I also definitely feel like there is—and this is universitywide, this is just not our department—is that as a male, the burden of a child is not considered as great." He later went on to elaborate:

In those early months, where, as a woman, you have to deal with, "Are you going to breastfeed?" and "How much time are you going to take off?" I think it would have been a problem if I had said, you know, I'm going to take six weeks off to spend with my wife and my newborn. I think there would have been some people going, "Why do *you* need to take time off? You know, you're the man."

This father pointed to the dilemma that exists for faculty at Southern University. While policies are ostensibly gender neutral, a belief remains that child rearing is more a concern for women than men. As this professor pointed out, the arrival of a child is framed in terms of physical demands on the woman, which for many explain why she needs to take leave. However, by continuing to rely on notions of difference, parenthood remains a woman's concern, leaving no space for men who wish to be involved fathers. In part these assumptions might arise from the university's location in the South—arguably one of the more conservative regions of the United States. And, faculty spousal employment patterns confirm this division of labor: nearly half were or had recently been in marriages in which men served as breadwinners and women as caregivers. Not surprisingly, then, administrators and other faculty assumed that work/family issues remained a larger concern for women than for men. Although Southern University and Eastern University provide family-friendly policies, neither has succeeded in becoming father-friendly campuses. However, Western University and Midwestern University come closer to meeting that ideal.

Western University: Working Toward a Father-Friendly Culture

At first glance, Western University and Southern University seem to have few differences. Both offer progressive family-friendly policies. Both have supportive administrators. However, Western University has transformed itself into a father-friendly campus whereas Southern University adheres to more traditional parenting roles. Of course, Western University is not a gender utopia; men still express frustration with gender bias and perceived marginalization of fathers' needs. I discuss the policies and actions of administrators that help earn Western University the label of father-friendly. However, one significant difference between the two institutions is the town in which each is located.

LOCATION

Western University is located in a quintessential college town. With fewer than 100,000 people, the town provides a safe place for faculty to raise their children. Many, in fact, remarked that the town is an easy place to raise children, both due to its size and family-friendly events that the town and campus host. Unlike Eastern University where faculty work far from home, Western University is so small that faculty can get to work in as little as 10 minutes. As one professor noted, "I live in a community that is small and daily life is easy enough. . . . I could pick up kids in five minutes from here." Such a small town allows these fathers to be more involved with their children's day-to-day care than fathers at Eastern University. Fathers on this campus were more likely to pick up children after daycare or school because they had such a short distance to travel.

Some of the Western University fathers also commented that the town provided a safe environment for their children. One father said:

> In my perspective, [this town] makes raising kids very easy, because from like third grade or second grade, they can ride their bikes autonomously around. And when we moved here, our son was in fifth grade, and you know, there was . . . an after-school program that was very cheap compared to what we could get in [the big city where we used to live].

This father appreciated that the cost of childcare was less expensive than in larger cities. Like this professor, other fathers also noted how the bike-friendly nature of the town was just a small part of its appeal:

> It's great to live in a town where you can ride your bicycle to work, the streets are flat, 6-foot bike lanes, right? Sunny every day. Very safe. Low amount of crime. Lots of parks all over the place. Schools where the parents are really, really involved. . . . It's just a really easy place to live to raise a family.

Many of the professors painted an idyllic picture of life in the town. Living there made being a parent easier in ways that life in other cities did not. Many also noted that the town and university had regular events that were of interest to families, including an annual campus open house. Several fathers noted that the town's twice-a-week Farmer's Market, complete with musical entertainment and activities for kids, was an event to which many parents regularly brought their children. The town itself was organized around family life in ways that life at Eastern University was not. However, many faculty reported that housing prices had skyrocketed in the previous decade, making home purchases more difficult for many younger faculty.

While faculty at both Southern University and Western University commended the regions in which they lived for family-friendliness, Western University faculty differed from their counterparts at Southern University in that far more men reported having wives who worked outside of the home. Of the 16 men interviewed, only 2 at Western University had a stay-at-home wife. Of the remaining 14, 4 worked part time while 10 worked full time. Some worked in a nearby city while others had employment at Western University as faculty, administrators, or researchers. Their wives' employment had implications for the kinds of work men did inside the home. For its part, Western University seemed to provide policies that supported men and women in being active parents.

POLICIES AND PROGRAMS

Western University provides a comprehensive portfolio of family-friendly policies. Like both Eastern University and Southern University, the campus allows faculty to extend the tenure clock for one year for major life events. Of difference, however, is that faculty are eligible to extend the clock twice, in the event of multiple children or other precipitating events. The campus also provides two policies related to the birth of a child: childbearing mothers are eligible for one quarter of paid leave while faculty parents of either gender are eligible for a one course teaching release for one quarter. (Given that teaching loads at this campus typically have tenure-line faculty teaching no more than four courses a year, faculty are usually able to guarantee a complete release from all courses for the quarter.) The campus also provides multiple quarters of leave in the event of the birth of twins or triplets. Unlike Southern University, this campus provides funds to cover replacement teaching costs. Western University also provides one quarter of leave to a parent of either gender who adopts a child. While a father who welcomes a child into the home through his wife giving birth is only eligible for one quarter of modified duties, those who adopt are eligible for one quarter of leave plus one quarter of modified duties, which has caused some discontent among faculty.

In addition to these leave policies and the tenure-clock extension, the campus offers and publicizes a partner-hiring program. One of the fathers I interviewed was hired as a result of the partner-hiring program; his wife was given the first offer and the institution found him a tenure-track position as well. Like Eastern University, the university also offers a part-time tenure-track option (for part-time pay) for a limited period. The campus has a lab school as well as standard childcare centers. As on many campuses, faculty continually complain that not enough spots are available for children. Although not of use to faculty fathers, the campus is well known for its lactation rooms and breastfeeding support program. In addition to these standard programs, the campus has tried to integrate work/life issues throughout the campus culture by creating a program of work/life faculty advisors, comprising professors in departments across campus who serve as advocates for work/life policies. These faculty attend seminars once a quarter and are expected to promote existing policies. The campus also offers a series of brown bag lunches for assistant professors to explain existing work/life policies and to provide suggestions for navigating work and family. Unlike the first two campuses profiled, Western University has a staff member who is solely dedicated to promoting work/life issues for faculty. In their interviews, faculty often noted her actions as well as those of senior administrators as critical to creating a family-friendly campus.

CENTRAL ADMINISTRATION

In large part, Western University owes much of the success of family-friendly policies to support from current and past central administrators. Many noted that the vice provost played a significant role in creating a supportive culture. One faculty member shared:

> I'm heartened that our campus administration is very much on the side of being enlightened about this. [The vice provost's] office . . . I think their outlook is superb. They've gone out of their way to try to make this university a more work/life friendly place. They have somebody, a staff person, who's devoted to this area, and you know, will assertively, if not aggressively, seek proper redress for faculty who are denied what they deserve.

This faculty member was not the only one to point to the role of the vice provost's office. Another professor recounted thanking the previous vice provost for approving a request to extend the tenure clock:

I just said, "Hey, . . . I just wanted to say thank you for granting my request for adjusting the clock . . . because I had kids." And he said, "You don't have to thank me." He says, "I approve those routinely." And I said, "Well, I was informed that it would be a big deal for me, because I was a male." And he said, "Are you kidding me?"

This exchange points to several features of life at Western University. First, extension of tenure clocks and other family-friendly policies have become entrenched on the campus through the tenure of multiple vice provosts. Also worth noting, however, is that this professor was misinformed by others in his department: he was told that male faculty were not eligible to use the policy. While the early 2000s were marked by a handful of incidents in which incorrect information was shared, participants reported fewer occasions where they were misinformed about university policy in the latter half of the decade.

What remained constant was faculty members' appreciation for the work that the vice provost and the work/life staff member performed. While the state university system with which it is affiliated first began offering some family-friendly policies in the late 1980s, Western University began offering even more generous policies in 2003. In part, the policies were implemented after recognizing that the campus was hiring low numbers of women; in the late 1990s, only about 20% of new faculty hires were women. To help remedy this, a taskforce generated a series of recommendations, which included offering more family-friendly policies as a recruitment and retention tool. Although the policies were generated out of a need to recruit and retain women, the vice provost reported that men and women are now accessing the tenure-clock extension and other policies in equal numbers. The institution's efforts to become a leader in family-friendly policies were given additional assistance when the campus won a national award focused on work/life issues. While the majority of the campus's work/family programs predated the grant, they were able to use the grant to develop the work/life advisors program described earlier and to publicize existing programs, which served to further institutionalize family-friendliness into the campus culture.

As mentioned earlier, the campus does not simply have a policy that offers a release from teaching duties for one quarter. Of more importance, it offers central funding to provide a replacement instructor for the quarter for childbearing mothers and all faculty parents for one quarter of release from teaching duties. Administrators estimated that they have spent "several million dollars" since the program's inception providing replacement teaching funds. However, the administrators attribute the campus cultural change entirely to the fact that the campus provides the replacement funding. The

vice provost mused that a department does not experience any sort of financial penalty for having a faculty member on leave and thus has little reason
to resist.

While the administration is able to provide central replacement funds,
the cost of the program has kept the institution from providing paid leave
for one quarter for all faculty fathers. As the vice provost explained, "it's
not a question necessarily of whether it's the right thing to do. It's really a
question of whether we can afford it at the present time." The vice provost
further explained that individual departments are welcome to provide leave
to their faculty, but that the institution cannot afford to subsidize such a
leave. This discrepancy has rankled some fathers who feel that men are
being treated inequitably by not having access to the same leave policies.
One father explained the challenges that one of his colleagues experienced
when trying to access a leave:

> One of my colleagues just had a baby in October, . . . and he had to
> apply for parental leave, and that was a fight. There's been a series
> of fights here over whether fathers who are the primary caregiver
> can get something equivalent, and it's . . . you know, it reaches
> the absurd dimension, because if they had adopted this kid instead,
> they would've gotten a full quarter off, plus half teaching release.

Because the policy is not standard across the university, men have to make
arrangements with their individual departments to access a genuine leave.
While the administrators argue that they would like to provide leave to
men (as they do to all mothers), the financial climate precludes this course
of action. Some inequities continue to exist at Western University; most
fathers are not eligible for leave, although their female counterparts are.
For the most part, however, the campus has created an environment that
encourages men to use family-friendly accommodations in ways that are not
happening on other campuses. This support translates to the department
level as well.

DEPARTMENT-LEVEL SUPPORT

Faculty reported that their department chairs encouraged them to balance
work and family. As one professor said, "I don't think that the department, you know, short of not expecting us to do our jobs, could be much
more facilitating in relation to people having families and having children."
Another faculty member described his department as "unreasonably supportive." The department chairs and other faculty had created environments
that encouraged faculty to balance work and life. As at Southern University,

one professor reported that his department chair brought him the paperwork necessary to take the reduction in teaching duties. Other faculty reported that men taking leave had become the norm in the department.

In addition to supporting faculty with major life events, department chairs at Western University made a concerted effort to support faculty throughout all aspects of their children's lives. One department chair recounted an incident when one of his assistant professors needed to bring a sick child with him to a departmental presentation:

> One of my outstanding faculty members, he had to give a presentation . . . his secretary came running, whispering to me . . . his daughter was sick and she's here with him. . . . I said, . . . "I don't have any problem with him bringing his baby with him." She said, "The faculty's baby?" I said, "Why not?" She said, "Really?" I said, "Yes." . . . and she said, "Okay, I will tell him." So, . . . he came with his beautiful little girl, an absolutely adorable little girl. She was like 6 or 7. I think she was sick and she didn't go to school or something. This blond, beautiful little girl, she was so cute just sitting over there, and she'd . . . draw and she would say a few random things here and there, and everybody would chuckle. I thought it was amazing. It was beautiful. So, [the faculty member] came up to apologize. . . . I said, "What are you apologizing about? To me this is perfect. Just great." . . . So, I tell everybody, and I really, really mean that . . . that people should feel comfortable so long as it's their decision when they bring their kids here, to babysit their kids here if they want to.

The chair indicated that he wants his faculty members to feel comfortable bringing their children into the office. He recognized the importance of balancing work and family and put confidence in the faculty that they could do so. This chair's department was also heavily male-dominated, which further suggests the degree to which the campuswide culture at Western University has succeeded in transforming norms. As I discuss in the next chapter, male-dominated disciplines tend to be noted for being less supportive of those with children. However, at Western University, definitions of the ideal worker and by consequence, hegemonic masculinity, were being challenged and transformed. Whereas on other campuses bringing in a child might be viewed as a disruption, in this department and others at Western University, it was encouraged.

Faculty reported that their departments frequently created other opportunities to include children in departmental events. Many faculty reported that their departments held semiannual parties to which faculty were encouraged to bring their children. One department even rents bounce houses for children to play in at its picnics. Another faculty member had to leave our interview to go pick up his daughter to bring to a potluck in the department. Other faculty reported that children were often present at fall and spring receptions, although he worried that the events were "boring for the kids." (Apparently his department did not rent a bounce house for their entertainment.) However, not all faculty reported that their departments included children in events. There remain pockets at Western University that continue to separate work and family. One father and department chair recounted his experiences interacting with other departments:

> As nice as I've described it to you, I've heard people in other departments say very different things across the university. . . . There are some departments where there are much more provincial outlooks by the older male faculty who are not as tolerant of younger faculty, particularly women, giving birth, needing Active Service/Modified Duties, needing the time off. So, I think it's a mixed bag across the university with respect to parenting.

Such attitudes may come as a disappointment, but they are also well rooted in decades of expectations about the importance of separating work and family. Even on campuses that have created family-friendly cultures, not all members of a community will work toward the same goal.

On the whole, Western University has made strides to encourage both male and female faculty to balance work and family. The campus provides a number of family-friendly policies that men can and do use. Some men complained about the lack of availability of leave for fathers whose wives give birth, given that childbearing mothers were eligible for an additional quarter of paid leave. On this campus, women received extra assistance for which men were not eligible. Some might argue that such demands reinforce assumptions of the ideal worker with a division of gender roles while others might make the case that this additional assistance recognizes the physical demands that pregnancy and childbirth place on a woman's body. Despite this difference, Western University faculty found themselves working on a campus and living in a town that allowed both men and women to balance work and family. Some faculty at Midwestern University reported much of the same while others painted a different picture.

Midwestern University:
Family-Friendly Policies, Father-Friendly Departments

Much like Western University, Midwestern University has made tremendous strides toward creating a campus culture that encourages both fathers and mothers to use family-friendly policies. The similarities are striking: both universities are located in idyllic college towns, which makes life easier for faculty with children; both have received national grants to help make the campus more family-friendly; both offer a litany of family-friendly policies; both have many departments that encourage men and women to access leave. However, cultural change on this campus is not yet complete as fathers in some departments report feeling very supported in balancing work and family while others noted a profound absence of support.

LOCATION

Midwestern University is located in a small college town in the Midwest. With a population just in excess of 100,000, the town provides a safe environment in which faculty can raise their children. Many faculty commented that they were happy at Midwestern in part because of its location and the town's safety. One father reported how he loved that his children could walk anywhere that they wanted:

> What that's done has instilled a sense of freedom in our kids that if they want to do something—like they'll say, "I need a library book for school" or you know, "I'd like to go with my friends to get a piece of pizza," or something like that. And we say, "Well, that's great," and they get up and they walk out and they go do it.

Like the children of Western University faculty who often biked around town, children of Midwestern University faculty could explore their town on foot. Many other faculty reported that they lived close enough to campus that they would walk to and from work each day.

Other faculty also described how ideal the town was as a location to raise children. Said one father, this town "is family heaven and people tend to stay for their families." Some other fathers commented that they probably would not have settled at Midwestern University if they had not had children.

> We feel very lucky both to have been hired here and to be able to raise our family here. It's the best town in the world as far as I can see . . . to raise your kids. It's just great and we're really happy to be here for that. Both of us chafe a little bit at the limitations. . . . We are city people who'd rather live in the city.

Another father similarly shared that he missed living in a city, but also recognized how much easier it was to be a parent in a small town instead of a big city:

> I think part of the picture for us of a place like [Midwestern University] has been the notion of us moving to a place that we would settle, stay, raise our children—a maybe kind of a longer term choice about the kind of life we wanted to live, which very much included children. I left New York [City] in part because having kids in New York was just really, really hard or difficult, which is the practical perspective and it was just going to get harder.

This father had experiences like the Eastern University faculty who planned their lives around traffic and commute patterns and contended with a significantly higher cost of living. For this dad and many others, being at Midwestern University was a deliberate choice of lifestyle for the sake of family.

Many fathers also praised the town and university for their cultural and recreational resources. One father commented that he could never see himself living outside of a college town because "it just increases the quality of life, not just because of the sporting events, but also for the access to the parks and culture kinds of experiences that you don't get in a noncollege town." Much as at Western University, faculty at Midwestern University took advantage of a variety of campus offerings such as museums and botanical gardens as places to bring their children. Quite simply, life at Midwestern University was easier.

Among all four campuses profiled, Midwestern University boasted the largest number of dual-career academic couples. Of the 19 men interviewed, 10 had wives who were employed in academic positions at Midwestern University, some as tenure-line faculty, some as clinical faculty, and others in research positions. An additional professor's wife was a faculty member at a campus 50 miles away. All of the faculty had wives who worked outside of the home; four of the wives had part-time jobs while the rest worked full-time. These employment patterns are in contrast to those at Eastern University where faculty tended to be married to nonacademics, and at Southern University, where a plurality of faculty had a stay-at-home wife. And, as I discuss in the next section, in part these employment patterns might be attributed to the institution's well-established dual-career hiring program.

PROGRAMS AND POLICIES

For male faculty, Midwestern University's policies match and exceed those available to Western University faculty. The campus offers all faculty the opportunity to extend the tenure clock following the birth of a child. Male and female faculty can extend the tenure clock one time for one year, although they must indicate that they have substantial child-rearing responsibilities to be eligible to do so. Like Western University, the campus also

provides a modified duties policy in which faculty are released from teaching duties for one semester following the birth of a child. Much like the
tenure-clock extension, faculty must certify that they have significant caregiving responsibilities in the home. Faculty are eligible to take one semester
of release for each child born. If both parents are faculty, both are eligible
to access the modified duties policy. Given that Midwestern University was
noted for hiring a large number of dual-career academic couples, such a
policy is critically important for ensuring that both women and men have
access to leave policies and points to ways that the university is trying to
decouple gender from parenting. One administrator also shared that faculty
are able to use the modified duties policy for life events other than the birth
of a child, such as caring for a sick relative. However, these circumstances
were not noted in the written policy, making learning about this provision
more difficult for faculty in need.

Midwestern University also has a well-established emergency backup
childcare program in which any employee or student can call an outside
service to come take care of a sick child if the parent has a meeting or
obligation that cannot be missed. Unlike many of the other initiatives on
campus, this program is subsidized by the provost's office. Staff members in
the university's work/life office shared that more than 1,300 employees had
registered for the service and more than 100 had used it in the previous
year. The campus offers numerous other policies and programs, including a
group of faculty from the sciences and social sciences who conduct search
committee training to highlight the importance of family-friendly policies
in hiring practices.

Midwestern University was also noted for having a robust dual-career
hiring program that was operated both by staff at the provost level and
administrators at the college level. This web of responsibility was reflective
of other work/life issues on campus where many efforts were decentralized.
Unlike Western University in which modified duties were subsidized by the
provost's office, Midwestern University has decentralized much of the implementation of its work/family policies. Although leave policies are mandated
at the university level, the dean of each school is responsible for finding the
funding to pay for teaching replacements for a semester when faculty are on
leave. Such a structure makes campuswide cultural change more difficult.

As one administrator shared, the dual-career hiring program has been
relatively successful in that the campus was able to offer accommodations to
50% of all spouses looking for employment in both academic and nonacademic appointments. Furthermore, she shared that while dual-career hires
historically treated women as the "trailing" spouse, an increasing number of
women were the initial hires, seeking appointments for their husbands. Several of the fathers discussed how Midwestern University's dual-career hiring

practices ultimately ensured that they stayed at the institution. One father explained how he and his wife were both considered for jobs in another city, but "that didn't work out in the end because they didn't want to hire two people." In contrast, Midwestern University created a position for his wife. Not all of the dual-career hires are necessarily ideal positions; many tend to be short-term fixed appointments that rarely turn into tenure-track positions. Given its location in a relatively isolated college town, administrators at Midwestern University seemed to recognize that in order to recruit and retain outstanding faculty, the campus needed to offer employment assistance to spouses.

Family-friendly policies were evident throughout campus. A well-established work/life office runs several campus childcare centers that offer 500 spots to children of faculty, staff, and students. Furthermore, the office identified and trained additional childcare providers in the community out of recognition of the fact that the university's childcare center could not accommodate all interested employees' children. The campus also runs a Campus Helpers' program that matches students looking for work with faculty and staff who need help with childcare and other home projects. Through its leave policies and other programs, Midwestern University has created the conditions to facilitate a culture that supports faculty with families.

CENTRAL ADMINISTRATION

Midwestern University has relied on central administrators' support for family-friendly policies for more than two decades. In 1990, the then-president formed an advisory committee to provide feedback on how to improve policies directed at women and employees with families. Under that president's tenure, the group played a significant role in advocating for increased maternity leave and other work/family demands. While the committee still serves in an advisory capacity, its power seems to have faded as subsequent presidents have "kept a distance from it," as one administrator told me. While Midwestern University's president may no longer play as central of a role in advocating for work/family policies, there is still evidence of central support for family-friendly initiatives in various pockets throughout campus.

Many of the Midwestern University faculty were able to rattle off the policies that the campus provides. Although policies exist at the institutional level, their execution differed dramatically from school to school. Many fathers were aware of the policies available for their use and tended to characterize the general institutional climate as family-friendly. About three fourths of the fathers were aware of the policies such as tenure-clock extensions, modified duties, and emergency backup childcare. One father described the frequent emails he received promoting various accommodations:

I think I would call it a family-friendly institution because you often see emails again talking about the services for families. Those things are relatively prominently advertised. In fact I just got one last week about merging of family kinds of services that's going to happen over the next six months. They always send a very positive tone I think.

The fact that the university prominently publicizes its accommodations suggests that it has institutionalized family-friendliness into its culture. Another father explained how important the policies were to his happiness at Midwestern University:

The child-friendly policies of the administration . . . are now about 10 years old. Having them has made this kind of a utopia for raising kids at least in my view. I don't know what other places are like, but the ones I've encountered are not like this.

Many of the fathers felt that they were fortunate to work in an environment that both had policies on the books and encouraged faculty to use them. However, not all professors described the climate as family-friendly. One father in a professional school shared stories about the pressures that early career faculty face from more senior faculty about the necessity of prioritizing work over family. He described one female department chair who told a female assistant professor who had children: "You have to hire a babysitter and you need to be in here on weekends or you're not going to get tenure." The faculty father went on to conclude, "Those kinds of stories are common enough and exchanged enough so that, to me, the true transformation to sort of a family-oriented enterprise has not been accomplished." These conflicting narratives characterized life at Midwestern University. Unlike on other campuses, there was less discussion directly of the role of the provost or vice provost in enforcing policies. While certainly some staff members in the provost's office were critical in facilitating dual-career hires, the deans of various schools carried much more power in promoting the use of policies on the campus. As a result, there were some differences in climate based on school.

Like Western University, Midwestern University also received a national award to help the campus promote family-friendly practices. Unlike Western University, however, Midwestern University's grant only focused on faculty in particular disciplines. Initially, the grant focused on faculty in two schools: (1) arts and sciences and (2) engineering. Part of the grant involved the creation of the faculty group responsible for search committee training on the importance of highlighting family-friendly policies when speaking with candidates. This group initially only included faculty in the science, technology, engineering, and mathematics (STEM) fields, although later added faculty in the social sciences, and still later business. Faculty in the first two groups of disciplines have seen the most transformation, in part, an administrator suggested, due to school leadership:

> The two [Engineering and Arts and Sciences] . . . have been very invested in this program. The deans . . . have committed both resources and their leadership and time and all those things and I think the impact's been real. I think the impact anywhere else is very little because there isn't that kind of—partly they weren't always the target but I think in general there hasn't been that kind of leadership anywhere else.

This administrator went on to explain how these departments have used the grant to create a climate that supports family-friendly issues. This grant and its resulting effects proved to be pivotal in shaping the experiences of faculty at the department level.

Department-Level Support

Of all four of the institutions, Midwestern University departments evidenced the most variance by department or school. While there was variation at Eastern University, the variation was larger at Midwestern University simply because there were even more generous policies that faculty did or did not feel like they could use. Men in some departments felt quite supported in accessing family-friendly resources while some in other departments felt that only women were supported and some in still other departments felt that neither men nor women were supported. While not universally true, faculty in schools that had been involved with the implementation of the campuswide grant focused on family-friendly practices tended to report deans and climates that were more supportive of work/family issues for men and women while faculty from other departments were less likely to report as positive support.

The group of schools that struggled the most with work/family issues was the health sciences. An administrator described the culture of several of the health science schools as "awful" in terms of recognizing faculty members' outside demands. She partially attributed this characterization to the demands faculty were under to generate money (through research and seeing patients) that those in other disciplines do not face. Faculty members' descriptions tended to confirm this. One father felt that the university was family-friendly, but that his school was not. "I don't get the sense that the president of the university and the president's immediate executives are quite so money-oriented as this school is incredibly money-oriented. That really bugs me." This orientation had significant implications for how faculty felt that they should spend their time. I expand on these disciplinary differences in the next chapter, but suffice to say that even Midwestern University had pockets in which family-friendliness was a concept that applied to faculty in other departments, but not to their own.

On this campus, some departments' faculty equated family-friendliness with women's issues. Said one father in a basic science department:

> This particular department . . . is one of the best in . . . the entire university of having the high proportion of working mothers. . . who are tenured professors. In fact there are more females on our faculty than are males, which is quite unusual I believe. . . . So from that perspective, there probably would be more understanding of the role of parenthood in this department than in many others.

This father suggested that the high number of women with children in the department meant that the department had to be family-friendly. While such claims are not necessarily true, faculty in this department described the family-friendly events that departments often organized, including department parties. Such stories were the exception to the experiences of many others in these schools.

In contrast, those faculty who came from other disciplines reported that their deans, department chairs, and colleagues were quite supportive of men taking advantage of institutional leave. Several fathers used the modified duties policy in order to spend time with newborn children. One father said that "there wasn't even a blink" from his dean or colleagues about using the policy because "every single male junior professor—and there are several of them now with kids—has taken that paternity leave off." Fathers accessing leave in his school had become the norm. Similarly, a father in another department was told that he would not experience any consequences for taking paternity leave. Additionally, in his department, children make more frequent appearances and might even attend faculty meetings if childcare plans fall through.

In sum, the Midwestern University culture is not as consistent as cultures on other campuses. While faculty on each of the four universities reported variations in the existence of a family-friendly culture, differences were most pronounced at Midwestern University. All faculty agreed that Midwestern University and the town in which it is located offered a supportive environment in which to raise children. Living in a college town made child rearing easier. And, for its part, the campus provides a remarkable number of family-friendly policies. However, faculty across various schools reported varying degrees of being able to access policies. Were family-friendly policies targeted at women? At men? At no one? I turn to these disciplinary differences in detail in the next chapter. First, however, I review my portraits of these four institutions in light of Schein's (2004) framework and consider how the artifacts and values reflect different assumptions about the ideal worker and hegemonic masculinity and, by extension, suggest different degrees to which the gendered university retains its own hegemonic position.

Conclusion

In this chapter, I have presented portraits of the four universities and the ways in which fathers on each campus felt supported or constrained in navigating their personal and professional responsibilities. I primarily let the institutional portraits stand on their own, but in the concluding part of the chapter, I return to Schein's (2004) framework to examine what the various artifacts reveal about each university's values and assumptions related to the ideal worker and hegemonic masculinity; these levels of culture each reflect varying degrees to which constructs of the gendered university retain their stronghold on each of these institutions. Recall that artifacts might include physical environment, social environment, written and spoken language, and overt behavior. Furthermore, the literature has established that certain features reflect the father-friendliness of an organization, including the existence and past use of policies along with managerial and coworker support (Blair-Loy & Wharton, 2002; Bygren & Duvander, 2006; Haas & Hwang, 1995, 2007, 2009; Thompson et al., 1999). Each of these four elements (or artifacts, using Schein's [2004] terminology) was present on each campus and each artifact reflects differing values related to gender norms and faculty work. I first discuss these artifacts before considering how the differences in each reflect differences in values and assumptions, and ultimately, institutional culture.

LOCATION

The institution's geographic location played a role in shaping the degree to which fathers felt connected to their institution and colleagues. Certainly, each university's development is shaped by its environment. A campus in a small town will likely have different norms than a campus in a large city. And, in fact, Eastern University faculty reported seeking different types of support from their colleagues and institution than did faculty at Western

University. Many Eastern University faculty members explained that the institution's location in a large urban area meant that they did not come to campus as frequently nor did they seek to form close relationships with their colleagues. This lack of connection with colleagues also meant that they were less invested in each other's personal lives and families. Unlike Western University faculty who were noted for celebrating each other's major life events and including children in campus events, Eastern University faculty maintained a rigid separation between work and family. While location is an artifact, it also shapes other artifacts, such as collegiality and relationships among colleagues.

EXISTENCE OF POLICIES

As Schein (2004) suggested, written and spoken language reveals a great deal about institutional values and assumptions. What do policies suggest about each institution? All four campuses offer some formal policies to support faculty fathers. All offer fathers the opportunity to extend the tenure clock in the case of the birth of a child. All institutions but Eastern University offer faculty a release from teaching duties following the birth of a child. Midwestern University and Western University have additional policies and programs in place, ranging from emergency backup childcare to faculty advocates trained to discuss work/family policies. The existence of formal policies is the bare minimum that institutions need to be family-friendly. One might argue that by offering a tenure-clock extension as its only family-friendly policy, Eastern University is sending a clear message that the institution does not value family for either male or female faculty.

HISTORY OF POLICY USE

Having progressive policies is important, but policies are meaningless if individuals do not use them. On some of the campuses, male faculty reported a lengthy history of men accessing policies such as the release from teaching duties. In some departments at Midwestern University all early-career male faculty had used a release from teaching duties after becoming fathers. Similarly, many men had accessed the policies at Western University. Because faculty saw that their colleagues had used the policy without penalty, they were more willing to do the same. However, faculty fathers at Southern University reported feeling hesitant to use the policies, as if the policies were intended for women's use, and not men's. In part, I suggest that these fears might have been due to the institution's location and messages they received from others about parenthood.

SUPPORT FROM ADMINISTRATION, DEANS, AND CHAIRS

Managerial support proves to be particularly critical in shaping a man's willingness to access leave. In the university environment, this translates to messages received from central administration and department chairs. While some men reported positive support from department chairs, others reported feeling that only women should use leave. Statements from administrators at Southern University echoed these claims who felt that work/family matters were a greater issue for women than men. Though the policies were available on a gender-neutral basis, the campus culture was one that did not actively support fathers. Many faculty at Western University pointed to the important role that central administration played in promoting work/family policies, not only through rhetoric, but also through financial support. By providing funds to departments to pay for a teaching replacement during a new faculty parent's absence, the university has removed finance as an obstacle to creating a family-friendly environment. While rhetoric is important, such actions suggest that the adage of "putting your money where your mouth is" remains true. Administrators at Eastern University were noted for a profound lack of action. Central administration sent few messages of support about work/family issues, which left many to conclude that parenting was a task that male and female faculty should navigate on their own. Although faculty at Midwestern University had extensive policies at their disposal, there was less agreement about the support of administrators. While the president and provost's office provided assistance, they were less noted than administrators on other campus for frequent displays of support. Midwestern University's culture was one where support differed by school. Some schools were noted as having deans and department chairs who supported faculty who wanted to take leave and promoted family-friendly cultures while other schools were noted for a profound absence of such support. These differences point to the fact that culture, particularly in large organizations, may not be uniform.

SUPPORT FROM COLLEAGUES

Faculty colleagues also play a pivotal role in creating a father-friendly culture. Faculty at Western University noted that their departments frequently organized social events that included children. Faculty in some departments at Midwestern University suggested the same. In contrast, faculty at Eastern University reported that they felt a significant separation between their work and home lives. Due to the institution's location, opportunities to include families in department events were few, thus leaving parenthood to be an event navigated on an individual basis. At Southern University, many men reported a bias against fathers who wanted to use institutional accommodations after the birth of a child, which points to values inherent in both ideal worker norms and hegemonic masculinity, thereby suggesting that caregiving duties are best left to women so that men can attend to their professional responsibilities.

The institutional profiles confirm that colleagues and leaders along with the existence of policies make a difference. Although these elements were all present on each campus, they operated in different ways. I summarize these differences in Table 3.1 and consider how they point to different values and approaches to reaffirming or challenging the ideal worker and hegemonic masculinity.

As Table 3.1 illustrates, each campus either reinforces or challenges traditional values around fatherhood and academic work, which has consequences for assumptions of the ideal worker and for the degree to which traditional definitions of hegemonic masculinity are produced and affirmed through campus culture. At Eastern University, for example, the campus reinforces traditional values around parenthood by not providing comprehensive family-friendly policies. By providing fewer policies than its national peers—solely an extension of the tenure clock—the institution has taken limited steps to help faculty balance work and family. The campus administrator acknowledged that the university was not a leader in the work/family movement and, in fact, suggested that those who accessed the tenure-clock extension were less likely to be successful at the institution than their counterparts who did not. The message on campus is that using work/family policies means that the faculty member is a less-committed academic and, by extension, not an ideal worker. In environments where ideal worker norms are the model against which all others are judged, traditional definitions of hegemonic masculinity will be valued as well. If the male ideal worker is one who works all the time and does not take advantage of even limited work/family policies, he will almost certainly adhere to traditional gender roles. Across the broader campus culture of Eastern University, both the ideal worker and hegemonic masculinity remain intact.

For many faculty, this disinterest in work/family issues translated to the department level as well. While some fathers reported that their chairs supported requests to use a tenure-clock extension, most reported negative or, at best disinterested, responses from their chairs and peers. At Eastern University, through the lack of action on the part of the administration, the status quo is reinforced as are traditional definitions of parenting, which typically do not create space for men to be involved fathers. The institution's location in a major metropolitan area also shaped the degree to which fathers felt free to balance work and family. Due to the campus location, many fathers reported that they did not look to the institution for social or

Table 3.1. Artifacts, Values, and Assumptions across the Four Universities

	Eastern University	Southern University	Western University	Midwestern University
Artifacts				
—Location	Urban	Small city	College town	College town
—Policy existence	Minimal	Present	Comprehensive	Comprehensive
—Actions of administration/chairs	Not family-friendly for anyone	Supportive of women	Very supportive of men	Dependent on school
—Actions of colleagues	Not sought out for support	Not supportive of men	Supportive	Dependent on school
—Children included in department	Almost never	Rarely	Frequently	Dependent on school
Values	—Separation between work and family —Institution bears no responsibility for helping faculty —Those who use policies are not serious academics	—Work/family issues are a concern for women —Reaffirming traditional gender roles	—Value work and family —Important to encourage men to be involved —Parenting is a concern for men and women	—Important to provide work/family policies —Institutional culture trumped by school culture
Assumptions	Reaffirms ideal worker and hegemonic masculinity	Reaffirms ideal worker and hegemonic masculinity	Challenges ideal worker and redefines hegemonic masculinity	Some schools challenge ideal worker while some reaffirm; hegemonic masculinity remains in flux

family support. Instead, they navigated family concerns on their own. Since faculty were dispersed throughout a large metropolitan area, the institution did not play as much of a role in their lives as Western University and Midwestern University did for their faculty and communities. This reduced role might also suggest that, even if support were provided by administrators and other faculty on campus, the campus might ultimately be unable to play as central of a role in challenging ideal worker and gender norms. The values of this campus—separation between work and family, lack of institutional responsibility for helping faculty navigate parenting concerns, and a belief that those who used policies were not serious academics—reinforce assumptions about the ideal worker and hegemonic masculinity.

Southern University's location made it a far easier—and cheaper— place to raise children. Unlike the majority of faculty at Eastern University who had working spouses, nearly half of the men interviewed at Southern University reported that they currently or had recently had a stay-at-home wife. Such a stereotypical division of labor reinforces ideal worker norms and traditional definitions of hegemonic masculinity. If a faculty member can rely on his wife to perform the majority of the care in the home, he can devote more of his time to work and less to his children, thus reaffirming traditional gender roles. The large number of faculty with a stay-at-home wife may also explain why administrators and faculty felt that work/family issues were more of a concern for female faculty. Female faculty are less likely to have a stay-at-home spouse, thereby creating additional burdens in the home that their male colleagues with wives at home do not have.

While some men at Southern University reported that they had used institutional policies, the majority reported that policies existed solely for women. Some worried that using policies might call into question their masculinity and violate appropriate roles that men and women are expected to fulfill. As a group, Southern University faculty adhered most closely to traditional definitions of hegemonic masculinity. They were most reticent to take leave or to support their colleagues who did so, though they certainly supported their colleagues who were mothers. Similarly, ideal worker norms remain intact, although in different ways than at Eastern University. While Eastern University upheld the ideal worker by expecting both male and female faculty to separate work from family, Southern University reinforced the ideal worker as being congruent with a masculine identity. On both campuses, men with parenting responsibilities lose.

Of all the campuses, Western University came closest to creating a campuswide environment that was supportive of fathers. In part, one could point to the college town location as creating an environment that made family life easier. The campus also had comprehensive policies that were targeted to and used by both men and women. But of most importance at

Western University was the support from central administration for family-friendly policies and the financial support provided. Fathers in a majority of departments reported that policies were regularly used by men with little concern. Unlike at Southern University, men at Western University did not express similar concerns over challenges to their masculinity for obtaining a reduction in teaching duties. Instead, for faculty at Western University, parenthood was redefined to include the needs of both fathers and mothers.

In addition, fathers in many departments reported great support for their personal lives. Many departments regularly included children in their events and it was not unexpected to see children in the halls. Recall the chair of the science department who encouraged his faculty to bring their children in at any time. All of these occasions suggest that the institution supports faculty with their personal and professional concerns. Furthermore, support is not solely reserved for women, but is extended to men as well. While the dimensions of faculty work have not changed (faculty are still expected to conduct research and publish prolifically), Western University comes the closest to challenging the notion of the ideal worker and redefining hegemonic masculinity to incorporate caregiving into the definition of fatherhood; in so doing, the institution also adheres the least to Acker's (1990) conceptualization of the gendered university. By providing institutional accommodations to all faculty and creating an environment in which men and women are encouraged to balance their home and work lives, Western University sends a message that parenthood is not just a concern for women and is not expected to take a secondary role to academic work.

Midwestern University had pockets that resembled Western University. The campus provides generous family-friendly policies, including a comprehensive dual-career hiring program that was particularly useful for the many Midwestern University faculty married to other academics. Furthermore, both mothers and fathers at Midwestern University were eligible for a complete release from teaching duties for a semester following the birth of a child. The gender-neutral nature of these policies suggests that the institution is actively trying to challenge ideal worker norms and hegemonic masculinity and, by extension, the gendered university.

However, because university policies were only centrally mandated—not centrally funded—the entire campus was not family-friendly. The national grant that the campus received a decade ago helped to promote family-friendly issues in several colleges on campus. Men in those colleges reported support for accessing leave and attending to family concerns. In contrast, men in other schools that were not involved in the grant reported more conventional norms around parenting and faculty work. Those in the health sciences reported significant pressure to bring in grants, which feeds into the burden of the ideal worker. While the campus provided a litany of very progressive policies (in some ways, more progressive and comprehensive than those at Western University), the absence of strong declarations of support at the university level and the absence of a central fund for subsidized leave meant that only pockets of the campus supported involved fathers. These disciplinary differences were not present solely at Midwestern University, but simply more pronounced. As I discuss in the next chapter, while institutional culture is important, disciplinary culture and norms also shape work/family norms. Given that behaviors and actions on the campus differed among schools, the degree to which ideal worker assumptions were challenged similarly differed. Fathers in some schools reported shifting gender norms while those in others reported that traditional roles and the separation of work from family remained intact.

The different experiences of men on each campus reflect different gender norms and underlying assumptions about the ideal worker and adherence to hegemonic masculinity. Though enacted differently, assumptions of the ideal worker are evident on each campus. Men on each campus, too, strive to embody a particular form of masculinity, although the values associated with ideal fatherhood differ from campus to campus. At Eastern University, all faculty are expected to be the ideal worker; the institution provides little assistance to men or women who want to balance work and family. The university assumes that faculty will find ways to accommodate their parenting demands. As such, there is little institutional concern with challenging traditional definitions of hegemonic masculinity. Traditional gender roles are important for maintaining ideal worker norms. Of mothers and fathers, one might suspect that faculty mothers might be expected not to adhere so rigidly to traditional gender roles in order to fulfill the demands that the university places on them.

The personal lives of many Southern University faculty fathers are built on traditional gender norms and the ideal worker; men work while women provide care for children at home. Neither administrators nor other faculty on campus challenge ideal worker norms or hegemonic masculinity. Women are expected to be the primary users of family-friendly policies, thus reinforcing traditional divisions of labor. At Western University and in some pockets at Midwestern University, the ideal worker and traditional gender roles are being challenged as men are expected to access leave policies and be involved with their children. These environments have the potential to nurture a new definition of hegemonic masculinity, one that values caregiving as a part of fatherhood. Certainly, disrupting the ideal worker is challenging at a research institution, which is predicated on constant work and innovation by its faculty. Doing away with such norms may be the only way to achieve gender equality both inside and outside the home.

Given that ideal worker norms and traditional definitions of hegemonic masculinity are still present to some degree on each campus, none has truly succeeded in creating a nongendered university. At Southern University, for example, Acker's (1990) conception of the gendered organization retains its stronghold in that men express hesitation over using institutional policies for fear of having their masculinity questioned. Western University may come closest to disrupting the gendered university as the campus has moved toward a culture in which men who use institutional accommodations do not have their masculinity challenged by colleagues or administrators. In this environment, due to the disappearance of divisions along lines of gender and supportive interactions with colleagues, new identities—those that value a more inclusive masculinity and challenge the ideal worker—are created and reinforced and, in the process, help to disrupt gendered organizational culture.

However, a pessimist might suggest that Western University will never completely succeed at casting off the constraints of the gendered organization. This is partially due to the fact that the university still operates in a gendered world, interacting with other universities, agencies, and organizations that embody the gendered organization. The constraints of gender will also remain intact because culture is never uniform. Campuses will always have areas that diverge from the institutional norm. One particularly powerful difference stems from disciplinary culture, which is the focus of the next chapter.

CHAPTER 4

Disciplinary Culture and the Ideal Worker

Faculty members hold membership in a variety of cultures; they are simultaneously members of their profession and are affiliated with their discipline, institution, and department. Some faculty may also identify as members of subdisciplines or interdisciplinary workgroups. Although faculty members hold allegiances to several groups, many argue that faculty members hold primary allegiance to their discipline (Austin, 1990; Becher & Trowler, 2001; Clark, 1987; de Zilwa, 2007). As Becher (1994) suggested, "disciplinary cultures, in virtually all fields, transcend the institutional boundaries within any given system" (p. 153). While one might not readily be able to articulate the difference between faculty members at two state universities, the contrast between the chemist and the historian is much easier to pinpoint. Furthermore, the chemists at these two state universities will find themselves in similar contexts and contending with similar norms. To reiterate Becher, although they are physically located in different universities, disciplinary culture transcends institutional boundaries. Each discipline has a unique culture that conveys messages to faculty about what behaviors and attitudes are valued. Implicitly included in that list are norms about fatherhood.

In this chapter, I discuss the role that disciplinary culture plays in shaping the degree to which navigating family concerns is valued for male faculty. As in the previous chapter, I use Schein's (2004) framework of artifacts, values, and assumptions to examine the culture of each discipline and understand the degree to which gendered organizational norms reify the ideal worker and hegemonic masculinity. In this chapter, I highlight how artifacts related to social environment, overt behavior, written and spoken language, and technology both reflect and simultaneously shape values and assumptions.

The conditions of and expectations associated with faculty work in each discipline shape the degree to which men are free to take an active parenting role in their children's lives. In particular, the nature of faculty work, the department chair, and other faculty colleagues contribute to creating a disciplinary culture that either supports or undermines notions of involved fatherhood and the ideal worker. Before turning to the details of the lives of the men in this study, I provide an overview of the literature on important disciplinary differences related to the nature of faculty work and the role that department chairs and colleagues play in shaping culture.

STRUCTURE OF WORK

On a practical level, the type of work performed by the chemistry professor differs from the work performed by the historian. As Becher (1994) outlined, scientists tend to perform work in teams consisting of academics, postdoctoral researchers, graduate students, and undergraduate students. Conducting science cannot be a solitary undertaking. In contrast, faculty members in the humanities typically work in isolation, surrounded by texts. Such differences not only lead to differences in research productivity, but they also mean that faculty members are accountable to a myriad of constituents each day. While a biologist might need to be on campus to conduct her research in a lab and to supervise those who work for her, the English professor tends to write alone and might be more productive if he is surrounded by books in a library. While such distinctions are basic and frequently ignored, they have consequences for a faculty member's daily life.

Disciplines also differ in the degree to which faculty seek or depend on external funding to conduct research (Becher, 1994; Clark, 1987; de Zilwa, 2007). While the English professor does not need a grant to deconstruct a text, the biologist can conduct very little research without large amounts of funding. Some disciplines expect faculty to seek out external funding while others depend on external funding for daily operation. While disciplines in which faculty secure external funding typically have greater status than other disciplines, these demands often place additional stress on faculty members to prioritize work at the expense of home.

Research and teaching obligations also vary by discipline. While faculty members in the sciences are the most research productive, those in the humanities and social sciences typically spend less time on research. According to the 2004 National Study of Postsecondary Faculty (NSOPF), a significant discrepancy exists in the amount of time that faculty members in various disciplines spend engaged in teaching, research, and service (National Center for Education Statistics [NCES], 2005). At research universities, faculty members in the natural sciences spend nearly 40% of their time engaged in research while faculty members in education spend just 24%

of their time conducting research. These variations inevitably lead to differences in status; faculty in disciplines that are noted for conducting more research typically hold greater prestige than those in less research-productive disciplines. This emphasis on research productivity also has implications for the amount of time faculty members are able to devote to their responsibilities outside the academy, including their children.

Time spent teaching also differs by discipline. As one might guess, faculty in more research-productive disciplines tend to spend less time engaged in teaching. In his profile of faculty in different academic disciplines, Clark (1987) suggested that the typical biology professor teaches only one semester per year and often shares a course with a colleague. In contrast, the social scientist is more likely to have a full teaching load of two courses each semester. These varying teaching obligations have consequences for the way in which faculty can spend their time. Those in disciplines who teach less often produce more research, the currency that is valued by the institution.

PEOPLE IN THE DISCIPLINE

While the importance of the structure of work cannot be overlooked in shaping the culture of a discipline, the composition of a discipline also helps determine what attitudes and behaviors are valued. Particularly appropriate to this chapter is the gender composition of a discipline; male-dominated disciplines may embrace values different from female-dominated disciplines. Different disciplines are noted for having a preponderance of either male or female faculty. According to the 2004 NSOPF, engineering remains the most male-dominated discipline where 90% of faculty at four-year institutions are men. The natural sciences and business follow closely behind; men account for 77% and 73% of faculty in these disciplines, respectively. The humanities is approaching gender parity; 59% of faculty are men whereas 41% are women. In contrast, education is noted as being a female-dominated discipline where 58% of faculty are women (NCES, 2005).

The composition of a discipline ultimately leads each culture to embrace different values. In earlier work (Sallee, 2008, 2011), I argued that graduate students in engineering are socialized into a gendered discipline that values competition, aggressiveness, and women's domination. In contrast, graduate students in English are socialized into a discipline that values reflexivity and challenges gender norms. Students do not learn these norms in a vacuum; rather, they are transmitted to them by faculty and others in the discipline. These differences in gender norms also translate into different values placed on the importance of balancing work and family.

Several studies of nonacademic organizations have found that the percentage of men and women shapes how frequently employees access family-friendly policies (Blair-Loy & Wharton, 2002; Bygren & Duvander, 2006; Haas & Hwang, 2007). The general consensus is that men who work in male-dominated organizations are less likely to use leave (Bygren & Duvander; Haas & Hwang). For example, Haas and Hwang found that companies with higher proportions of women reported that managers and coworkers reacted more positively to male employees taking leave. Female-dominated companies created an environment in which men were encouraged to access family-friendly policies. In another study of one major financial corporation in the United States (Blair-Loy & Wharton), the findings were reversed. The authors found that women who worked in male-dominated workgroups were far more likely to use family-care policies than women who worked in female-dominated workgroups. These trends might be related to contrasting expectations and gender roles for men and women. These studies have particular implications for STEM fields and other disciplines traditionally dominated by one gender or another. These findings suggest that men in science and engineering may be less likely to take leave than their colleagues in the more gender-balanced English department.

In addition to the gender composition of the discipline, the literature also suggests that other faculty and the department chair play a considerable role in shaping disciplinary culture. As theories of socialization suggest, newcomers to an organization or a department are socialized to adopt appropriate norms, values, and behaviors in order to fit in (Tierney & Rhoads, 1994; Van Maanen & Schein, 1979). Theories of socialization have suggested that those who fail to adopt appropriate norms will not succeed or will choose to leave the organization. Existing organizational members play a critical role in the socialization process. In colleges and universities, other faculty members are noted for their roles in helping to transmit values and reinforcing existing norms.

As I discussed in the previous chapter, the department chair, in particular, is frequently noted for playing an important role in shaping culture. As the link between administrators, faculty, and students, the chair is responsible for advocating for the needs of faculty to administrators and transmitting administrative directives to faculty in the department (Seagren et al., 1993). The chair also plays an instrumental role in faculty hiring and evaluation (Hecht et al., 1999; Seagren et al.). Although faculty may have considerable autonomy in shaping their work lives, chairs can exercise authority in faculty evaluations. Through their support of some faculty and resistance to others, chairs can send powerful messages about what behaviors are valued in the department.

In sum, each discipline is populated by faculty and staff with distinct identities. The types of work performed in each discipline and reliance on external funding lead disciplines to develop their own distinctive cultures. The engineering faculty member who works in a predominantly male department and conducts much of his research in collaboration with others finds himself in a different department than the foreign languages faculty member who is in a more gender-balanced department and spends her time conducting research in isolation. These differences both shape and are shaped by disciplinary culture. But what of work/family balance? How might disciplinary culture shape the degree to which navigating work and family issues is valued by other faculty and how might disciplinary culture reflect and reinforce assumptions of the ideal worker and traditional norms of masculinity?

For the purposes of this chapter, I grouped participants into one of three broad areas: the humanities and social sciences; sciences and engineering; and the professional schools. Professional schools included a diverse cluster of schools, including law, business, medicine, and dentistry. I follow in the footsteps of Becher and Trowler (2001) who suggested that disciplines could be placed into one of four categories—hard-pure, soft-pure, hard-applied, and soft-applied—based on the nature of knowledge in each discipline and scholars' concern with application of findings. Becher and Trowler suggested that these differences lead faculty members in various disciplines to organize their lives and their work in different ways. As the stories in this chapter suggest, these differences do indeed lead to different ways of thinking about the compatibility of work and family.

In total, 21 fathers came from the humanities and social sciences, 27 from the sciences and engineering, and 22 from the professional schools. Faculty members' institutional location determined in which of the three categories they were grouped. For example, at one institution, several faculty members were in a basic science department that was housed in a medical school. As a result, these faculty members were categorized as professional school faculty. In contrast, faculty members in the same basic science discipline on another campus were not located in a medical school and therefore were categorized as faculty in the sciences and engineering. I ultimately made the decision to categorize faculty in this way because the culture of the college or school plays a significant role in shaping faculty work lives and attitudes.

Although I join a long line of others who posit that disciplinary culture is the primary organizing feature of faculty life (Austin, 1990; Becher & Trowler, 2001; Clark, 1987), institutional location also shapes faculty experience. As I explored in the previous chapter, engineering faculty at Eastern University had different experiences than their counterparts at Western University. Clearly, institutional location matters. However, my aim in this chapter is to explore discipline as another location of importance. Given that disciplinary culture transcends institutional boundaries, my contention in this chapter is that the culture of a discipline matters nearly as much as the culture of an institution.

Some might find it helpful to analyze men's experiences at an even finer level—such as comparing the experiences of Eastern University engineers with Western University engineers. But the data could be disaggregated even further—as computer engineers find themselves in a different context than civil engineers. However, due to space limitations along with limitations of my sample, I have categorized men into larger disciplinary groupings. I contend, however, that the differences between the civil engineer and the computer engineer are minimal compared to the differences between the civil engineer and the management professor.

As a whole, men in the social sciences and humanities reported working conditions and colleague support that facilitated their involvement in the home. In contrast, many men in the sciences and engineering as well as the professional schools contended with workdays and disciplinary norms and values that precluded similarly active parenting. While there are certainly some similarities within each disciplinary grouping, there are also some differences among fathers' experiences. Not all men in the humanities and social sciences reported working conditions that facilitated their involvement in the home whereas some men in the sciences and engineering found ways to structure their days to engage in care. In this chapter, I present portraits of life in each discipline. I highlight the role that the structure and nature of work along with department chair and colleague interactions play in shaping the degree to which participants are able to balance work and family and the extent to which norms of hegemonic masculinity are reified or challenged. To provide further evidence of the differences between the lives of faculty in each discipline, I begin each section with narratives highlighting the experiences of two professors, both on campus and in the home.

Humanities and Social Sciences

Simon, a full professor in the social sciences, became a father later in life. He has two daughters, one in preschool and the other in elementary school. He typically wakes up at 6:00 A.M., about 45 minutes earlier than the rest of his family, to get a start on administrative work, such as answering e-mails from colleagues and students. From 6:45 to 7:30 A.M., which he labeled "the point of no return," he helps his wife get his daughters ready for the day and off to school. He then heads to campus where he spends time preparing for class, doing research, and performing administrative work. Two days a week, he stays on campus until 5:00 P.M. before heading home while the other three days he leaves either at 1:30 or 3:00 P.M. to take care of his elder daughter and shepherd her to piano lessons and other after-school activities. While he occasionally performs a few hours of work in the evenings, he says that he works far less than he did before becoming a father.

Simon described his department as very family-oriented. There are a lot of faculty and graduate students with school-age children. When the department has parties, many children attend—so many, in fact, that the department now rents a bounce house for them. The parties, he explained, "are very kid-friendly events." He also mentioned that parents occasionally bring young children to department seminars and lectures. Simon described the department as very flexible in terms of scheduling teaching times and being cognizant of people's schedules when scheduling meetings. As he summed up, "I don't think that the department . . . short of not expecting us to do our jobs, could be much more facilitating in relation to people having families and having children."

Antony is an assistant professor in the humanities with a toddler daughter and another child on the way. The semester of our interview, he was on a research leave guaranteed to all assistant professors in his discipline. His days typically start between 6:30 and 7:00 A.M. when his daughter wanders into the room to wake her parents. He and his wife spend the morning making breakfast and getting their daughter ready for daycare. Due to financial constraints, they can afford to have their daughter in daycare only between 9:00 A.M. and 4:00 P.M. Antony typically takes his daughter to daycare at 9:00 A.M., returns home to research and write, with an hourlong break for lunch, before leaving at the end of the day to pick her up. He tends to spend time on the weekends catching up on department e-mail or reading an occasional article, but does not spend a lot of time writing.

Antony was exceedingly positive about his department's climate toward parenting and children. He recalls telling his department chair about his wife's second pregnancy and being greeted with support. "I thought he was going to do cartwheels. He was just so cute. He jumped out of his chair, hugged me, and [cheered] 'Ahhh!' " His colleagues have been similarly supportive; faculty in the department often host baby showers for expectant faculty mothers and fathers. They also bring food to each other after the birth of a child. Antony felt very supported by his colleagues, though he worried that there was some bias throughout the larger campus culture toward fathers who used parental leave policies.

These two professors' experiences point to some commonalities among the experiences of men in the humanities and social sciences. First, participants were likely to adhere to a nonstandard work schedule. Note that neither man was in the office from 8:00 A.M. to 5:00 P.M. In addition, both spoke about the support they received from departmental colleagues and leaders to create an environment that they felt supported them in navigating personal and professional demands. I use their experiences as a starting point to discuss those of other men in these disciplines.

Structure of Work

Faculty in the humanities and social sciences have considerable flexibility in how they schedule their workdays. They were the most likely to report non-standard work hours and engaging in childcare during the day. Six of the 20 fathers in these disciplines reported scheduling their work hours in ways that were most conducive to their productivity and to their family's needs. The faculty reported that they needed to plan only around their teaching obligations because they could conduct their research from most places. Unlike their peers in the sciences and engineering and many of the professional schools, those in the humanities and social sciences tended to teach two classes a semester.

Despite these fixed teaching obligations, fathers in these disciplines were less likely to report being in the office from 8:00 A.M. to 6:00 P.M., but rather arrived slightly later in the morning and left slightly earlier in the afternoon. Many of these same men reported working for several hours at night on a regular basis. Neither Simon nor Antony maintained standard hours in the office; however, both reported working outside of standard work hours as Simon did in the mornings and Antony did on weekends. In some ways, these fathers both adhered to and reframed ideal worker norms. Although they may not have been in the office throughout the workday, many continued to work after hours, thus fulfilling the ideal worker contract. However, many simultaneously challenged the ideal worker by taking care of their children at times that many of their peers were at work.

While several of the humanities and social sciences faculty reported leaving work mid- to late afternoon several days a week to care for their children, several others shared that they were responsible for childcare for several full days each workweek. One father worked on campus from 8:00 A.M. to 6:00 P.M. three days a week and took care of his infant son the other two days. During those days, he reported that he did not get much work done.

> MARGARET: So, you said that you watch him two days a week. . . . Are you getting any work done on those days? [The father laughs] Sorry, that was a silly question.
>
> FATHER: Uh, . . . no . . . he's also not sleeping a lot right now, because it's a pretty exciting time. So . . . I used to be able to get

like a few things done. Like I taught this summer too, and I could get some, you know, like grading or whatever done. Stuff that basically doesn't take an enormous amount of [intellectual energy]. . . . Like, my work is not like the kind of work that some people do. It requires like blocks of time . . . undisturbed, where it's thinking time.

While this professor was able to structure his time to care for his son, he found that he sacrificed productivity, both on the days he engaged in care and on other days when he was in the office due to sleepless nights. Another father commuted from out of state and was in the office only three days a week. Another father with three young children was able to be on campus only from 9:30 A.M. to 3:00 P.M. daily because his childcare responsibilities demanded more of his time. While these men's experiences may seem like exceptions, they point to the fact that the humanities and social sciences allow men to conduct their work anywhere. An English professor may very well be off campus but still working, whereas the same may not be true of the biologist. This flexibility in where they perform work gives these fathers more leeway in shaping their schedules to be more involved in their children's lives without penalty.

PEOPLE IN THE DISCIPLINE

It was not simply the flexibility of their workdays that allowed fathers in the humanities and social sciences to be more involved with their children, but also the support they received from department chairs and faculty colleagues. Of the three groups of disciplines studied, the humanities and social sciences faculty reported environments and interactions that were most conducive to balancing work and family. Recall Simon who described that his department parties were so family-friendly that they included bounce house rentals and Antony who reported that colleagues brought meals to each other following the birth of a child. Similarly, many faculty reported that their department chairs were supportive. Such characterizations were common across all four campuses.

Department chairs were generally noted as being supportive in three ways, by (1) making public declarations of support about parenting; (2) encouraging faculty to use institutional accommodations; and (3) making small shifts in procedures that helped alleviate work/family conflict. Antony's chair reacted with excitement after learning that Antony and his wife were expecting their second child. Antony described how the same chair made an announcement at a department retreat about the birth of Antony's first child.

> After everybody had introduced themselves . . . he said, "Oh and there is a new arrival in the department, our latest member," and then he mentioned [my daughter] and I thought that was pretty cute because to remember to mention this in a somewhat impromptu fashion, it means that somehow he cared enough to and even if he prepared ahead of time—to say I need to do this—(1) it's not easy to remember, and (2) it showed me that it was important enough to him that it would be appropriate to mention in an academic setting at that particular moment.

For Antony, having his department chair publicly acknowledge his daughter's birth sent an important message that family was and would continue to be valued in his department.

Second, fathers praised their department chairs for encouraging their faculty to use institutional work/life accommodations, such as extending the tenure clock for a year or, on some campuses, gaining a release from teaching duties for one semester. One faculty member applauded his current and past chairs for their efforts in advocating for faculty to use the institutionally available release from teaching duties. As he noted, the release from teaching duties "has now become fairly standard. You know, people don't ask questions about it. They just see it as a standard way [of operating]." While this comment might be true for his department, it was not always true across other disciplines. Another professor explained how his department chair did not give him the option not to use the institution's tenure-clock extension:

> It wasn't really a choice. The chair at the time said, "you get this—you'd be a fool not to take an extra year." There's no added workload or there's no change of opinion of a person for taking that year so he's like—basically it was weird—he came down and said, "I basically signed you up for it. Just sign the bottom here please. Why wouldn't you do it? They're offering this—this is the university policy."

This department chair helped his faculty member navigate the requirements to take leave by preparing the paperwork to be signed and articulating his support for the professor using this policy. Not all chairs, even in the humanities and social sciences, were as supportive of their faculty. One faculty member lamented that his chair did not inform him about a tenure-clock extension policy on his campus, despite the fact that the chair knew about the recent birth of the professor's child. While it might not necessarily be the department chair's responsibility to inform faculty of existing policies, his lack of information stands in stark contrast to the actions of the supportive department chairs noted earlier.

Third, in addition to supporting faculty's use of policies, chairs were noted for intervening in other ways to accommodate logistical demands of daily life. One chair was praised for shifting teaching schedules to accommodate a faculty member's family demands. The professor had been asked to teach a 9:00 A.M. class on Mondays, Wednesdays, and Fridays, but doing so would conflict with getting his children to school and allowing him to be at work on time. Understanding this, his department chair allowed him to shift to teach at 9:30 A.M. on Tuesdays and Thursdays, creating a course option where one did not exist before. Simply shifting departmental structures in small ways allow faculty members more control over their work and home lives, which challenges the notion that the ideal worker norm must always prevail. Many of these chairs clearly communicated to faculty that making space for family in their lives was acceptable. In these cases, organizational structures shifted to accommodate personal responsibilities rather than expecting faculty to adjust their personal lives to meet the needs of the organization.

While department chairs play a significant role in shaping the departmental climate, so too were other faculty noted for promoting an environment where parenting was accepted. Faculty support was delivered in two ways: via conversations with colleagues about the challenges in balancing competing demands and through more formalized events, such as baby showers and other festivities, which conveyed that children were valued. Overall, most faculty in the humanities and social sciences suggested that their departments were those where children were welcome—and, depending on the time of year, faculty children just might be seen in the hallways.

Many fathers in these disciplines discussed how much they valued being able to talk to their colleagues about being fathers and professors. As one man explained, he felt better knowing that others in the department had similar experiences:

> There are a lot of parents here, and there are a lot of father professors whose wives also have careers, just like me. So I don't have to explain myself. It's very obvious to most of my colleagues what's going on, and they are very understanding.

Simply knowing that others were in similar situations brought this faculty member relief. Another dad shared how he often compared parenting notes with his colleagues:

> Some of my best friends are also my colleagues [and] have kids of the same ages as mine. And, there are many of us in the same situation here. So, that leads to an environment where most of them are facing similar problems, and then you compare notes with your

kids and what do you do with your kids, and at school, and things like that, so in that regard it makes life easier.

This dad discussed how he valued chatting with his colleagues about work issues, but turned to the same group of men about parenting concerns. Another professor turned to a colleague for advice when he found out his wife was expecting:

> When I found out my wife was pregnant, one of the first people I talked to was another male colleague who has kids, and I talked to him about, "So like, what did you do?" "How was this for you?" "What should I be thinking about?" And he's the one who gave me the idea of doing what seemed crazy, of teaching right after the birth. He said, "you'll kind of get by on fumes, and then you'll have more time later," and things like that.

Having a colleague in the department with whom to discuss family concerns helped this father figure out how to craft a schedule after his son's birth that made the most sense for his family and his career. It also underscores the ways in which gender and masculinity are constructed in concert with others. These men all reported that their colleagues served as sounding boards about their parenting concerns, which suggests that these men valued incorporating caregiving into definitions of hegemonic masculinity. At the very least, it suggests that taking a more active role as fathers was valued in these disciplines.

In addition to having conversations about parenthood, participants also discussed the ways in which their colleagues mobilized to support each other during happy and difficult times. Several professors noted that their colleagues had developed a tradition of having baby showers for expecting mothers and fathers, as Antony shared about his own department. In one department, colleagues frequently brought meals to the new family. Several faculty members reported feeling supported by their colleagues in taking advantage of formal and informal institutional accommodations after the birth of a child. One professor, who became a father during his second semester on the faculty, shared how his colleagues stepped in:

> Everybody said, "listen, we'll cover your classes. Take at least two weeks for you to get yourself situated and sorted out." I know it doesn't sound like a lot, but when you're trying to get your classes up and running and figure out who you are or where you fit in in the department. . . .

Although it is lamentable that this professor was not able to draw on an institutional accommodation for a release from teaching duties, he was still grateful for the fact that his colleagues provided help, sending a message that becoming a father was a fact to celebrate. Each of these examples underscores the ways that faculty in these disciplines embraced fatherhood as a part of faculty life, thus subtly challenging traditional notions of masculinity that call for a separation between the breadwinner and caregiver roles.

Many faculty across these disciplines shared that seeing children in the department, both for formal and informal events, was not uncommon. Some departments, like Simon's, even rented a bounce house specifically to entertain the children. Others simply created environments where children were welcome. In addition, some faculty reported that they occasionally brought their children to the office, particularly during school breaks. One father described how both faculty and staff in the department have brought children in:

> We have a new faculty who has a kindergartener; we have [another person] who has got a kindergartner and a 1-year-old. I've got my three guys. The graduate students bring their kids in. It's fine. It's not distracting and we all work pretty hard. In fact, one of the admin assistants—she has her son in today. So I think we're really good about making sure the guys stay engaged and don't go running up and down the halls and [being] distracting, but people don't—I've never heard anyone complain and say. "What are these kids doing here?" It's definitely not that kind of department.

This father described his department as one in which children were welcomed and regularly appeared with minimal impact on the productivity and work environment of others. While this department seemed to have a more constant presence of children, faculty across departments shared that it was not unusual to see children walking (and occasionally running) through the halls.

In summary, the culture of the humanities and social sciences is one that allows fathers to be involved parents. The flexible structure of their workdays and the fact that many can perform work from home allow men to shape their daily schedules around those of their children. In addition, department chairs and faculty colleagues play pivotal roles in creating environments in which parenting and professing simultaneously is valued. While men in these disciplines certainly performed work, they may challenge the notions of the ideal worker and traditional gender roles that are both deeply entrenched in academic work. Not every faculty member in these disciplines had positive experiences, such as the one faculty member whose chair knew nothing about parental leave policies. However, most faculty reported feeling supported in navigating work and family. The same sentiment did not translate to the faculty in other disciplines.

Sciences and Engineering

Adam is a full professor in the sciences and engineering. He and his wife, who has a high-level position with the state government, have a 13-year-old son. Because working for state government is far less flexible than academia, Adam notes that he is responsible for their son in the late afternoon. To accommodate these demands, Adam typically wakes up at 5:00 A.M. and is usually in the office by 6:00 or 6:30 A.M. before his wife or son are awake. Like many faculty in the sciences and engineering, Adam has a light teaching load and does not teach every term. The term of our interview, he was not teaching and was writing papers and grant proposals to garner more funding. He typically stays on campus until about 4:00 or 4:30 P.M. when he heads home to drive his son to one of the many sports and music activities in which he participates. Adam noted that he used to coach his son's sports teams when his son was younger and would leave work midafternoon. But since his son's expertise has now surpassed his own, Adam has been relegated to the role of chauffeur. After his wife gets home from work and makes dinner, Adam helps clean up and then both husband and wife help their son with homework—Adam with math and science and his wife on-call for writing, social studies, and Spanish. After homework, the family typically goes to bed and starts again the next day. Adam finds that he is generally too tired to perform too much work at night, but will occasionally work on weekend mornings.

Adam praises the flexibility of the faculty career for allowing him to be as involved with his son as he is. He remarked, "Because I have this schedule, it's allowed me to do some things that other fathers don't. . . . His friends' dads, who I know well, they just wouldn't have time to coach, in some cases." However, children rarely make an appearance in the department, either physically or in discussions. He mentioned that faculty members almost never bring their children in, other than briefly, when picking up something. He also said that there are rarely discussions of the impact of parenting on faculty work and demands. As Adam stated, "I think most of my colleagues have done a pretty good of balancing things well enough so there's not a discussion of [how family affects their work]." Work/family issues are left to the individual to navigate and figure out how to keep family from conflicting with career. Despite the significant role that he plays with his son,

Adam discussed family-friendliness in relationship to the challenges the few women in the department face.

Henry is an assistant professor in the sciences and engineering with a preschool-age daughter and an infant son. His wife works full-time as a scientist in a nonacademic position. Because he has such young children, Henry finds that he spends much of his time wishing for more sleep. He typically wakes up with his children between 5:30 and 6:00 A.M. He and his wife spend the next two hours getting the children ready for the day before they each leave for work; his wife brings their son to one daycare while Henry brings their daughter to another. Because they live in the metro area of a large city, his commute typically takes about 45 minutes, putting him at work around 8:30 A.M. He spends his day managing students in a lab, writing grant proposals, and preparing for classes, and laments that he never has enough hours in the day to get everything done. He typically leaves work around 4:30 P.M. to pick up his daughter and make the grueling drive home. Many faculty at his institution reported planning their lives around traffic. Once home, his wife cooks dinner and they get the kids ready for bed. They switch off nightly on who does the bedtime routine with each child. Henry's daughter likes for him to stay until she falls asleep, at which point he does, too. He reports that he typically will wake up anywhere between 11:00 P.M. and 2:00 A.M. and work in the middle of the night to catch up on work tasks. As a result, as he described, "my sleep schedule is completely . . . there isn't a sleep schedule." Since the demands of rais-ing two children have made working on weekends close to impossible, Henry reports that these middle of the night sessions are the only time when he can get extra work done.

Henry is wildly effusive about the family-friendliness of his depart-ment. He described that many other male faculty (there were few female faculty in the department) have children and that others face the chal-lenges of balancing work and family. Henry frequently talks with one of his colleagues about raising children; the two lament that their lives would be easier if their wives did not work, as was the case for some of the senior faculty. Henry's department chair informed him that he would be expected to use a tenure-clock extension policy; his chair took care of the paperwork for him. Despite this support, children rarely made an appearance in the halls of the department or at department events. As Henry said, "there's more of a boundary between the personal and the workplace."

These narratives already point to differences between the lives of men in the sciences and engineering and those in the humanities and social sciences.

Men in the sciences and engineering report adhering to a more standard workday. Even though Adam leaves campus at 4:00 P.M.—a rarity among many of his colleagues—he is typically in the office by 6:30 A.M. Unlike their colleagues in the humanities, both Henry and Adam discussed the importance of applying for grants as requisite parts of their work. There were some significant differences in the degree to which each man described his department as family-friendly; Henry felt that his department was quite friendly and his chair had encouraged him to use a tenure-clock extension while Adam noted that there was simply an absence of discussion of work/family issues in his department. Despite these differences, both men felt that their departments provided them with the leeway to be successful in their careers. In the remainder of this section, I again discuss the structure of a typical workday and interactions with department colleagues and chairs as indicators of the degree to which the culture of the sciences and engineering supports or thwarts men interested in balancing work and family.

STRUCTURE OF WORK

Men in the sciences and engineering reported working traditional work schedules, arriving in the office around 8:00 A.M. and leaving around 6:00 P.M. For example, one father biked his children to school on the way to work, arriving around 8:45 A.M. He typically stayed at work until 6:00 or 7:00 P.M. An assistant professor reported arriving at work at 6:00 A.M. and leaving at 5:00 P.M. Other dads worked from 8:00 A.M. to 5:00 P.M. with a few additional hours of work in the evenings. However, 5 of 26 scientists reported leaving work around 3:00 or 4:00 P.M. fairly regularly to go care for their children. One father coached his daughter's softball team and left work at 4:00 P.M. three days a week to get to her 5:00 P.M. practice. Another scientist left work at 3:00 P.M. two days a week to go swimming with his son. These fathers are in the minority; the majority of their peers did not report making similar modifications to their schedules. The scientists and engineers were more likely to maintain typical hours in the office than their counterparts in the humanities and social sciences.

In part these differences might be attributed to the nature of work in the sciences and engineering; unlike the types of research that many social scientists perform, scientists and engineers are more likely to conduct research in labs and with large cadres of graduate students and postdoctoral scholars. For example, one assistant professor had a lab with two undergraduates, a graduate student, a postdoctoral researcher, and a technician; parts of his days are spent providing guidance to various lab members and answering questions. This professor, like others, needs to be present and available in order to keep his research going. In addition, many scientists described the demands they faced to bring in large research grants. Adam described devoting his time to writing grant proposals to bring in new funding. Other fathers reported similar pressures. As one professor explained:

> the pressure of this job, I think, is a lot different than maybe just other academic positions, in the sense that I have—as somebody said—mouths to feed, and if I don't bring those grants in, you know, potentially my door's shut.

While scientists might be able to write grants from any location, many felt an added pressure to bring in funding as a requisite part of maintaining a scientific career. These extra demands may compel faculty to spend more time working than their counterparts in other disciplines, thus continuing to fulfill the norms of the ideal worker.

People in the Discipline

While many of the faculty in the humanities and social sciences reported supportive department chairs and colleagues, there was less commonality among the scientists and engineers. Some reported supportive chairs and colleagues, whereas others shared stories of chairs and colleagues who discouraged them from using institutional policies. In some ways, these contradictions make sense as many faculty described their departments as neither supportive nor unsupportive.

When asked to describe the department climate regarding parenthood and children, many faculty concluded that the department was positive simply because some of their colleagues had children. For example, one professor explained, "I think [the department climate] is good, actually. . . . Everyone I can think of right now has raised kids. . . . We've got some people on the younger side now too, who've got kids." Similarly, another professor stated, "I think just about all of my colleagues are parents." For these men and others, the family-friendly department is one in which faculty have children.

Other male faculty equated queries about family-friendliness with women's issues. Several professors in different engineering departments proudly touted that their departments had high numbers of women. Their responses suggested that women-friendly meant family-friendly. Another father explained his perception of the family-friendliness of the department. "I think it's quite understanding. I actually haven't talked to too many mothers in the department about that situation. But, they seem pretty comfortable with it." Although all fathers were asked about their perceptions of the family-friendliness of their department, for some this was clearly an issue that was predominantly associated with women, thus underscoring traditional gender roles in which parenthood simply meant motherhood.

Overall, however, departments might be characterized as being neither overtly supportive nor unsupportive. As one science and engineering faculty member neatly summed up, "I can't say the department climate is one that's not supportive. I just think it's not explicitly supportive." Another professor in the same discipline echoed the sentiment:

> I think our department has been able to sort of take a very relaxed approach with no questions asked, no consideration of that. There's not pressure to do one thing or the other. We don't get snide comments about someone not keeping up their side of the bargain. So, it's just almost an absence of discussion, really. . . . There's a clear bar of what you have to do to . . . advance, and . . . it's publishing and do grants to a lesser degree.

As this participant noted, familial obligations did not enter into the conversation. Rather, colleagues assumed that faculty members would be able to balance their own commitments and not have their work affected. However, by not having conversations about work and family demands, ideal worker norms and norms of hegemonic masculinity remained intact as the status quo continued to apply. Another father described the department climate as "very accepting of and fostering of people with parental responsibilities, but in a very casual way." Faculty in these departments did not report department chairs making overt statements in support of balancing work or family nor did any discuss baby showers being thrown for new parents. Instead, the support was reserved for tragic circumstances.

Department chairs in the sciences and engineering were described in conflicting ways. Some faculty noted that their chairs encouraged them to use institutional accommodations, as Henry's chair did. Another professor reported that his chair encouraged him to use his institution's semester's release from teaching duties. (The faculty member opted not to because he did not want to give up teaching the class and risk losing the class forever to a colleague.) Another father reported that, like his counterparts in the humanities and social sciences, his chair allowed him to adjust his teaching schedule to be more conducive to his childcare obligations in the mornings by shifting a course from 8:00 to 9:00 A.M.

While some department chairs encouraged their faculty to use institutional accommodations, others discouraged them from doing so. An assistant professor recounted his conversation with his department chair who was unaware of the automatic one-year tenure-clock extension policy available to all assistant professors who became parents. The faculty member reported that his chair discouraged him from using the policy, and he had to convince his chair that requesting to use this policy was not out of the ordinary, but standard for the campus. Another assistant professor shared how his department chair gave him incorrect advice about university expectations for the tenure process:

> When I had my kids, my department chair, who has two kids him-self . . . he said, "You should teach a normal load of classes. You can do whatever you want, but make sure you teach like you're supposed to, so when you go up for promotion, we can write a let-ter that says you taught what you were supposed to teach, right?"

Such advice directly contradicts the institution's recommendations that suggest that faculty take a release from teaching duties for a term to allow parents to bond with their children and, if possible, spend some time on their research, the real currency involved in tenure and promotion. Instead, this chair advised his faculty member to maintain his teaching load to appear as if he were continuing to perform as an ideal worker. As these examples suggest, while some department chairs pushed for their faculty to use institutional policies, others provided misinformation or balked at policy use.

While few faculty reported chairs or colleagues as overtly supportive like their counterparts in the humanities and social sciences, faculty noted that both department chairs and colleagues were supportive in extreme and tragic circumstances with their children. Several science and engineering faculty contended with their children's serious illnesses and praised their department chairs for their support. One father spoke appreciatively of his colleagues who brought meals to his family after one of his children was hospitalized:

> It actually was kind of nice to come home and have a meal that was delivered. So, people in the department were taking a round for making those types of meals, including the department head and stuff. . . . I really did appreciate it and respect that.

Another faculty member praised both his department chair and his colleagues for their support when his newborn was hospitalized and subsequently died:

> [My department chair] basically said, "Just tell me what you need." So, in a sense, I mean, I guess that's a blank check. But, so you know, he said, "If you need people to cover [your classes], you know we can do this." . . . He basically said to me, "Let me know and just give me the book and if I have to, *I'll* go teach it."

The faculty member was exceedingly grateful for the support. He shared that his colleagues also were supportive:

> The department basically said, "Tell us what you need." So, they were great in that respect. Granted, that's sort of an extreme situation as opposed to a normal kid's birth, so under sort of stressful times like that, you sort of see people's true colors, and I thought the department did well in that respect. Under extreme duress, they definitely . . . came through. And that wasn't the chair, that was everybody—most of the people in the department.

This professor offered praise for his colleagues and chair for supporting him in unimaginable circumstances. But what should be noted in these stories is a pronounced absence of celebration of positive life events. There were no stories of baby showers or meals brought to new parents. For the scientists, parenthood was an event that everyone needed to learn how to navigate on their own.

Much as there was an absence of celebration, so too was there an absence of purposeful inclusion of children in department events. Some departments had adult-only socials. A few faculty reported that children and families were welcome at department parties. One department had occasional gatherings at a bar to which parents brought their children. However, no department reported going to the extremes of some of the humanities and social sciences of creating child-focused department parties.

Similarly, there were mixed reports whether faculty in the sciences and engineering felt that they could bring their children to work. One father reported that his children would be "too disruptive." Another father said that people were "too busy" to bring their children in and "have them sit somewhere for any prolonged time." Adam reported that he never saw children in the department whereas some fathers reported that occasionally mothers might stop by with their children to say hello. In these departments, work and family remained separate; when children did appear, it was often briefly and with their mothers, thus reinforcing traditional gender roles.

However, some fathers noted that they had no qualms about bringing their children in to meetings or during school vacations. One father described bringing his children to department seminars and meetings:

> When my oldest son was very young, I just brought him along to meetings all the time. I think at that time because I was chair of [a campus group] I had meetings out of town, all around the state. . . . I just dragged him along when he was a baby and I was chair of lots of committees here, so he would just lie quietly.

This father later reported that while he had no problems bringing his sons with him to meetings, he had spoken with women who did not feel as though they had the same privilege. Another father brought his one-year-old to a department meeting that he could not miss. Although his department chair said it was "not a problem" for him to bring his son, the professor reported that his son was fussy, so he had to step out of the meeting. "I think," he said, "most faculty members were probably okay with that, but it was distracting and I would not do it again." For many fathers, bringing children to campus was an option of last resort and not one that others in the department necessarily supported.

To sum up, the sciences and engineering have a distinctly different culture from the humanities and social sciences. Since some departments are supportive and others are not, one might conclude that the disciplines are defined by an absence of discussion of family-friendly issues. Faculty fathers are free to structure their time in the manner that they see fit to balance work and family, but only within the constraints of the standard workday and the demands of bringing in grants that are imposed on this group of faculty. In other words, as long as faculty continue to live up to the expectations of the ideal worker, they are free to structure their familial obligations in any way they feel appropriate. However, with the absence of support toward shifting organizational and gender norms, both remain intact.

Professional Schools

Kenneth is a first-year assistant professor in a basic science depart-ment located in a medical school. He and his wife, a research assistant professor in the same department, have an infant son. Kenneth's days start at 6:30 A.M. when he gets up with the dog and makes coffee for his wife. He tries to spend at least 30 minutes with their son in the morning before leaving for work. He tends to arrive in his lab between 8:00 and 8:30 A.M., and he spends time setting up experiments and supervising his small but growing staff. His wife arrives in the lab a few hours after he does; the two of them work together until 5:00 P.M. when Kenneth leaves to pick up their son from daycare. His wife stays a bit later. These staggered schedules allow them both to get work done. They spend time together as a family in the evenings. After putting their son to bed around 8:30 P.M., the two professors pull out their laptops and work for a couple of hours. Both he and his wife tend to go into the lab at least an hour each day Saturday and Sunday. As Kenneth explained, "the lab's still small enough now that I usually go in for at least an hour each day over the weekend, just to check things out, make sure nothing's exploded, the freezers are still running, stuff like that."

He and his wife often bring their son with them on the weekends and switch off watching him while the other person works. While both of them work a lot, Kenneth reports that they work far fewer hours than they did as postdoctoral researchers. Nonetheless, he, along with other faculty in the department, feel the pressure from the dean of the medical school to focus on "funding, funding, funding."

Kenneth is very positive about the department, labeling it "subjectively very positive." He mentioned that many other assistant professors in the department—both male and female—have young children and senior faculty have older children. As a result, he said "everyone knows what it's like to be in that position." Children are frequently invited to department parties and they often bring their son to department seminars. They have occasionally had to juggle childcare demands for department events, such as graduate student recruitment, at night and on weekends. Sometimes, he and his wife bring their son with them and experience no repercussions for their decisions. Despite the family-friendliness, Kenneth is unaware that the institution provides policies such as tenure-clock extensions if they decide to have a second child.

George is an associate professor in a school of business. He and his wife, who is a stay-at-home mom and active volunteer in the schools, have two sons in elementary and middle school. Like many of his colleagues across the professional schools, he could be working in industry and making significantly more money but has chosen a career in academia to spend more time with his children. Nonetheless, he maintains an exhausting schedule. He typically wakes up early in the morning and comes to campus early. Given that he has some administrative responsibilities, his days are filled with department meetings, research meetings, teaching obligations, and interactions with industry. He makes sure to go to the gym on his way home from work, arriving home around 5:00 P.M. He makes dinner for the family, helps his children with their homework, and spends a few hours working before going to bed. As part of his job, George frequently travels for work to meet with business leaders and to collect data. The month after our interview, he expected to be gone for at least 12 days.

George is enthusiastic about the culture of the department. "There's some people here that not only run [the department] like a business, but run it in a very, very collegial way," he said effusively. He described the department as one in which colleagues worked very hard; he estimated that most faculty work upward of 60 hours a week. It is not uncommon, George suggested, for colleagues to e-mail ideas back and forth at 10:00 P.M. Although faculty work hard, they also put a focus on family and fulfilling obligations to children. Department parties regularly include

children. George is not aware of the institution's family-friendly policies,
though freely admits that he has never had occasion to use them.

Kenneth's and George's narratives paint stories that both echo and differ
from the stories of their colleagues in other disciplines. Both men maintain
fairly traditional hours in the office and work many hours at night and on
weekends. George's experiences are similar to many faculty in the professional schools in that he compares his job with potential career options outside
of the academy, concluding that faculty life allows far more opportunities to
be involved with children. Both men reported that their departments were
supportive of faculty with families and regularly included children in department events. However, neither man was particularly knowledgeable about
family-friendly policies the institution provided. Yet, as the experiences of
these two men and their peers across numerous professional schools attest, in
some ways these disciplines still provided ways for faculty to accommodate
their work and family demands. I again consider the nature of faculty work
in the professional schools along with the ways in which department chairs
and colleagues predominantly support, but sometimes hinder, faculty fathers'
efforts at balancing family and career.

STRUCTURE OF WORK

Faculty in the professional schools tended to mimic their colleagues working
in nonacademic professions by maintaining a fairly typical work schedule.
Whereas almost half of faculty in the humanities and social sciences maintained hours outside of a typical 8:00 A.M. to 5:00 P.M. schedule, nearly all
of the professional school faculty—18 out of 20—reported keeping to fairly
traditional work hours. Aside from occasionally staying home from work to
care for a sick child, few reported devoting any time during standard work
hours to child-rearing responsibilities.

What was particularly notable for men in the professional schools
was their gratitude for the flexibility and autonomy that the faculty career
afforded them. Many argued that they were able to spend more time with
their children than if they had worked outside the university in a number of
fields, including law, business, and medicine. As one law professor succinctly
stated, "I certainly spend a heck of a lot more time with my son than I
could as a practicing lawyer." Another law professor concurred:

> I think it's less challenging than if I had stayed and been a practic-
> ing lawyer. I think that would have been far more difficult, and I
> would have been coming home consistently at a much later hour,
> and spending less time with the kids.

Faculty in other professional schools also noted that their academic careers allowed them more time to spend with their children, as did this father in a business school.

> So maybe I'd be in a consulting job and earn much more, but then I wouldn't have the time to interact with my kids. So I think the value that I put on that is much higher. So I'm very happy about the job that I'm doing.

In addition to praising the faculty career for allowing them time to spend with their children, many faculty in the professional schools also noted that they relinquished the opportunity to earn higher salaries by turning their backs on the private sector.

On top of gaining more flexibility, many professional school faculty noted that they had more autonomy in academia than they would in other professions. One former practicing lawyer noted that, in his previous career, he "had little control over [his] life on a day-to-day basis . . . in small petty ways." He had to respond to the demands of his supervisor and did not have the freedom to pursue projects that interested him. Another faculty member in business also noted that he appreciated not having to answer to a supervisor as he would if he worked in the corporate world.

Although working in academia has its benefits, some of the structures of the professional fields continued to influence life for many faculty members in these disciplines. Faculty in these disciplines were far more likely to report having meetings and teaching obligations in the early mornings or late afternoons and evenings. Several faculty in various health-related fields reasoned that meetings had to take place after hours to accommodate the schedules of clinical faculty. One professor explained:

> We are revamping the curriculum so the meetings are between 5:00 and 6:30 in the evenings or between 7:00 and 8:00 [in the mornings]. . . . I don't think it's malicious or anything like that. The problems are because they are teaching the clinic, the faculty, that's the time they can have everybody together, before the clinic starts or after the clinic finishes. So that's the reason [for] that, which I understand is very practical. But at the same time, it shows very little sensitivity to people with children.

Because this father worked in a field with both research and clinical faculty, the only meeting time that everyone could agree on seemed to be times inconvenient to people with familial obligations. Other faculty noted similar concerns. Recall the faculty member from chapter 2 who tried to change the start time of a meeting from 7:30 to 8:00 A.M. with other faculty with no success.

In addition to after-hours meetings, some disciplines are increasingly offering courses at night and on weekends. One faculty member has accepted this new schedule as the new normal:

> Everybody teaches at all hours. We teach on weekends, evenings and that's something the market controls. If demand is there at those times and people are working and they want to take classes in the evenings, you have to go and teach in the evenings. . . . And I think those are market factors and so if you really want to be out there competing for the institution dollars, you have to do those things.

As this father noted, faculty in his discipline teach at all hours in order to respond to market demand. Such a schedule may lead to institutional competitiveness, but it certainly has consequences for faculty members' personal lives. It also suggests that faculty have no familial responsibilities, or at least can depend on their wives to provide childcare. Asking faculty to be ideal workers and teach outside of the standard workday has consequences for their ability to be involved fathers. Despite the intense work schedules that many faculty in these disciplines maintained, the majority held that they were satisfied with their work. In part, this might be attributed to their colleagues and chairs.

PEOPLE IN THE DISCIPLINE

Most faculty in the professional schools reported positive interactions with their department chairs and colleagues. While chairs were not noted for making public declarations in support of work/family issues as some of their counterparts in the humanities and social sciences did, these chairs were appreciated for inquiring about faculty members' children and supporting policy usage. Whereas the family-friendly department in the sciences was one where faculty had children, professional school faculty required a little more agency on the part of chairs. For example, several faculty noted that they appreciated how their department chairs would inquire about their faculty's children. As one professor shared, "the department chair asks me, you know, at least weekly what everybody's doing, how everybody's getting along. He keeps track of what season [of sports my kids are playing in]." This professor valued that his chair cared enough to inquire about his children.

Several faculty noted that their deans were particularly supportive. (Given the size of some of the professional schools, deans often took the place of chairs.) One faculty member took advantage of a release from

teaching duties after the birth of his child and recalled the response he got
from his dean when asking if he could use the policy: "I e-mailed the dean
and . . . he phrased his response in such a way as to not be just as 'so noted'
but 'that's great! Of course you should take paternity leave!'" This professor
felt well supported in using this institutional accommodation.

However, not all professional school faculty received such positive
support from their chairs. As one professor explained, colleagues warned
him that the department chair would react negatively if he were to have a
child. He described having to negotiate with his chair in order to not be
in the office full time after the birth of his daughter:

> We'd be out talking and we'd hear him say things about when he
> was a new parent, and his wife has never worked, and it was just
> never an issue. "I don't think I could do it again," is one thing I've
> heard him say. So, I knew and people had told me, . . . "You've got
> to be worried about how he's going to be when you have a child."
> But, luckily for me, . . . I really had a great relationship with him
> by the time that came around. I was his transition person. He said,
> "This can't work." [And I responded,] ". . . You'll see no change
> in my output. I will never keep you hanging on a project. But, I
> might not be here working on it." I'm willing to do it on my time
> at home at night, you know, whatever as long as I could go home.

The department chair adhered to traditional norms that expected faculty
members to be in the office with a spouse at home to take care of the children. This professor was able to circumnavigate these expectations and used
the relationship he had developed with his chair to work at home. However, the faculty member did not take leave after the birth of his daughter.
Rather, he continued to perform as the ideal worker, but simply worked from
a different location. The stories of overtly supportive or overtly negative
department chairs in the professional schools were few and far between.
Faculty were generally pleased when department leadership showed even a
passing interest in family-friendly issues.

Faculty colleagues in the professional schools were also remarked on
for being generally supportive of families, although less overtly than humanities and social sciences faculty. As one professional school professor stated,
"I don't want to say it's 'pro-family,' but it's 'appreciate family.'" Colleagues
indicated in many ways that they appreciated each other's families. Like
their counterparts across campus, some faculty reported valuing conversations with their peers about the challenges of raising children or the importance of family. One professor noted how his colleagues would intervene if
they saw that faculty was spending too much time with work to the neglect
of their children:

> If we were not spending time with our kids, I can think of at least
> five people that would sit down and argue with you for an hour or
> two to get it through your thick head that that's what you should
> be spending your time doing. . . . You know, it's just a lot of people
> who really value you. . . . And, they've been there, [they've had
> kids], so they understand and they get it, and say, "Well, of course
> you would need to go to that event."

Professional school faculty work long hours, but there was an always an
undercurrent of appreciation for their roles as parents.

Another professor noted that he frequently talked with his colleagues
about the challenges of raising children:

> I've had lots of conversations with people here about the chal-
> lenges of balancing. . . . To some extent I'm a little more open
> with women than men. Maybe that's like gendered or sexist on my
> part, I don't know. But there's an extent to which I haven't had as
> many of those conversations with men.

This professor sought out others in his discipline to discuss the challenges of balancing work and family. He is one of the few professors across
the entire sample to mention that he preferred having conversations about
balancing work and family with women. This preference might be due to
the fact that this father assumes a majority of the childcare in the home,
doing more than other fathers. Perhaps his concerns, therefore, resonate
more with those of other parents who are the primary caregivers, which in
most cases is women.

The majority of positive interactions were rooted in conversations.
In some cases, they were also rooted in actions. In many of the professional schools, faculty suggested that children frequently made appearances
at department events, but less frequently made appearances in the department. One professor mentioned that his department dedicated a play area for
children who come to department parties. Another faculty member reported
that a colleague hosts parties twice a year for the entire department at his
home, which is on a lake. He described the party as:

> a big cookout and volleyball and football and Ph.D. students are
> invited. Family is invited. Kids are encouraged to come. We try to
> do that kind of thing. Not as much as I think we should. We need
> to do more, but I think we work ourselves too hard sometimes.

This faculty member wanted the department to host more frequent events,
although he was pleased that there was some focus on family.

In addition to being welcome at department parties, children also occasionally made appearances in the departments themselves. Remember Kenneth who brought his son to his lab regularly. While such frequency might have been out of the ordinary, other faculty still reported that children could often be seen in the halls. One faculty member said that children "are a presence here. Lot[s] of people have them. People bring them around." Another professor noted that his colleagues had recently been asking when he was next going to bring in his young daughter. As one dad explained, "kids come in and see where their parents are working fairly frequently." As in other disciplines, some faculty mentioned that parents might bring their children in when a child was sick or scheduling conflicts prevented alternative arrangements.

For all of the faculty who discussed that children were welcome in the department and at department events, others suggested that their departments and colleagues were not at all family-friendly. One professor shared that many of his male faculty colleagues have unreasonable expectations about work and family life:

> I do think there are male faculty either who don't have kids, but even male faculty who do have kids but have wives that don't work, who have an expectation that . . . basically that your children shouldn't interfere with your work and you should be available and around regardless of the family responsibilities, which I think is ungenerous and not an accurate reflection of what their lives are like.

This professor discussed a split between the younger generation of faculty who tended to be in dual-career couples and more senior (male) faculty who had stay-at-home wives. This arrangement left some faculty with different expectations about how acceptable it might be for a faculty member to be an involved parent, thus underscoring how ideal worker norms in concert with hegemonic masculinity continue to define expectations for academic work. Some faculty in other professional schools mentioned that children were not welcome in the department or at department events. However, more frequently, departments reported welcoming the presence of children—either their physical presence at events or their presence in discussions.

Across professional schools, many faculty members evidenced a zeal for and, often, an all-encompassing commitment to their work. Yet how do these fathers differ from those in the sciences and engineering? In part, they are distinguished by their ties with professional fields. Although some men had never worked outside academia, they all had the specter of Life Outside of Academia as a point of reference. Many acknowledged that they were able to spend more time with their children than they could in other professional roles. Even though they tended to work as much as their colleagues across campus, they seemed to reflect a sense of gratitude that their choice to pursue an academic life freed them to embrace family life.

Conclusion

I began this chapter by describing the ways in which disciplines have frequently been thought of as cultures. Research has pointed to the ways in which the nature of work (Becher, 1994; Clark, 1987), the emphasis on external funding (Becher, 1994; Clark, 1987; de Zilwa, 2007), and the people within disciplines (Tierney & Rhoads, 1994; Van Maanen & Schein, 1979) each contribute to creating a disciplinary culture that values some attitudes and behaviors over others. Framed differently, each of these artifacts reveals different values and assumptions of the discipline. Among faculty fathers, I found that the structure of workdays along with behaviors of department chairs and colleagues simultaneously reflected different values and shaped the degree to which a discipline valued faculty making space for family. In other words, artifacts are both reflections of a culture's values and assumptions and simultaneously shape those values and assumptions. Such a statement aligns more with Acker's (1990) theory of gendered organizations that points to the ways in which individuals shape organizations just as organizations shape individuals. In this section, I consider how the experiences of these fathers underscore previous findings about differences in disciplinary norms and the ways that assumptions of the ideal worker as well as hegemonic masculinity continue to shape faculty life. As in chapter 3, I first discuss various artifacts across the disciplines before considering how differences in the artifacts point to different values and assumptions related to the ideal worker and hegemonic masculinity. I conclude by examining how these values and assumptions suggest the continued presence of gendered organizational values.

STRUCTURE OF WORK

As the portraits of fathers in these disciplines should make clear, faculty work differs across campus. A father in the business school will have different expectations on his time than a father in engineering. I use structure of work to consider a discipline's emphasis on external funding as well as how and where research is conducted. All of these issues are examples of Schein's (2004) artifact of technology, which focuses on how inputs are transformed into outputs (or, in this case, how research is transformed into publications). Some disciplines more than others rely on external funding

in order to conduct research. Fathers in the sciences and engineering discussed how constant pressure to bring in grants created additional stress
and demands on their time. To produce the research necessary for tenure
and promotion, faculty need to bring in external funding. Faculty in the
humanities and social sciences did not face similar pressures as most his-
torians and social scientists can write books with minimal funding. While
men in both disciplines face tremendous pressure to publish, those in the
sciences and engineering need to put in extra work to have the funds to
pursue publication.

The way that research is conducted in each discipline also points to
different values about work. In the sciences and engineering, the majority of research can be conducted only in a lab with other scientists and
scientists-in-training, whereas faculty in the humanities and social sciences
often conduct their research in isolation. These differences have significant
consequences. Because faculty in the sciences and engineering rely on a
team of individuals to conduct research, many men reported that they felt
additional pressure to keep bringing in external funding to support those
whom they employed. In some ways, this replicates stereotypical notions
of men as breadwinners discussed in earlier chapters. Additionally, because
scientists are frequently tied to their labs to conduct their research, they
have less flexibility in their daily schedules. Many also felt that they needed
to be present in order to provide guidance to their research teams. Note the
number of humanities professors and social scientists who reported that they
regularly left campus before 5:00 P.M. Men in these disciplines can and do
conduct their research anywhere, which gives rise to different disciplinary
cultures.

Finally, the structure of work in professional schools includes after-hours
demands placed on faculty time. Several of the men noted that their departments offered courses in the evenings and on weekends. Others noted that
their departments held meetings in the early mornings or in the evenings.
These practices all suppose that the faculty member has no other demands
on his time. Although many of the men in the professional schools objected
to this practice, they all felt grateful that their lives in the academy were
more flexible than their lives would have been if they had been employed
in the private sector.

PEOPLE IN THE DISCIPLINE

The people who compose a discipline play an important role in shaping
its culture. I contend that the degree to which a discipline is male- or
female-dominated shapes the degree to which fathers feel able to make
time for family. As I discussed earlier, the sciences and engineering along

with professional disciplines have been noted as being among the most male-dominated in the academy, whereas the humanities and many social sciences have more women (NCES, 2005). One might expect that disciplines with more men would be less concerned with parenting demands. Perhaps it is no surprise, then, that the humanities and social sciences were generally noted as being more family-friendly than the professional schools and sciences and engineering.

The socialization literature suggests that faculty within a discipline play a critical role in shaping the culture and transmitting messages about what behaviors are valued (Austin, 2002; Tierney & Rhoads, 1994). Faculty across the disciplines noted the ways in which their department chairs and colleagues either supported or thwarted work/family balance efforts. Faculty across all disciplines characterized their departments as family-friendly. In some departments, a supportive culture was one in which other faculty had children. Simply knowing that one could simultaneously be a father and a professor was enough for some. Others labeled their departments as supportive when their chairs inquired about their children's well-being, as noted by some faculty in the professional schools. For other fathers, such behaviors were important, but were not necessarily enough. Rather, disciplines that were noted as most supportive—typically in the humanities and social sciences—were those in which department chairs regularly advocated for faculty to take advantage of institutional accommodations and made frequent statements in support of families. Supportive departments were also noted as those in which children were welcomed into the department and faculty supported each other through frequent celebrations. While some faculty in both the humanities and social sciences and the professional schools noted that children might be seen in department halls, there was an added degree to which children were centered in the humanities and social sciences. Centering parenthood—and fatherhood, in particular—challenges the ideal worker by recognizing that being an involved parent is not a negative reflection on one's capacity as an academic. After Table 4.1, I discuss what the artifacts of each discipline reveal about the values of each discipline and assumptions regarding the ideal worker and hegemonic masculinity.

As Table 4.1 illustrates, the behaviors of faculty and structure of work in each discipline simultaneously point to and give rise to different values and assumptions. Before proceeding, it is once again worth underscoring that while artifacts point to different values and assumptions, they simultaneously shape those values and assumptions. For example, the fact that faculty in the humanities and social sciences have great flexibility in where they conduct their work allows different values related to work and family to bloom. As should be clear from the narratives, the humanities and social sciences are the disciplines that allow male faculty the most freedom

Table 4.1. Artifacts, Values, and Assumptions across the Disciplines

	Humanities and Social Sciences	Sciences and Engineering	Professional Schools
Artifacts			
—Structure of work	—Flexible work days —Research can be conducted anywhere	—Standard work days in office —Emphasis on external funding —Reliance on labs to conduct research	—Standard work days in office —After-hours teaching and meeting schedules
—Gender composition	Approaching gender parity	Heavily male-dominated	Nearly all male-dominated
—Actions of chairs	Evidenced support through (1) public declarations of support; (2) encouraged faculty to use policies; and (3) shifting procedures to alleviate work/family conflict	Mixed—some supported policy use while others did not	Mixed—evidenced support through (1) inquiring about children and (2) some encouraging policy use
—Actions of colleagues	Evidenced support through (1) conversations about family and (2) celebrations inclusive of family	—"A relaxed approach" —Other faculty had kids —Some equated family issues with women's issues	—"Not pro-family, but appreciate family" —Discussions with colleagues about family
—Children present in department	Frequently	Almost never	Occasionally
Values	—Important to encourage men to be involved —Faculty work and parenting are not in conflict	—Competition and hard work —Individual responsibility —Separation between work and family —Reaffirms traditional gender roles	—Autonomy is important —Family is important, but so is work —Faculty need to find ways to accommodate encroaching work demands
Assumptions	Challenges ideal worker and hegemonic masculinity	Reaffirms ideal worker and hegemonic masculinity	Reaffirms ideal worker and hegemonic masculinity

to navigate personal and professional responsibilities. In addition to the freedom faculty have to conduct their work anywhere, these disciplines are also marked by greater gender parity. These facts helped to create cultures with different values related to parenting and work. Faculty in these disciplines noted that their department chairs and colleagues supported both men and women who took on active caregiver roles. Department chairs were noted for recognizing births and for encouraging their male faculty to take advantage of institutional accommodations. Children were frequently included in department events and visited their parents at work. Many faculty appreciated that they could discuss work/family concerns with their colleagues. Given that gender is created through interaction with others, many of the men in these disciplines interacted in such a way to promote a new type of masculinity that incorporated caregiving into its definition. The culture in the humanities and social sciences is one that values men as active parents. Those in the discipline do not seem to see parenting and work as two domains that must necessarily be in conflict. In this way, the values and artifacts of the discipline suggest a challenge to assumptions of the ideal worker and hegemonic masculinity.

In contrast, the sciences and engineering along with the professional schools both adhere to more traditional values and, as a result, reaffirm ideal worker assumptions and hegemonic masculinity. Both the structure of faculty work along with the behaviors of those who populate each discipline help reinforce these values and assumptions. Faculty in the sciences and engineering typically need to be on campus to conduct their research they are tied to their labs in ways that their counterparts in other disciplines are not. These faculty also face tremendous pressure to bring in external funding. Such demands point to the value that those in the discipline place on competition and hard work. Faculty need to garner grants in order to do their jobs. Such constant stress feeds into assumptions of the ideal worker as an organizing structure for faculty life; hard work is how one demonstrates one's worth. Given that the sciences and engineering are largely male dominated, the absence of women creates a culture in which stereotypically masculine demands prevail.

Chairs and colleagues in these disciplines were not noted for either positive or negative behaviors related to family demands. Some faculty reported support from their chairs while others reported negative reactions. Whereas faculty in the humanities and social sciences praised their colleagues for celebrating personal events and discussing children, science and engineering faculty simply noted that their colleagues had children. The fact that one could be both a parent and a professor at the same time led faculty to label these departments as family-friendly. Some also suggested that their departments were family-friendly because women had children.

Equating parenthood with motherhood punishes fathers who want to take more active roles with their children by failing to challenge traditional gender roles and hegemonic masculinity.

Although some might have described the department as family-friendly, just how family-friendly the discipline truly was remains unclear. Children were rarely present in the department and major life events were rarely celebrated. In part, the nature of faculty research in the sciences and engineering made it less safe for children to be present. However, children were not just physically absent from these disciplines; they were metaphorically absent. This lack of consideration of family demands also points to the ways that family was considered to be an individual responsibility that needed to be navigated without help. By failing to provide support, those in the discipline simply reaffirmed traditional gender roles, thereby lending strength to the ideal worker construct. Of all the disciplines, the culture of the sciences and engineering supports both tenets of the ideal worker; faculty are expected to work at all times and to create a separation between work and family that reifies hegemonic masculinity and a gendered division of labor.

The culture of the professional schools also is one that fails to challenge the ideal worker or hegemonic masculinity. The structure of work in the discipline does not allow men the flexibility to engage with their children. After-hours meeting and teaching schedules encroach on personal time, but are considered to be a requisite part of the discipline. There was again mixed evidence as to whether chairs and colleagues in these disciplines supported men who were involved parents. Some chairs were noted for encouraging their male faculty to access institutional accommodations while others were noted for discouraging their faculty from doing so. Some men simply appreciated that their chairs inquired about their children. What loomed large for men in these schools was the fact that life in academia allowed far more personal and professional freedom than life in the corporate sector would have. Faculty in these disciplines valued the autonomy their academic careers brought them. For many, this value of autonomy translated to their personal demands as well. Despite ever-increasing demands on their time (such as after-hours meetings and teaching), faculty were expected to find ways to accommodate their personal responsibilities. Faculty in these disciplines felt that family was valued. However, this support often took the form of rhetoric that was unsupported by action. As a result, the notion of the ideal worker remained unchallenged.

Norms of the gendered organization remain evident throughout all three disciplines, although faculty in the humanities and social sciences came closest to challenging those norms. Given that gender is enacted through interaction, interactions among colleagues and chairs in various departments sent particular messages about the importance of faculty balancing work and family. In the humanities and social sciences, there was some acceptance of men being involved fathers. Policy use was supported by chairs and colleagues alike; men reported talking with their colleagues about how to balance work and family. The organization shifted in order to accommodate parental demands. While these disciplines are housed in particular gendered institutional contexts, the norms of each suggested progress toward disrupting the ideal worker, hegemonic masculinity, and by extension, the gendered nature of the university.

In contrast, the sciences and engineering along with the professional schools remained mired in gendered organizational contexts. Simply by being a heavily male-dominated discipline, the sciences and engineering almost had no choice but to remain gendered. Inside the academy, strict divisions remained along lines of gender as just a handful of women were employed in some departments. There were few signs that families were valued in these departments and when family-friendliness was acknowledged, it was often labeled a woman's issue. Conversations with colleagues and chairs reinforced this lack of support. Faculty were free to structure their own time in ways that were conducive to their personal demands as did a small group of scientists who regularly left work midafternoon to spend time with their children. However, they did so in the absence of support from their colleagues. Their efforts defied disciplinary culture and norms about appropriate roles for academics and men.

Similarly, the culture of the professional schools maintains a strict focus on constant work, which inevitably reinforces norms of the ideal worker and, by extension, the gendered university. Faculty in these disciplines maintained more standard hours in the office than their counterparts in other disciplines. Additionally, many reported working at all hours, such as George who exchanged e-mails with his colleagues late in the evenings. Although a few of these men's interactions revolved around fatherhood, such as the men who reported that their colleagues inquired about their children, the intensity of the faculty work schedules reinforce notions of the ideal worker, hegemonic masculinity, and the gendered university. Simply by being able to engage in work at all hours of the day points to the fact that these men have significant help with their child-rearing responsibilities. Additionally, such expectations suggest that others in the discipline are not interested in shifting the norms to accommodate external demands. Instead, through constant interaction with their colleagues, ideal worker norms and gender norms are created, re-created, and reified as institutional values.

The portraits that I have painted here suggest two conclusions. First, significant differences exist across the disciplines, which reflect an academy that, while united by an academic culture, is composed of many smaller subcultures. These disciplinary cultures ultimately create environments that either promote or hinder faculty efforts to be engaged parents and point to the ways in which the notion of the ideal worker remains dominant in many pockets of the university. Second, while faculty in the humanities and social sciences are in a discipline that permits more parental involvement, the situation is not yet one of equity. Although the discipline may be more father-friendly, disciplines are housed in larger institutional and national contexts. A father in the humanities and social sciences will have different experiences at Western University than at Eastern University. Furthermore, even the Western University professor is influenced by national disciplinary norms that play a considerable role in shaping the values on each campus. Until parenthood is valued across genders, disciplines, and institutions, the ideal worker and hegemonic masculinity will retain their stronghold on academic work and the identities of those who perform it.

CHAPTER 5

How Family Life Affects Faculty Life

In the previous chapters, I considered how various cultures shape men's ability to be involved parents, or how work affects family. In this chapter, I reverse the lens to consider how becoming parents affects men's work. Due to an increasing workload, the challenges may be more difficult than they once were. Today's faculty member is expected to teach courses, conduct research, perform service, seek grants, participate in professional organizations, and complete many other duties. As part of this increasing portfolio, tenure expectations have also increased (Youn & Price, 2009). Faculty members also work more than a standard 40-hour workweek. According to the 2004 National Study of Postsecondary Faculty, faculty members at four-year institutions reported working an average of 50 hours per week (NCES, 2005). As the increasing expectations and long work hours make clear, faculty work is indeed a "greedy institution" (Coser, 1974) that takes up a large amount of academics' energy. However, parenting is also a "greedy institution," which demands a significant amount of an individual's time. Faculty fathers may feel pulled in two directions—toward the expectations of the academy and toward the expectations of home. While early chapters considered how faculty norms shaped men's experiences as fathers, this chapter considers how men's status as fathers shapes scholarly engagement and work.

As I soon discuss, some fathers frequently compared themselves to their childless peers in terms of their research productivity. There was simply no way, they argued, that they could produce as much scholarship as those unfettered by familial responsibilities. For some, this comparison led to the conclusion that faculty work was incompatible with family life. An individual could not simultaneously be a good father and a good academic—or an ideal worker. One father shared that he "struggled with the fact that [he is] suboptimal in everything" he does. Another echoed these conclusions that he simply was not able to do a good job at being professor and parent:

> Well there's a sense of doing a B to B+ job at everything . . . if you've grown up being successful in academic endeavors and professional endeavors and being thought of as somebody who is good at what they do, you want to keep that up. And there is a great pleasure in being good at what you do and there is a great pleasure being at the table in interesting discussions and there is a great pleasure in your students liking the job you do and giving you good ratings and getting good feedback. . . . Similarly it is a happy, pleasurable, etcetera, thing to be—to feel like you're being a great dad. And guess what? You can't do both of those things to the A+ level. News flash! That for me has been one of the most significant complications of parent- and fatherhood.

This father believed that he was unable to excel at both of his roles, which led him to feel that he was not succeeding in either academia or the home.

Another father reiterated the ways in which home and work responsibilities influence each other:

> If you want to make it and you want to be the top in your field . . . I can't really see how you can successfully manage a healthy or functional family. I can't see it because you constantly have to be on the go. You constantly have to be reading and, at least in my field, you have to be out there and it's almost 24/7. There's people that do it and man I applaud them, but something has to give in that equation.

As this father points out, faculty seem to need to make a choice: either they can choose to be highly productive academics and less involved fathers or reasonably productive academics and involved fathers. Having children takes time away from work. Less time to work might mean, for some, less time to produce scholarship.

While every man who participated in this study was both a professor and a father, some wondered whether fatherhood was compatible with an academic career. In part, these musings were related to the experiences of most of the men who found pointed changes in their productivity after becoming fathers. While a few faculty found that they were more productive, many others lamented that they had less time to work and pursued markedly different lines of research than they had or would have if they were childless. It is these conflicts that I explore in this chapter. After I review the ways productivity and scholarly output might be defined, I turn to the experiences of the fathers who reflected on how their professional lives had changed since becoming parents. The changes in their productivity illustrate challenges to the norm of the ideal worker and, by extension, norms of hegemonic masculinity. I turn more explicitly to these concerns in this chapter's conclusion.

Defining Productivity

Many white-collar jobs, such as faculty work, gauge employee success not in terms of the number of hours an employee works per week, but in terms of measurable outputs, such as articles published, students taught, and so forth. And yet, often efforts seek to regulate how many hours a faculty member is in the office. Occasionally a university appears in the national news after a combative president or state legislature seeks to mandate how many hours a faculty member must be on campus. However, faculty work does not solely occur on campus during standard work hours, but often occurs at odd hours and on weekends. As such, there are often efforts to try to measure how many hours faculty members work. For example, for several decades, the National Study of Postsecondary Faculty measured how many hours faculty work per week and what percentage of their time they devoted to teaching, research, advising, and other activities. The last iteration, deployed in 2004, found that full-time faculty at doctoral-granting institutions reported spending 31% of their time engaged in research, 46% of their time engaged in teaching, and 24% of their time engaged in other undefined activities (NCES, 2005). Although faculty spend less than one third of their time on research-related activities, tenure and promotion decisions are based almost entirely on research output. Perhaps this explains some of the stress that faculty experience in trying to find enough hours in the day to produce scholarship.

While hours worked is one measure of productivity, publication count is a far more common measure of research productivity for faculty in most disciplines. Previous scholarship has defined productivity in different ways: some count solely the number of peer-reviewed articles published over a period of time (Fox, 2005) while others include conference proceedings, chapters, books, and other types of publications (Fairweather, 2002; Kyvik, 1990). The evidence from previous studies is mixed at best in terms of impact of children on research productivity. Some have suggested that children have no effect on productivity (Bellas & Toutkoushian, 1999; Cole & Zuckerman, 1987; Sax et al., 2002). Others have suggested that children increase productivity, either for all faculty (Stack, 2004) or for women only (Kyvik). And others argue that children reduce research productivity (Hunter & Leahey, 2010; Kyvik; Stack). Some scholars even have found contradictory findings—that children can increase or decrease productivity depending on faculty gender and children's age. I briefly review some of these studies to contextualize these fathers' experiences.

Some researchers have found that becoming a parent leads to increased productivity. Using data from the 1995 Survey of Doctorate Recipients, Stack (2004) found that the presence of children in the home is correlated with increased research productivity. Others have found that this increase in productivity may not occur for all faculty or occur for only a short period of time. Although their studies were conducted more than 20 years apart, both Cole and Zuckerman (1987) and Hunter and Leahey (2010) found that faculty members' productivity increases in the years surrounding the birth of a child. Cole and Zuckerman's participants experienced an increase in productivity over a three-year period from 1.5 to 2.7 papers per year. Hunter and Leahey's participants experienced similar gains during that period, leading the authors to speculate that such an increase might be due to extra effort to complete research in anticipation of reduced time to work postchildbirth.

Not all faculty experience gains in productivity after the birth of a child. While some scholars have found that children have a negative effect on all faculty members' productivity, others have found that the effects are more detrimental for female faculty. Kyvik (1990) found that women with children younger than age 10 produced 47% fewer publications than men with children in the same age group. Stack (2004) also found that women with young children published less than other women. In contrast, Hunter and Leahey (2010) found that children have a negative impact on all faculty members' productivity, although women may experience more long-term effects.

Scholars have also examined productivity by measuring the quality of particular publications, such as the rank or impact factor of a journal (Hasselback, Reinstein, & Schwan, 2000). Articles published in more prestigious journals are often assumed to be of higher quality and a greater contribution to research knowledge. Researcher productivity might also be measured by counting citation rates, or the number of times a particular article or book has been cited. In their study of productivity among faculty parents, Hunter and Leahey (2010) sought to determine what they labeled as the visibility of faculty members' research. The authors constructed a model that provided greater weight to publications that appeared in high-impact journals and to those cited by subsequent scholars. As with using impact factor as a proxy for quality, a high citation rate assumes that a particular publication has had a greater impact on the field. The authors found that becoming parents inhibited faculty members' rate of publishing articles in high-impact journals. Over their careers, those with children had 88% as many publications in prestigious journals as faculty without children. The authors suggested that while faculty may experience an increase in productivity immediately following the birth of a child, the long-term consequences for both men and women leads to fewer publications in high-impact journals over time. In sum, research productivity might be determined in several ways—in terms of number of hours faculty spend engaged in research, in the number of publications (peer-reviewed or otherwise) produced, or in the perceived impact of a particular publication. Each of these metrics has implications for the work of the faculty fathers in this study. I discuss them in the remainder of the chapter.

Hours Worked

Many faculty reported that they had less time to work after becoming fathers. The arrival of children into the home necessitated a shift in the number of hours faculty worked and the type of attention they were able to give to their careers. For example, one participant noted that before having kids, he regularly worked from 8:00 A.M. to 8:00 P.M. Another father said, "When I wasn't married, I tended to be something of a workaholic. I wouldn't say completely over the top, but you know I worked quite a bit, and it didn't really matter to me." This passion for work was present in many fathers' responses, such as this one: "Before my kids were born, . . . I worked every Sunday. . . . I mean I just regularly wanted to work and it didn't really matter, because it wasn't like I had much else to do during that time." Another said that before he was married, he spent six or seven days a week in the office:

> I would be at the office at like 6:30 A.M. in the morning and not leave until 9:00 and 9:30 PM. Looking back, I'm like, "What was I thinking?" I mean, that's extreme. Six days a week comfortably. So, I probably would be doing more of that [if I didn't have kids], and that would be a miserable existence, if you're asking me.

While this father similarly had a passion for work before his kids arrived, he also expressed gratitude that work was no longer the singular focus of his life. And while many of his peers shared the same gratitude for becoming fathers, they still noted that they had much less time to work than they once did.

However, the ideal worker norms of the academy suggest that faculty gain their worth by working long hours at night and on weekends. Although the number of hours that many participants worked after becoming parents decreased, they nonetheless reported working early in the morning, late at night, or on weekends. As I noted in chapter 2, 31 of the 70 participants reported working in the mornings before their children woke up or in the evenings after they had gone to sleep. Fifty-one participants reported working at least one weekend per month, and more typically at least one day every weekend. While faculty felt that they had less time to work, they tried to squeeze in every available opportunity to work around their parenting obligations.

More often than not, many of the faculty reported that their after-hours work occurred at home. As a result, many struggled with the types of work they could reasonably perform. Some suggested that the only work they could complete at home was administrative work or other work that required less concentration. One faculty member explained:

> I don't do as much heavy thinking at home as I used to. . . . I find by the time that it's 8 or 9 o'clock at night, I'm mentally exhausted. And so, I do a lot of kind of rote work at home, [such as answering e-mails].

This father was not the only participant to note that he tried to continue working, but realized that the types of work he was capable of performing would have to change:

> I try to work at night, but I often find that by the time I've got the kids in bed and have the kitchen cleaned up, it's 9 o'clock or later and I'm just too exhausted. So if I have things that are not too cognitively demanding and I have to take care of it, I'll just go off and do that in the evening. But I'm not able to write as much in the evening as I would like to.

Another father distinguished between the demands of his job and the "real work" at home in discussing why he did not perform much work in the evenings:

> Especially when the kids are very little, it's very demanding to be with them, and then for example after a typical day at work and you go home, and that's when the real work starts. So, it's not that you can say, "Well, I'm going to rest a little bit and then I can work more." That's when you get really drained. So, you get a break in that regard. Whereas if kids were not around, I think it would be much easier to have more of a constant day of intellectual activity. Your brain wouldn't be as fried as it is with kids.

Unlike popular rhetoric that often characterizes paid work as difficult and child rearing as easy, this father argued that taking care of children is exhausting. As a result, he felt unable to perform intellectual tasks in the evenings because he simply did not have the energy left to do so. His actions suggest that he is not living up to the expectations of the ideal worker, as he spends time engaged with his children in the evening instead of working. Similarly, by being involved with his children's care, he does not adhere to traditional definitions of masculinity.

These fathers' comments represent the sentiments of most of their peers. Faculty fathers constantly feel the pressure to work and yet frequently are unable to engage in the intellectually demanding tasks required of research and writing. As a result, though many continued working at odd hours, they often performed the other functions of faculty work (teaching preparation, article reviews, and answering a constant stream of e-mails) to fulfill the obligations of their jobs. While number of hours worked is one way to measure productivity, the academy values more concrete outputs, such as grants obtained or articles published. Many fathers reported that becoming fathers affected their research productivity. Paralleling existing literature, there were two diverging schools of thought as to whether fatherhood made participants more or less productive.

Fatherhood Leads to Increased Productivity and Efficiency

Few fathers denied that having children had an impact on their careers. However, 11 participants argued that becoming parents led them to make wiser choices about how to spend their time more efficiently, which ultimately led to increased productivity. As one father bluntly stated, "before I had a child, and I could spend as much time as I wanted working, I was very inefficient. I've become more efficient since I've had a child." Another described how similar demands on his time have led him to work more efficiently:

> It does help me be more productive when I am working because I know that I have a limited number of hours. I can't just say, "Well I'll just do it later tonight or this evening" because I'll be busy with [my kids]. So I try to get things done when I can get them done because I have other demands on my time. . . . It helps me really value the hours I do have available that much more.

Both participants felt that the demands of fatherhood led them to use their workdays more wisely.

Other participants explained appreciatively how time with their children led them to ultimately produce better scholarship. Many suggested that being forced to step away from their work, even for short periods of time, allowed them to be more productive. One father explained how being a father positively affected his scholarship:

> On some level it helped me focus more. . . . I feel like it like hollowed me out quite a bit. Like I always have . . . four hours in the evening, where I'm just not thinking about work. And in general, I think that's been helpful for balance, because it's easy to become a workaholic.

As this father pointed out, spending time away from work allowed him to focus more while he was engaged with it. Importantly, this father, like many others, challenges both notions of the ideal worker and hegemonic masculinity; he spends less time at work, but produces more scholarship and he is engaged with his children, which also contradicts traditional gender norms. He was not the only father to challenge the assumptions undergirding the ideal worker and hegemonic masculinity; another participant discussed becoming a father during the year he lived abroad in a country that provided generous parental leave. As a result, he only worked 30 hours a week and yet managed to publish five papers during that year.

> I spent 3 days a week, 10 hours a day, whatever it was, with the kids and they were babbling and blowing spit bubbles and in the back of my head I actually thought about the experiments I was doing and I planned better. And, it became really clear to me that you made more intelligent progress when you worked less. And the tendency is to force people into working more and into putting in more face time, if you want to put it that way, and I feel that my research suffers when I do that.

This participant was able to translate the lessons he learned while living abroad to his faculty life in the United States and was one of the few assistant professors who rarely worked nights or weekends. Instead, he was able to be quite productive in fewer hours.

This group of professors suggested that the amount of time they dedicate to work does not necessarily matter. For some, putting in less time than their peers led to increased productivity. Like the previous participant who suggested that "face time" was problematic, another faculty member pointed out that the number of hours worked did not matter as much as the degree of effort.

It's not the amount of time that you put in. It's that . . . and it sounds a little trite, what I'm going to say, but it's the quality of time out of all the time that you put in. And it's the quality of effort that you put it in. . . . So, if I didn't have kids, I would have been spending a lot more time at work, . . . but I don't know if I would have been more productive.

These fathers recognized that their work patterns had changed since having children. However, they all argued that they maintained or even increased their productivity because they had learned how to work more efficiently, thereby challenging one of the basic assumptions of the ideal worker, which suggests that the most productive employee is the one who works the most hours. Although many of the fathers acknowledged that they had fewer hours to work, not all agreed that this reduction in time was detrimental. While some felt that their careers and productivity had suffered, others felt grateful that this forced balance between their lives and careers.

Fatherhood Leads to Decreased Productivity and Scholarly Engagement

Although some fathers felt that becoming parents had made them more productive, many others looked wistfully back on their days without children as being a time of greater productivity. While many stated that they valued their children over their work, they also felt that the amount and type of work they performed had changed. Some, in particular, worried that they could not measure up to their childless peers. One participant explained:

I compare myself with some folks that don't have kids. They are much more disciplined. Disciplined and they have a very disciplined schedule and they are also more productive. I have not been very productive. . . . But if I didn't have kids, then I probably could do a lot more research.

This participant noted that he simply was unable to produce at the same rate as some of his colleagues. Although he did not tie his lack of productivity to any penalty to his career, other participants explicitly suggested that their parenting responsibilities meant that they could not be as successful in the workplace:

Before we had the kids, I was very aggressive. My research was very good. I went straight through tenure without [problems]. . . . But the minute we had kids, my production level went way, way down.

It's been difficult for me to petition for full professor. I've just had to take my losses there. I can only spread myself so thin.

This professor later explained that he had plateaued at the associate level and had found himself a target of many in the department for failing to meet research expectations.

Twenty-six fathers suggested that their careers had suffered as a result of becoming parents. Participants noted a variety of ways that their careers had been impacted, including turning down career advancement opportunities, being less involved in professional organizations, reducing conference attendance, and producing fewer publications. Such findings are not unique to fathers; several studies of faculty mothers have found that women experience similar career penalties post-motherhood (Sallee & Pascale, 2012; Ward & Wolf-Wendel, 2012). Several men discussed not pursuing particular career options, for the sake of their families, such as this father:

I've had a number of opportunities to do administrative work— high-level stuff: department chair positions, associate deans, etcetera. And I turned them down . . . for two reasons. One is I don't want to make my life any more complicated professionally than it is and frankly I want to stay focused on the things in the profession that I really enjoy doing. But I bet that if I didn't have kids, I probably would have been more likely to accept a position like that.

This father shied away from administrative responsibilities both because such positions would take him away from conducting research and out of respect for his children. Another professor discussed how he had declined a position at another university because the institution could not find a suitable position for his wife. He went on to say that "since then, there have been a couple of opportunities that I might have applied to if I didn't have kids." While this father had turned down these opportunities, he did not seem to regret his decision.

Other fathers discussed how they had pulled back from significant involvement in professional associations. One new father described how he was suddenly less interested and involved in his professional association:

Two years ago . . . I was really involved in our discipline at the national level, and I cared a lot about, you know, all kinds of discussions that were going on at the national level. . . . I just don't care [now]. . . . I've probably like disappeared from a lot of different spaces.

He described that he was once invested in national conversations, but he had chosen to redirect his energy toward his son, which stands in direct contrast with the valued traits of hegemonic masculinity and the breadwinner/caregiver dichotomy inherent in the ideal worker. Another father described his reasons for turning down the opportunity to chair a major conference for his field:

> I had been invited to chair major conferences in my field and so forth and those are basically invitations that I've deferred because they just—that's not a very high priority for me. It's a nice honor and I could see that it would lead to certain things, but I'm not that interested in it relative to the amount of time I would have to spend, particularly away from home.

This father argued that the costs of being away from his family outweighed the professional benefits that he might accrue. Importantly, this father was a full professor and an associate dean in his school; while he may have turned down opportunities that took him away from his family, he did not have the same concerns as the professor described earlier who steered clear of administrative positions. Although their situations differed, both men turned down professional opportunities for the sake of their families.

Like the men who turned down leadership positions, 22 fathers discussed reducing conference attendance or other travel opportunities after having children. Some fathers reported that after earning tenure, they reduced the number of conferences they attended, like this father:

> I did stop attending conferences and submitting abstracts, especially the international conferences and that had really a lot to do with the fact that I just didn't feel like taking big chunks of time off and gallivant around Europe. . . . When I was younger, it was much clearer to me that that was an important part of my job, that's what I did. . . . Now that I have tenure and don't sort of need to do it to maintain my position, it seemed like something I couldn't afford.

This father felt that he was able to reduce his conference attendance because tenure gave him the protection to do so. Some other fathers noted that they attended fewer conferences when their children were younger, which coincided with the early part of their careers. Said one father with a particularly large family:

> There were times when I did not go on many of the conferences. . . . I thought that I could [not] just leave my kids at home

with my wife and she had to deal with the smaller baby and so on
and so forth. So I used to rarely travel when the kids were really
small. I went on maybe one conference. Now I go to maybe four
or five conferences a year.

He made a conscious decision to reduce his conference attendance when
his children were younger and now that they were older, he felt that he
was able to increase his involvement.

Other fathers discussed that they tended to shorten the amount of
time they spent at conferences or spent traveling. Several fathers reported
only attending parts of conferences and taking overnight flights to cut down
on their absence from home. Others reported avoiding international conferences due to the amount of time such events took them away from their
families. In both cases, these actions suggest that fathers are not willing to
conform to the norms of the ideal worker at the expense of their families.
One father explained how he made travel work:

> I went to Japan, but I left on a Saturday afternoon and came back
> on Wednesday so I only stayed there for two days. And I travel to
> the West Coast and I usually take an evening flight out and come
> back on the red eye so I'm usually two days on the ground and I'm
> gone two and a half or three days. So I try to minimize the time
> that I have to travel.

Like the previous father who did not want to spend too much time away
from his children, another father described the time he gave a presentation at a conference in Scandinavia when his son was an infant: "I think
it was a 54-hour trip. . . . So basically, I was out, gave the talk, went to
the dinner, hopped on a plane, and then made the whole trip back again."
These are the types of choices that many of the fathers made on behalf of
their children, which contradict expectations of both the ideal worker and
hegemonic masculinity. While they cut down on conference attendance
and invited presentations, many realized that they could not completely
withdraw from the circuit or suffer career repercussions. One father described
how he found his professional fortunes change once he reduced his travel
due to his children:

> For the first year of our son's life, whenever I would travel, disasters
> would happen. [My wife would] lock herself out, the kid was sick
> and so on. And so I got to the point where, for instance, once I
> was invited to give a talk in Boulder, Colorado. I flew to Boulder,

gave my talk, flew back. . . . So it just gets too ridiculous. So I started to say no and once you get off the circuit, you're sort of forgotten. You're no longer the flavor of the month for anybody.

For this father, the frequent and short trips around the country to give talks proved to be too much for his family and so he opted to retreat. He did not feel that he could be the ideal worker—available to work and travel at all times—because it had significant consequences for his family life. However, choosing his family over his career and making himself less available had long-term professional consequences.

In addition to reducing travel and turning down other professional opportunities, many participants imagined that they would have been able to publish more if they had not children. One father explained:

Having children is a huge commitment and a huge investment in time. And . . . if I didn't have to make those investments and those commitments, that energy might have been channeled into writing more papers and getting more grants and having more graduate students.

Another participant imagined that he "would've written all these great books by now" if he had not become a parent. Another explained that he had not published any articles in the previous two years, and he felt that his career was "on hiatus." He explained his dilemma:

I've found it easier to continue to feel really strongly about my commitment to being a good father than I have to my commitment to being a good scholar and so my scholarship has really suffered. Although I mean I'm not very happy about that, . . . I think my positive self-image—and I don't think that it's terribly unreasonable—involves me being both a good father and a good scholar.

These participants described various ways in which they felt that their careers had been impacted. Their sentiments point to beliefs about the impact children have on their productivity, but also underscore the ways that participants felt they were failing to live up to their professional potential.

Another father reflected on the difficulty he had writing since the birth of his two children. As he describes, he was able to find adequate momentum to write enough to earn tenure, but found that his significant responsibilities meant he was unable to produce as much as he would like, and certainly less than his childless peers.

After the birth of my [older son], for awhile I didn't publish anything for a few years, except for one article. And then I published quite a bit of stuff as my tenure was coming, I sort of wrote . . . really pushed it, and then I came out with a lot of articles. And right now, I feel like I had just had that momentum of producing a lot, but then the second one was young. So, I feel I actually could continue that momentum and publish more and sort of make a more recognizable name for myself by pushing a few more things around, but I can't do it, because you know, I have to end my day more or less around 4:00 P.M., whereas other colleagues who do not have some of these responsibilities, actually can go later. I can't stay up all night because in the morning I really have to get up at 7:00 A.M. and take care of the kids and make sure they get to school. So, the kinds of extra things that one could do, doesn't have to do, but one could do for, you know, if you have a little bit more ambition, those things I cannot do.

This father was less productive than he wanted to be due to his familial responsibilities. He would like to be able to invest more time to "make a more recognizable name" for himself, but simply does not have enough hours in the day to do so. In part, he is at a disadvantage because, as he notes, he cannot compete against his childless peers who are able to work into the wee hours of the morning. However, this father also takes a more active role in his children's lives than has been traditionally expected of men. As he notes, he leaves work every day around 4:00 P.M. to pick up his children from school and spends the afternoons and evenings engaged in care. Such actions mark him as divergent from expectations of the ideal worker in the academy and traditional definitions of fatherhood.

This father was not the only one to compare himself and his productivity to his childless peers. Noted another:

I'm sure that I could have done more. Because every now and then, you kind of look around at your colleagues and friends in grad school [who] don't have kids and you kind of see what they're doing, and they seem like they get more papers published in the average year than you do. I know they do.

A couple of fathers suggested that faculty with children should receive some acknowledgement of that fact or, as this father, explained "a handicap":

I probably would have had more publications than I do [if I hadn't had kids]. Not that I'm behind in any way, but I said to my wife the other day, "When you have a family, you should get a handicap. If you're a mother you should get a handicap because it's just different." And people will say, "Well it's your choice to have a family." Yeah I understand that it's your choice, but I know that if I did not have kids, I would be working—I would just work a lot more than I do. I'd go in more often.

Another professor shared similar concerns:

If you're a workaholic, if you don't need much sleep, if you don't have children, you can crank out so much work. And in the end, my value as a scientist is gauged against all the other scientists. And, of course, you always look to these super high performers, and you look at their life and you say, "Sorry." I mean, I wouldn't want to have their life really. I want to have children, and I want to have my family life. But if my productivity as a scientist and as a researcher gets gauged against people who have nothing in life. . . .

As this participant so aptly pointed out, parents seem to produce less than their childless peers. And yet, all individuals are measured by the same metrics, which puts those with children and significant child-rearing responsibilities at a disadvantage. Rightly or wrongly, the academy does not account for an individual's parental status in evaluating a faculty member's contribution. Research expectations continue to increase and expect all faculty members to be ideal workers, always working and always productive. Many participants felt that their research productivity had declined since becoming parents. Others suggested that while they had fewer hours each day to work, they found that they had become more efficient. However, productivity is not simply measured by numbers of publications, but also includes the quality of work produced. Some participants noted a distinct change in their research and capability to engage in intellectual work after becoming parents.

Intellectual Attention and Scholarly Work

One unanticipated finding revolved around changes in the types of research men conducted after becoming parents. Some participants suggested that becoming fathers led them to engage in "safer" research. Others also suggested that they no longer had the time or space to engage in deep intellectual thought. Both have consequences for the quality of research produced.

Many fathers spoke regretfully about not being able to find time to engage in sustained intellectual thought. While many found ways to attend to teaching and administrative duties, they found that they simply did not have enough focus to devote to scholarship. One new father described trying to find time to engage in research:

> [The challenge is] getting some momentum going on some of the intellectual work. It's not so hard to come in and do things like meet with students or comment on their dissertation draft, or read e-mail and stuff and respond to that sort of thing or chat about grant ideas, but you know doing writing or designing a research study . . . I've been trying to design a little study . . . and I almost know what it should be, but it's really hard to kind of find the block of time and attention to, you know, dig into the articles that I need to to kind of push myself further.

Other participants spoke about missing sustained blocks of time for thinking about ideas. One participant worried that he no longer had the "intellectual acumen" to bring to his scholarship. Another suggested that due to his obligations to his children, he could never find enough time to think and write:

> Research requires an amount of time that you can concentrate on the work. If you have interruptions occurring over and over again, it's very counterproductive for doing concerted research. It's not something like, "okay I'm taking two hours off and I will work one hour and then I'll take two more hours off." . . . You need to have a good window of three to four hours where you are not disturbed so that you can think and do your writing or conceptualization and things like that.

This father felt that he was only able to be productive when he had uninterrupted blocks of time. Other fathers noted that their obligations to their children meant that they often had enforced start and stop times to work. One father described waiting for "the muse" to arrive, only to find that he had to stop working and switch into "dad mode":

> Any academic parent probably has had to do the same thing—that our work has to rev up and to some extent you depend on the muse visiting you and are you going to get into a flow or not. And when you do, it's . . . aggravating and unfortunate to have to leave it and just drop it just because the clock says it's time.

This father points out what is often glossed over in discussions of faculty work and productivity. Doing good research and scholarship requires time and intellectual engagement. Fitting in work around other obligations is possible, but often does not allow faculty the time they need to develop their ideas. While most fathers noted the limitations of time on their scholarship, one father suggested that he was able to use short concerted blocks to be productive:

> Often the conflict come[s] out about decisions each day and the conflict of whether to try to finish something before leaving or leave and hope that you might finish it later at home or the next day. It adds to inefficiencies in your system. Sometimes the most efficient bit is that last half hour when you're trying to finish something off. Or when you come in the next day, you're not as focused.

Unlike many of the other men who felt constrained by the clock, this father argued that the last part of his day often provided him a forced burst of energy to finish the tasks he was working on. Each of these participants pointed to the fact that while they are able to find time to work, performing work that requires less intellectual attention is often easier. For some, that entails focusing on teaching obligations. Even when participants wanted to focus on research, they often felt that there were unable to muster the type of intellectual investment that they once had.

Some participants discussed that, as a result of this reduced intellectual investment, the types of research they pursued had changed. Some of the social scientists discussed that they no longer had the time to engage in deep philosophical thought, such as this participant:

> There's a paper I published [that came out the year after my kids were born] . . . that's just a think piece, that's sort of a philosophy of science. It's unthinkable to me now to imagine that I could spend that kind of time developing those thoughts. I could never do something like that now, you know. So mostly it's the things that I have some obligation to do because—or I feel that because students are coauthoring with me or things like that or I have deadlines.

This professor noted a distinct change in the types of work he performed before and after becoming a parent. Before becoming a father, he was able to spend time developing a philosophical argument. Since becoming a father, he has had to push such intellectual musings to the side and has instead focused on publishing research with his students. Such research tends to lead to more immediate rewards.

Participants in other disciplines noted a similar tendency to pursue safer lines of inquiry. One participant suggested that had he not become a parent, he would have "spent more time on difficult projects than [he does] now." Another participant suggested that he, too, would have pursued different projects:

> I might have taken more risks and that's a possibility. . . . I cannot tell you that I wanted to do this and I didn't do it because of the kids, . . . but it is obvious that you look for more stability when you have kids.

As the father correctly noted, he cannot say with certainty that his research would have been different if he had not had children. (Indeed, this is simply not a possibility that one can measure.) But he did point to the importance of pursuing research and career choices that would not put his family's future in jeopardy.

Several fathers discussed making purposeful decisions to shift the focus of their research to be less disruptive toward their families. For example, one faculty member opted not to conduct research outside of the United States, despite wanting to do so.

> I'm an anthropologist, but I've done all my work in the U.S. I did my initial work in the U.S. . . . And it's possible I would've pursued some foreign field work. . . . I had kept saying I was going to do something either in Europe or Japan, but that just became impossible.

This father did not feel that he could leave his family for long periods of time and so opted to pursue different lines of inquiry. Similarly, another professor discussed how he shifted his research site from overseas to within an hour's drive of his university after becoming a parent:

> I didn't want to do . . . a lot of international travel. So that's why I chose to do field work [nearby]. . . . So that was a very much family/child decision that I made when I joined [the university]. I would shift my research sites closer to home.

This father had traveled overseas significantly in a previous position and was uninterested in continuing that level of travel, particularly after his children were born. None of these changes necessarily led these fathers to have unsuccessful careers. However, they all provide evidence that making choices for family has implications for the types of work faculty can perform. In some ways, none of these men were ideal workers as they all chose their families over particular aspects of their careers.

Another father regretted not having the time to explore interesting ideas in the way that he might have if he had not become a father:

There are probably projects that I would pursue if I didn't have kids, just because I had the time to do it. But, in the end, those might be the projects that are less likely to ever come to fruition. You know, you just kind of do it because they are, maybe, high-risk, high-reward–type projects. . . . So I guess it becomes a philosophical question, "What is productivity?" I think it is very important to measure productivity, not just in the output of quality articles, or students taught, or Ph.D.s produced. But there's more to that and that is just, you know, developing ideas, exploring ideas, and to the point where they fail, in which case the outside community would say, "Well, that wasn't productive at all." But, I think for the person who was working on it, it may have been very productive time, just being able to say well, I tried it and now I know the answer. It doesn't work. . . . Yeah, if there was one thing I wish I had more time for, it is exactly that.

This lengthy excerpt sums up several issues that characterized fathers' experiences. First, like others, this professor pointed out that he felt unable to pursue the same types of ideas that he might have had he not become a parent. Second, he underscored the fact that some of the ideas that are not pursued are those that are most likely to be "high risk." Becoming parents seemed to lead some men to pursue safer lines of inquiry, due to shortened workweeks, lack of time to engage in intellectual thought, and fear of putting their families at risk. Given their responsibilities as breadwinners, regardless of whether they shared such responsibilities with their wives, these fathers did not want to put their families in financial jeopardy by pursuing the unknown. Finally, the father also challenged conventional definitions of productivity. While he acknowledged that "quality articles" are important, he also suggested that one way to produce such articles is to allow faculty to explore uncertain lines of inquiry, which could lead to either the next big breakthrough or to findings of no significance. Due to the high stakes in the academy and the demands of fatherhood, many such projects are never explored. Given that colleges and universities have traditionally been sites of innovation and discovery, these constraints have significant consequences for the future of knowledge production in the academy.

Conclusion

While productivity is occasionally measured in terms of the number of hours devoted to work, more often faculty productivity is measured in terms of research output, either purely by counting publications or in terms of the degree of impact a publication has on the field. Previous research has led to conflicting conclusions on the impact of parenthood on faculty productivity.

Some have found that parenthood has a positive effect on productivity (Stack, 2004); others concluded that parenthood has a negative effect on productivity (Hunter & Leahey, 2010); and still others suggested that it has no effect (Bellas & Toutkoushian, 1999; Sax et al., 2002).

The experiences of these fathers reveal similar tensions. Many men reported that the hours they worked had changed after becoming fathers. They similarly reported trying to find any available time to get work done—after their children went to bed at night as well as on weekends. Some men suggested that becoming fathers had led to a negative impact on their careers. Recall one father who had been highly research productive as an assistant professor. Upon becoming a parent, he found his productivity decline to such an extent that he has never been able to transition from associate to full professor. Not only did fathers discuss the ways that their careers had been affected, but they also suggested that reduced productivity led to negative feelings of self-worth. If value in academia is measured in terms of research output and norms of masculinity suggest that men are to be high performers, it is no surprise that these fathers felt battered and demoralized by reduced productivity.

Just like the contradictions within existing literature, not all men concluded that becoming fathers had negatively affected their productivity. Some suggested that while they had fewer hours to work per day, the reduction in time available to devote to work had led them to be more efficient. Some men adhered to fairly structured work schedules, trying to mirror the norms of a standard workday. Realizing they only had so many hours in a day to get work done and not the same availability of time to work at night as some of their peers led them to make wiser choices in how they spent their time. Such reduced time to work had positive consequences in that these professors were forced to step away from their work. Take, for example, the father who was able to produce five papers in the year in which he only worked 30 hours per week. By being forced to spend less time working, he was able to gain fresh perspective and bring a new approach to his work. These fathers' experiences call into question the norms of the ideal worker; if time away from work makes employees more productive, perhaps norms need to shift. In some ways, the experiences of these faculty fathers echo the findings of previous studies. Some fathers felt that their productivity was positively affected while others suggested that the effect was more negative. Perhaps these divergent findings point out that the impact of children on productivity depends on the faculty member. Like previous studies, it also underscores that productivity wanes and waxes throughout a faculty member's career. For example, one professor indicated that after the birth of his son, he had a short period where he wrote only one article. As he approached tenure, his research output increased. Post-tenure, it subsequently decreased. Other fathers discussed that their attendance at conferences shifted throughout their children's lives. Whereas some fathers reported going to fewer conferences overall, other men reported that they had scaled back their conference attendance while their children were small, gradually increasing their attendance as their children got older. The experiences of these men indicate that fatherhood does indeed impact productivity, but that the impact is different for each individual.

Men experienced more than just a change in productivity after becoming parents; some also reported shifts in their choices about the kind of work they pursued. Fathers suggested that due to changes in their time and priorities, the types of projects pursued were different. In part, some fathers suggested, this change in projects was due to a lack of available time for sustained intellectual thought. Many fathers discussed needing significant blocks of time to engage with their research. However, teaching, administrative, and parenting demands made such time blocks elusive. In addition, these men suggested that they no longer had the time or the courage to take on high-risk or intellectual projects with no certainty of payout. One father reflected on the luxury of being able to spend time writing a purely philosophical piece before having children. Another suggested that he was unwilling to pursue projects that had a high risk of failure out of concern for his obligations to his family.

These changes in work reflect the tensions men feel in living up to ideal worker norms and hegemonic masculinity (Connell, 1995). While the ideal worker suggests that employees must be always available and engaged in work, the norm does not dictate the types of work that must be performed. Faculty have realized that they can ensure stability for themselves and their families by producing types of research that will get them tenure and continued appointment. To some extent, any publication is better than no publication.

Hegemonic masculinity underscores appropriate roles for men, including serving as breadwinners for their families. However, long-term and high-risk projects have the possibility of leading to no reward. A faculty member could spend months or years pursuing a promising line of inquiry, only to find that it leads nowhere. Such failures could put a professor's job at risk. Even if a faculty member has already earned tenure, continued failures have consequences for post-tenure review, merit raises, and the less tangible metrics such as reputation. To avoid disrupting their families and challenging their reputations as breadwinners, some men chose to stick to safer arenas.

I suggested earlier that men who were more efficient after becoming fathers challenged the trope of the ideal worker by illustrating that working longer hours does not necessarily produce better scholarship. One might also argue that men whose productivity decreased after becoming fathers are similarly challenging ideal worker norms in the choices they make about their personal and professional lives. The ideal worker may spend all of his time working, but the ideal worker is not ideal for families. By choosing to put limits on their professional obligations, these fathers are challenging deeply entrenched norms about work and family.

Of course, changes in some of the fathers' productivity may be troubling as they confirm some detractors' claims that high professional standards and parenthood are not compatible. However, eliminating all parents as potential candidates for faculty jobs is simply not possible. And, continuing to support a work environment in which faculty are expected to focus the majority of their attention each and every day on work is not good for families. Instead, as I discuss in the concluding chapter, the experiences of these fathers suggest that the notion of the ideal worker needs to be reframed. Some participants suggested that they produced the highest quality work when they worked fewer hours and had the time and space to do so. Perhaps institutions might consider that the ideal worker is not necessarily one who is always working, but rather one who has achieved a proper balance between work and parenting demands so that he (or she) might do a good job at both.

CHAPTER 6

The Ideal Worker Inside or Outside the Home?

The majority of literature on faculty parents focuses on how the structures and cultures of the academy shape their experiences on campus. Indeed, much of my focus in this book has been on experiences in the workplace. However, what happens in the home has significant implications for an individual's productivity in the workplace. A faculty member who is caring for an aging parent, raising young children, and has a partner who works full-time outside the home likely has different demands on his time than a single faculty member with no children. Similarly, the married faculty member with the working spouse likely has different demands on his time than a married faculty member with a stay-at-home wife. As I discussed in the previous chapter, men experience a variety of changes to their scholarly engagement after becoming parents. However, what of their domestic engagement? How might the work they perform inside the home differ from that of their wives and, furthermore, how might their wives' employment status shape the kinds of domestic labor they perform? It is these questions that I explore in this chapter.

Although my focus in this chapter is on work performed in the home, Acker's (1990) theory of gendered organizations and consequently ideal worker norms and hegemonic masculinity are implicit in the experiences of these fathers. I focus my analysis on two areas: (1) the gendered division of labor between the fathers and mothers in this study; and (2) the differences in these divisions between men whose wives work full-time outside the home and those whose wives stay at home at least part time. While many men and women continue to divide their labor into traditional gender roles, the experiences of these faculty fathers suggests that those with wives who work full-time outside of the home are more likely to engage in household labor than those whose wives stay home. While the structure of academic work introduces flexibility into men's lives, which might allow them to be more involved than a typical father, the experiences of these faculty fathers suggest that stereotypical gender norms maintain a stronghold on men's and women's behaviors. As the experiences of these fathers suggest, the gendered culture of the academy does not simply affect what happens on campus, but also affects what happens in the home. Stated differently, the gendered expectations placed on faculty fathers in the workplace are related to the gendered division of labor in the home. There can be no permanent shifts in one domain without subsequent shifts in the other. Such shifts require redefining the ideal worker along with norms of hegemonic masculinity.

I begin the chapter by providing an overview of past research on gendered divisions of labor, reviewing the types of work that men and women typically perform in the home and factors that influence this division of labor. Although there have been shifts in the past several decades in men's interaction with their children, the evidence suggests that women remain predominantly responsible for their children in the home, despite women's increasing representation in the workplace. I then discuss how the faculty fathers in this study described the ways that they divided labor in their homes with their wives. Due to the design of the study, I rely on the men's descriptions of their wives' work. While the women might have described their tasks differently, the fathers' descriptions point to significant differences in who does what. Men tended to perform less housework and more fun activities with their children while their wives performed the necessary tasks to keep the households functioning. I conclude by discussing how task allocation differed between couples with full-time working mothers and couples with stay-at-home moms. While traditional divisions of labor were present in all couples, they appeared more entrenched in couples where the woman did not work full-time. I conclude the chapter by discussing how such divisions of labor reinforce norms of the ideal worker as well as hegemonic masculinity and the implications these divisions have for men, women, and the workplace.

Shifting or Reinscribing Gender Norms?

Ideal worker norms are predicated on the division of labor between breadwinner and caregiver. Although such norms may be dated given women's increasing participation in the labor force, they still hold sway over the division of labor in the home. Although the time they spend engaged in care and performing housework may be increasing, men perform significantly less work than women in the home. In this section, I discuss past studies on the types of work that men typically perform in the home and the factors that shape the provision of care. As one might expect, most studies suggest that men whose wives work outside the home are likely to perform more work in the home.

MASCULINE PROVISION OF CARE

Although work inside the home was traditionally women's domain, men's time spent performing childcare and housework has increased over the past half century (Bianchi et al., 2000; Coltrane, 2000; Sayer et al., 2004). Despite increases in men's household labor, women still perform significantly more care and other work in the home than men (Bianchi et al.; Coltrane, 1996; Kazura, 2000; Shelton, 1990; U.S. Bureau of Labor Statistics, 2013). Household labor may be used to describe a variety of tasks including care-giving, cooking, and cleaning, to name but a few. The distinction between childcare and housework is one of importance as some have found that men do not consider housework and particular cleaning tasks to be part of parental responsibility (Brandth & Kvande, 1998; Coltrane, 1996). For example, while Coltrane (1996) found that about half of household cleaning tasks and meal preparation were shared equally between men and women, women remained solely responsible for performing about one quarter of all household tasks, including laundry and meal planning. In their study using time diaries from 1965 to 1995, Bianchi et al. found that although women's time spent performing household tasks had decreased while men's had increased, women still remain responsible for far more household tasks than men. In 1965, married women spent 33.9 hours per week on all household tasks, including cooking meals, cleaning, and doing laundry. In 1995, women reported spending 19.4 hours per week on the same group of tasks. In contrast, men's time spent engaged in the same tasks increased from 4.7 hours a week to 10.4 hours a week in the same timeframe. Yet, as the authors pointed out, women still spend nearly twice as many hours per week as men on the same tasks.

A more recent study found that 82% of women versus 65% of men spent time on a daily basis engaged in activities including housework, cooking, and lawn care (U.S. Bureau of Labor Statistics, 2013). The findings are particularly gendered in that 19.8% of men versus 48.4% of women performed housework on a given day while 39.2% of men and 64.9% of women engaged in food preparation and cleanup on a particular day (U.S. Bureau of Labor Statistics). These studies suggest that men are far less likely to participate in home maintenance tasks than their wives. The results of Gerstel and Gallagher's (2001) study suggest why; the authors found that men were far less likely than women to perform tasks that they deemed as feminine, such as preparing a meal or engaging in childcare. These trends extend into the academy as well. Nakhaie (2009) found that female academics perform 20% more housework than male academics. Both inside and outside the academy, the evidence is fairly convincing that men perform less housework than women.

While men seem to shy away from cleaning, they are more likely to engage in care in the home. Time spent with children can take several forms, as Lamb et al. (1985) suggested. Involvement might include: (1) interaction, which involves caregiving and other opportunities for direct contact; (2) availability, which refers to being present and therefore having the possibility of interaction; and (3) responsibility, which refers to "the role the father takes in making sure that the child is taken care of and arranging for resources to be available for the child" (p. 884). A father who is responsible for his child might call to arrange a doctor's appointment or schedule a play date. While men's interaction and availability may be increasing, women tend to maintain responsibility for their children (Lamb et al.). Pleck and Masciadrelli (2004) found that fathers' level of engagement was about 43% of women's while their accessibility was about 66% in the early 1990s; in contrast, studies between the 1960s and early 1980s set men's engagement at one third and accessibility at one half that of women's. As research suggests and the experiences of faculty fathers underscore, women tend to maintain greater responsibility for their children than their husbands.

Although men are spending more time with their children, they are most likely to engage in play with their children over all other types of activities (Craig, 2006; Lamb & Lewis, 2004; Pleck & Masciadrelli, 2004). One study found that 39% of all paternal engagement takes the form of play or companionship, followed by caregiving at 28% (Pleck & Masciadrelli). Another study found that fathers were far more likely than mothers to engage in "physically stimulating and unpredictable play" (Lamb & Lewis, p. 276). Other studies have reported that men value being companions and playmates for their children (Brandth & Kvande, 1998). While men perform childcare, they frequently engage with their children through activities and other fun play.

FACTORS THAT SHAPE THE PROVISION OF CARE

Several factors impact the amount of childcare and housework a man performs, including the employment status of his wife (Coltrane, 1996; Deutsch, Lussier, & Servis, 1993; Lamb & Lewis, 2004; Williams, 2000). Lamb and Lewis argued that men who worked fewer hours or whose wives worked more hours performed more care in the home. Similarly, Coltrane, in a study of married couples, found that the more hours a woman worked at her job, the less work she performed in the home and the more work her husband performed in the home. While most studies have found that a wife's employment status shapes her husband's propensity to engage in work in the home, some, like Shelton (1990), argued that there is little effect on the amount of work that men perform. She found that while women who worked outside the home performed less work in the home than stay-at-home wives, the amount of work that men performed did not significantly differ in either configuration. However, most agree that employment demands on both members of the couple have implications for what goes on inside the home.

A few other factors have been noted for shaping men's work in the home, including gender ideology, age, and class-based ideology. Some have found that men who subscribe to a more egalitarian gender ideology are more likely to perform work in the home than those who hold more conservative beliefs (Bulanda, 2004; Crompton & Harris, 1999; Deutsch et al., 1993; Matta & Knudson-Martin, 2006). In contrast, Gerstel and Gallagher (2001) found the opposite to be true; they argued that men who hold more egalitarian ideals are less likely to provide care in the home. While Nakhaie (2009) found no relationship between professors' gender ideology and men's work in the home, he did find that men who subscribed to a more egalitarian class-based ideology were more likely to perform more housework while women with such beliefs reduced their housework. While the evidence from these studies is mixed, enough data exist to suggest that personal attitudes and beliefs may play a role in shaping the type of work a man performs. Above all, however, the wife's employment status plays the biggest role in determining the degree to which a man will engage in childcare and perform housework. With the review of existing studies in mind, I now turn to the experiences of faculty fathers to consider the ways in which they mirror and differ from their nonacademic peers. Their experiences suggest that while their wives may perform more work in the home, they enjoy playing with their children and being otherwise active.

Care in the Home

Life in a home with children is characterized by constant activity. Many of the fathers described their days as filled with a variety of activities, from waking their children in the morning to taking them to activities to putting them to bed at night. Often, the fathers discussed activities that they performed alongside their wives. However, there were some tasks that fathers described engaging in more and some that they suggested that their wives did more. The fathers-only tasks tended to involve more fun while the mothers-only tasks were more likely to involve routine work that kept the household going. I begin by discussing the types of tasks that emerged as regular responsibilities for both parents, before turning to the gendered divisions of labor that also emerged. This initial portrait illustrates all of the tasks that are required in an involved parent's daily life. Importantly, these tasks occur before, during, after, and occasionally simultaneously with the demands required of faculty work.

THE EXHAUSTING DAY

Many fathers started their days before 6:00 A.M. when their children first awoke. Nearly all of the fathers were involved in some way in their children's care in the mornings. One father, for example, described his role as the "waker-upper." Other fathers were in charge of feeding their children breakfast. One father described his routine with his two daughters:

> I get up at 6:30. I have two daughters [who are] 8 and 6. [The 8-year-old] gets up . . . just as soon as the alarm goes off—she's up and ready to go. So, she gets herself dressed. [The 6-year-old] is a heavy sleeper, has a hard time going to sleep at night, and then a hard time waking up in the morning. So I usually get her dressed. Then I carry her downstairs. I make the girls breakfast.

Other fathers discussed the chaos of simultaneously getting the children ready in the morning, preparing breakfasts, preparing lunches, and getting children out the door for school, like this father:

> So I have a middle school kid and let's see a 7th grader and a 5th grader and they have to wake up to catch the bus at different times. So my wife and I alternate who gets up earlier with the bigger kid. So, for example, I got the later shift [today] so I woke up, went downstairs, had breakfast, made breakfast for my younger daughter, woke her up, took a shower, shaved—that kind of stuff, came downstairs, made my lunch and her lunch and got her on the bus.

This father discussed the number of tasks that he accomplished before arriving at work; such tasks differed depending on the child for whom he was responsible. Many parents reported taking the divide-and-conquer approach. In families with multiple children, often one parent was responsible for getting at least one child to school or daycare.

However, some fathers reported that they were solely responsible for bringing their children to daycare or school in the morning due to their wives' work schedules. One father, with young children, described his family's morning routine:

> My wife leaves about quarter to seven in the morning and so I actually have some time to spend with the kids. Part of it is me yelling at them, "let me read the newspaper," and "leave me alone." But particularly in the summer, I try to get outdoors and go to the playground or something before coming to work. They're both in preschool. Their preschool doesn't open however until 8:45. So I drop them off at 8:45 and then I come [into work].

While this father joked about trying to get some peace and quiet in the mornings, he also reported what turned out to be fairly standard across fathers' narratives: many reported playing a significant role in facilitating play activities for their children and many also reported being involved in driving their children to school, daycare, and the now ubiquitous after-school activities.

Twenty-six fathers discussed frequently driving their children to activities, including sports practice and games as well as music, dance, and language classes. The list was long and varied, but many reported how much they valued the time with their children in the car. One dad described how he had made a conscious effort to increase his share of driving the children to activities since his wife went back to work. Doing so allowed for some good conversation, he said, "So, quiet time, talking with them individually, car rides are probably some of the best times. It's usually close proximity. You know, as long as they don't have their cell phones busy." This dad appreciated these opportunities to connect with his children in ways that were not always possible outside of the car. Several fathers had children who participated in high-level sports teams that required frequent practices and many games. Another father spoke fondly about taking his son to an out-of-state sports tournament:

> So with [our son], my role in the family division of labor is to get him to soccer games and get him to soccer practices, which involves a lot of driving and hanging out time, which I'm really glad for. I think as he gets older he's more and more bored with it, but that's totally appropriate, totally cool. So on Sunday there was—I had to drive him Saturday night [to a city 250 miles away] for a soccer tournament. I went to his soccer game and turned around and drove back the next day. It was actually fun. We had a good time when we do these little road trips together.

This father took advantage of these grueling travel demands to spend time with his son while he still could. While longer trips were often reserved for the fathers, very few fathers reported that they were solely responsible for their children's transportation to all activities. Rather, these were activities that were often shared between the parents, even in some families with mothers who did not work outside the home.

The list of parental tasks continued well into the night. Some fathers reported cooking dinner. Many reported helping with homework. Several reported that their roles as academics led them to take a particular interest in their children's schoolwork. Noted one father:

> I try to be really engaged in their education. Not surprising being an academic, you know, I put a lot of emphasis on that in our household. So I'm right on the front line helping with homework and not just math and science stuff . . . that an engineer would be inclined to do. I enjoy the language arts and helping them with that, although my wife is more gifted than I am.

Another father reported that he often used homework time as a teaching opportunity for his children, a fact that clearly bothered them:

> I help them out with their homework and I try to teach them. I'm probably the most annoying dad ever because they'll ask me a question and I won't answer it. I'll do the Socratic thing and they'll say, "Dad, just tell me the answer," and I'll say, "Let's walk through this. Where can we find the information?"

This father viewed helping with homework as an opportunity to teach his children the tools to find the right answer. He went on to share that he intentionally created opportunities for his children to teach him things as well.

> So I think probably one of our biggest interactions is probably what I would call homework, but it's more about learning. Homework tasks that could take 10 minutes, I drag it out and it's 45 minutes. But it's interaction time. I let them teach me things occasionally. Like they'll get a video game and I'll ask them, "How do you play this?" and they'll try to teach me and so they'll see that not everybody has the same skill set and that their dad might be pretty good at math and whatever and helps them out, [but] is a total clod when it comes to this.

This father tried to shift the way that his kids thought about learning, by helping them develop the tools to solve problems themselves. He also wanted his children to know that they had skills he did not and encouraged them to teach him how to play video games and other activities in which they—but not he—excelled.

Video games popped up as popular activities in some households as did reading. Many fathers reported reading to their younger at bedtime or reading alongside their older children. In fact, reading was often a staple in bedtime routines, which for some families were performed together while other families reverted to the divide-and-conquer approach. One father shared, "we consciously try to swap the bedtime routine. Otherwise my son is always with my wife and my daughter is always with me." Recognizing that one child frequently gravitated to a particular parent, this father and his wife built in routines so that each parent spent time with each child several times a week. Another father described how he and his wife regularly shared the ritual of putting their three children—twin toddlers and an elementary-school aged daughter—to bed.

> The boys get a bath. I'll sit with them during the bath and [my wife] is making the bottles and then she'll come up and we'll move into the bedroom and try to put the boys—so then we do a bottle, brush their teeth. I hold their hands while [my wife] tries to brush their teeth. It's very hard. She's very noble with this and has been bitten and yelled at and all kinds of things. Anyway then we lay them in their cribs. I sit with them for just about five minutes, not more. I come out of the room at about 8:30 and begin to—that's kind of a nice time. [Our daughter] is about to go to bed. I'll start to clean up and do the dishes. . . . Then I'll go up and I'll—we'll sort of put [our daughter] to bed together, [my wife] and I. She'll read to [our daughter] and I'll sit up there too and massage [my wife's] feet or just be up there in the room.

After the chaos of getting two young children ready for bed, the moment of peace for this father came when he and his wife put their older daughter to bed together. Many fathers discussed these moments and the ways in which they provided a cap to often harried days in which they had put in long hours at work and long hours as involved fathers. But with few exceptions, none of these tasks emerged as being particularly in the realm of fathers or mothers. Rather, these were activities that both parents tended to share, although potentially parents split their attention among multiple children. However, some tasks emerged as belonging purely in the domain of fathers or mothers.

FUN AND GAMES

While many fathers reported participating in the daily routines of family life, three tasks emerged as falling within men's realms of responsibility: physical play, outdoor activities, and coaching sports teams. One might argue that all three of these activities are more fun than activities of daily life. Seventeen fathers mentioned that they were far more likely than their wives to rough-house or engage in physical play with their children. Such play started from an early age as a father of infant shared that he played with his son "a little bit more vigorously" than his wife. Another father stated that he "tickled and wrestled around" more than his wife. Yet another father described his role with his son:

> I think I do a lot more of the physical stuff with him. He just can't control his energy and he's learned not to jump on my wife, but he hasn't learned that with me. So he's very physical and I sort of give him that outlet for jumping on things and elbowing things and kicking them, which he wouldn't otherwise have and I can't really train him not to at this point. I don't know why. So we do more of that kind of thing. He likes to run; he likes to pretend. He wants me to pretend like we're both robots or dinosaurs or something.

This father was not the only one to note that he played differently with his children than his wife did. Another father described how he was deliberate in his choice to play with his daughter in such a physical manner:

> I read all the stereotypical stuff [to prepare for having a child]. They said don't ever shy away from playing rough with your daughters even though people might look at you and tell you that. . . . We wrestle. . . . I'm her jungle gym. So, I'll lay on the floor and she plays, she slides down my leg, that's her favorite thing to do now. Runs across the room and jumps on me. I mean, it's just our . . . stuff [my wife] would never want to do.

This man noted that fathers tend to treat their daughters differently than their sons. However, much like the other fathers described earlier, he liked to roughhouse with his daughter. Such behaviors reinforce gendered expectations about appropriate behavior; fathers could be the "fun" parents while mothers performed other tasks. As this last father pointed out, such gender socialization often starts from an early age because men are often dissuaded from "playing rough" with their daughters.

In addition to roughhousing, many men discussed that they were more likely to engage in imaginative games with their children, such as the dad earlier who explained that his son liked to pretend that they were robots or dinosaurs. One father described his son's elaborate role play:

> One of his favorite things to do . . . is have battles where they're built around one or another of the fantasy games. . . . So he's into

Bakugan and Pokémon and super action heroes and so we have these and he usually wants me to be the bad guy and he's the good guy and we have to choose roles and then we have these super weapons. And then we—we basically wrestle together and we play battle music, which is usually like 80s punk rock from my iPod. He has pretty strong opinions about what makes good battle music. . . . So I sort of dance around and we—then we throw pillows and I tickle him.

Even in this elaborate role play of good guys and bad guys, physical play is central. Many fathers shared such stories of playing with their children in a manner the mothers would be less likely to do.

In addition to roughhousing, many fathers also suggested that they were more likely to play with their children outside, either playing sports in the front yard or taking them on outings. One father of a high school athlete said that he frequently worked with his son on soccer or basketball skills at their home. Another dad said he was more likely to take his children to the playground. Another father shared that he might do "impromptu" activities and throw rugby balls or baseballs with his children. All such activities reinforce traditional definitions of masculinity, which value athleticism as part of the male identity (Connell & Messerschmidt, 2005). These behaviors are acceptable for men to participate in with their children because they adhere to traditional gender roles.

While some activities were centered closer to home, many fathers shared that they were more likely to take their children on outings. Several fathers said that they took their children to local nature centers or on hikes. One father catalogued all of the tasks he was more likely to do with his elder son:

> I'm more likely to make him run around, or play soccer, or go for a hike, or go to [the nature center] or go to the swimming pool or something like that. I'm usually the one who will take him swimming or something like that for instance or, you know, is more enthusiastic about taking him to soccer practice or something like that.

While this father felt that he was more likely to engage in more physical activities with his son than his wife, other fathers reported that they planned occasional outings with their kids, such as one dad who took his son on a father-son ski weekend. Another father reported that he was trying to cultivate in his children a love of his favorite sport: mountain biking:

> I'm really into mountain biking. It's one of my favorite things to do. And so, my kids like to do that as well. Not quite as much

as I do . . . you know, suffering up a hill for an hour and a half isn't their idea of a good time, even though it is for me. So, we do that kind of stuff.

This father continued to find time for his own passion while spending time with his children. His experiences resemble those of many of his peers who also reported that they tried to find ways to be outside and active with their children whenever possible.

Men were also more likely than their wives to coach sports teams, another activity that allows men to draw on traits and behaviors inherent in hegemonic masculinity. Much like the father who mountain biked with his children, many fathers were able to continue their passion for sports they had enjoyed playing as younger men. Thirteen of the fathers coached or were involved in youth sports; in contrast, only one father noted that his wife had coached their children's teams. Several of the fathers served as referees or umpires. One father who used to coach his children's sports teams now serves as the statistician for his son's high school basketball team. Others were coaches or assistant coaches. One father noted that he coached both basketball and baseball, despite preferring one sport over the other. "I've coached his basketball team for 10 years now. . . . I coached my other son's baseball team—that gives it some balance. I really don't like baseball that much, but I still did it." This father, like many others, has invested a significant amount of time over many years coaching sports for his children.

A father of three discussed the commitment he felt to coaching, and the benefits that being a coach brings:

> I coach soccer so that I can arrange for the practice days and times of the games and if I have control, then I can circle around my work. . . . I did it for the 16-year-old and I've been doing it for the 6-year-old and I'll continue until he goes to high school and then I will do it again for the other one. I enjoy it. It's a way to help the community because not many people have the time. . . . They're always asking for coaches, right? I just think it's important. I just do it.

Much like the previous father who had coached his son for more than a decade, this father of multiple children planned to coach for many years as a way for him to give back to the community. He was also strategic in that coaching allowed him to set a practice schedule that worked for his professional obligations and other demands for the family. He was not the only father to point out this benefit:

> One of the benefits of coaching a soccer team is that you get to determine when the practices are. Well, it's actually really important, so what I do is I find out when my oldest son's practices are, and what I'll do is I'll slot my practice in an hour before. So, he'll go with me to the youngest's practice, and he'll actually help me with the practice. And when the practice is done, we all go to his practice.

This father also planned coaching obligations to accommodate the schedules of both of his children who play sports. Such planning proved to be critical for many families who were juggling multiple after-school activities with the demands of careers. Fathers reported a variety of ways that they engaged with their children. Most of this engagement took the form of physical activity: physical play and roughhousing, physical exercise, or coaching sports. All of these behaviors are those that are valued by traditional definitions of hegemonic masculinity. Few fathers reported that their wives engaged in any of these activities with their kids. Instead, the tasks that women were more likely to perform were similarly gendered—and perhaps far less fun.

The Daily Grind with a Side of Nurturing

Fathers reported that their wives were more likely to be responsible for activities that kept their homes and children's lives running. Women were responsible for coordinating schedules and appointments, making sure the children were clothed, and sought out as their children's confidants and soothers. In these ways, the work that women performed often adhered to traditional gender norms.

Many of the fathers recognized that their wives performed more routine work in the home. For example, one father stated:

> She does a lot of just like maintenance parent time. She does bedtime with him every night. She cooks dinner for him most every night. . . . It's really mostly her and stuff like that. So they have this . . . sort of daily grind kind of bond.

Several fathers also noted how their wives recognized that the work that they performed was less "fun" than the tasks typically delegated to their husbands. One father explained:

> [My wife] often feels like I end up having more fun with them and she is more sort of doing un-fun stuff with them. She picks them up at 3:30 so she'll be there with [our son] making sure he

> gets homework done and that kind of thing and so that time that
> she's with them from 3:30 until after dinner is often her kind of
> managing these kind of things like homework and stuff and I bathe
> them and get them ready for bed and there's things like that. . . . I
> know that she feels like I end up having a lot of the fun stuff with
> them and that can be difficult.

Although both this professor and his wife work full-time, his wife's schedule
as a teacher allows her to spend time with their children in the afternoon,
which typically meant that she was in charge of helping kids with homework
and other tasks until the professor was able to come home from work. As
such, she felt that her husband was often able to do more fun activities
with the children because he did not have to negotiate discussions over
homework. This man was not the only to note such discussions in the
household:

> My wife would say the rules are that she feels like I'm able to play
> more than she is, and she kind of resents that at times, where I
> come home and part of it's my nature, and so a part of it that she
> feels as her role began with the manager of the home, that she sort
> of stays in that role. She's not real playful by nature, so. . . . But,
> she's kind of, . . . "But, I want to be the playful one." And I'm
> like, "Well, go for it. Be the playful one." And she's like, "I'm too
> busy thinking of all the things we've got to do, and I don't feel like
> I've got the time or energy." And I'll say, "What can I do?" And so
> we wrestle with that. How can I take over the management stuff?
> And if I do, I don't usually do it well enough.

This father discussed several aspects of the division of labor in his home.
First, his wife felt that he gets to be more playful with their children. And,
while this playfulness is motivated by differences in personality, she still
wished that she could be more playful. Second, his wife performed more
"management" in the home. And when the father tried to assume some
of that responsibility, things did not run smoothly. He and his wife have
adopted a distinct set of roles that may keep the household running more
smoothly, but such an arrangement leaves her in charge of the less-fun
activities.

Many fathers, in fact, noted that their wives were far more likely than
they to coordinate their children's activities, including doctor's appointments, haircuts, and playdates, confirming past empirical studies that point
out that women are typically more responsible for the daily activities of their

children than are men (Lamb et al., 1985). Said one father, "[My wife] is far likelier to be negotiating with other parents about certain playdates or play opportunities than I would be." Such division of labor was common in homes regardless of parental employment status; even in homes where both parents worked full-time, the mother still tended to be in charge of routine daily activities. Many fathers attributed this division of labor to a natural division of traits: their wives, they suggested, were much better at planning and organization than they were. These three fathers each used such language:

> My wife is more of a details kind of person. I'm more of a bigger picture kind of a guy. So, [my wife and kids] talk about specifics. "So, at school we have to do this, we have to do that by such and such date." My wife is excellent at that. She's like an operations kind of a person. I'm not like that. You know, I forget details. I forget dates or whatever.

Another father described his wife's role with their son similarly:

> She definitely likes to go to all the school events and doctor's appointments and things like that. I say "like" because she does. . . . She just likes to know all those things, and I'm much more laid back. And she's much more of a planner, and really likes having all the knowledge, so I usually don't ask enough questions and then she needs to call people up and check.

This professor's wife, he suggested, was far better at organizing while he typically neglected to ask the appropriate questions. And so, in this family, too, scheduling fell to the mother. Another father explained the role that his wife played in organizing their children's lives:

> I would say that the majority of the child rearing falls on my wife's shoulders. She is the one who is active with the PTA. She is the one who is active with the synagogue. She is the one who really keeps in touch. Here we have in our school, we have this thing online and basically you could log in and see exactly what your kids are doing and where your kids are on a real-time basis. She is the one that is on top of that—much more on top of that than I am. She also pays the bills. I can't handle that. She runs the house and I help. I try to help as much as possible and not take it for granted.

Each of these fathers was married to women who worked at least part-time outside the home. Despite the fact that each member of the couple had professional obligations to fulfill, the majority of scheduling still fell to the woman. The narratives that the men used to describe their wives suggested that being engaged with their children and running the household were traits that came naturally to women rather than necessarily being behaviors that women are socialized to perform. In this way, although gender norms may slowly be shifting in the workplace and the home, traditional norms still play a significant role in influencing men and women's behaviors.

In addition to being responsible for the details of daily life, women were far more likely to be responsible for going clothes shopping for and with the children. Even in families where men reported doing more caregiving than their wives, women still remained responsible for buying clothing. One father in such an arrangement explained, "She's more likely to . . . take him shopping, make sure he has clothes and shoes, and she's much better about even buying toys and gifts and things like that than I am." Another father who performed significant care in the home acknowledged that his wife was responsible for making sure their daughter had clothes that fit for the summer. Many other fathers reported a similar division of labor, usually framing the task in a negative way. Said one father, "[My wife] will take them shopping usually. I don't. If I can escape that, I'm happy." Another father reported, "I hate going to the mall. She'll take them to the mall." And another: "Well, there is a stereotype here. She does more of the serious shopping with them. I go along, but I just can't get into it as deeply." And still another:

> She does a lot more shopping with them than I do. I'm sort of the negative shopper in the sense that I consider it a successful shopping trip if I go and look at things and determine that there's nothing worth buying, and that's not a very satisfactory solution for . . . especially my older daughter, who has become quite a healthy consumer. So that's one activity that they do a lot together.

Each of these men discussed how clothes shopping was a task that they had left to their wives. Each of their responses, too, coded shopping as a feminine activity and not one in which men enjoy engaging. Such attribution relates back to norms of hegemonic masculinity, which prescribe appropriate behaviors in which men are to engage; shopping typically does not have a place on that list.

Mothers were noted for performing a few other tasks more than fathers. Some fathers suggested that their wives were more likely to serve as their children's confidantes and nurturers. The father of a preschool-age child reported that his wife was their son's "comforter." Another reported that his children frequently sought out his wife for help, though were willing to go to him if she was unavailable:

> Any crisis that happens for [my daughters] or anytime they're upset, their first person to approach is their mother. Now, if their mother isn't around, it's not that they have any problem approaching me. That's quite clearly the case. But, she is the person to whom they are more likely to seek immediate redress.

In this family, too, the mother was the one who helped children with their problems. In yet another family, a father described how his wife was more attuned to problems going on with their teenage daughters. "My wife . . . [monitors] bigger sort of issues between mothers and daughters. Like my one daughter broke up with her boyfriend, whatever that means. She still hasn't told me, but I learned it through my wife." Again, in this family, the mother played the role of confidante during personal crises. This father also suggested that such a role might be natural for relationships between mothers and daughters. While such a statement might be true, it also points to the institutionalization of gender norms and roles. Girls are expected to be better able to relate to their mothers as they are socialized to adopt different traits from boys. However, even in families with sons, mothers were noted as being the one more likely to be sought out for comfort in difficult times.

While men and women performed some of the same tasks with children throughout the day, they also performed different tasks that point to gendered divisions of labor. Men's unique tasks tended to revolve around fun and physical activity while women's unique tasks fulfilled more feminine roles as caregivers and shoppers. In addition, women were far more likely to be noted for performing the daily scheduling tasks that are necessary to keep lives moving forward. In short, while men may interact and engage more with their children than in the past, their wives still retain greater responsibility (Lamb et al., 1985). While I have discussed gendered differences in tasks across all households, men noted some pointed differences in the division of labor in the home based on the division of labor outside the home, or based on whether women worked outside the home. It is to these differences that I now turn.

"Support Staff" versus Coparent

Of the 70 fathers interviewed, 10 were married to women who were full-time stay-at-home mothers; 13 were married to women who worked part-time outside of the home; and the remaining men, save a handful who were divorced, were married to women who worked full-time outside of the home. Men with wives who worked full-time outside of the home exhibited different behaviors in the home than their counterparts with wives who stayed home part time or full time, suggesting that sharing breadwinning responsibilities leads couples to also share caregiving responsibilities.

Many men reported that their wives had transitioned between different employment statuses throughout their marriage, which suggests that men's careers and children's needs took precedence over both the careers and needs of women. For example, three fathers at Southern University reported that their wives had stayed home with their children until just a few years earlier. Other fathers reported that their wives who had worked full time had once worked part time and still others reported that their wives had worked part time, but now stayed home with their children. More often than not, the arrival of children prompted these shifts. One father recounted his wife's career shifts:

> It was an option for my wife to work or not to work. So, when we had kids, she was home for the first [few years], I guess until they got to kindergarten. Then she went to work half time. . . . When we went on sabbatical leave, she quit, and she hasn't gone back to work yet.

Over the course of a decade, his wife went from working full time to staying home full time to working part time to again staying home full time. Her career moves were influenced not only by the arrival of children in the home, but also by an opportunity brought by her husband's career. To allow the family to live overseas for a period of time, she gave up her job. This was not the only family to report that the arrival of children brought changes to the wife's employment. Another father reported that his wife quit her job to stay home full-time when their children were born. There were other fathers who reported that their wives went back to work after their children were older, which added a degree of chaos to family lives. One father recounted that his wife was very stressed with the demands of her new job, which necessitated that the family make some shifts to accommodate it.

In addition to staying home or reducing the number of hours that they worked, many men reported that their wives had shifted careers after having children. Some men explained that their wives were interested in tenure-track faculty positions, but had been unable to find suitable jobs in the same location as their husbands. One man's wife cobbled together three adjunct positions to make money. Several other men reported that their wives had once worked in high-powered professions, but had scaled back their jobs after becoming parents, such as one woman who used to be a lab scientist, quit her job to stay with the kids, and most recently went back to work in the service industry. Another mother had worked as a full-time museum curator, but took a part-time position as a childcare administrator after becoming a mother:

> Before we had our child, she had [a] full-time job as [a] museum curator. And after we had our child, she went back to work full time, briefly, in a different museum as a curator, full time. But . . . with us both working full-time, it was putting too much of a strain on our son to be in childcare so many hours a day. So, she eventually quit that job altogether. This is when we were living [elsewhere]. . . . When we moved [here], she at first didn't have a job at all, for the first year and a half, I think, of our being here. And eventually she took this part-time job and I think her hours have been gradually increased, but she still is technically working part time.

Much like the previous professor's wife, this man's wife has also transitioned through a variety of career changes and statuses: from full time in one career to staying at home to part time in another career. In each case, the wife's career path changed specifically due to the arrival of children.

Several fathers suggested that they made a gender-neutral decision about who would stay home following the birth of their children. One man described how the decision played out in his home. "We decided that when we had children, whoever had the most interesting and lucrative career opportunities, that person would work. We don't care who it is. Flip a coin. We don't care. She said, 'I'm done.'" Another father described how his wife, who holds a master's degree, came to the decision to quit her full-time job:

> She worked all the way up until . . . two years into my Ph.D. program. . . . So, we said, "You know what? It's a lot easier on everybody if she doesn't work and stays home." Because of [the demands of my] Ph.D. program, . . . it was much better for her to not be working to deal with day-to-day things.

Some of these decisions were described as gender neutral while others were framed around meeting the needs of the children; very few fathers actually acknowledged that such decisions were informed by societal gender norms that make it more appropriate for women to leave the workforce than for men to do so. National statistics suggest that 5% of academic women compared with 20% of academic men have stay-at-home partners (Schiebinger et al., 2008). While these decisions may have been framed as gender neutral, they clearly conform to a well-established pattern of many other families. Such decisions had consequences for both the man's and the woman's career. Men were able to rely on increased help in the home that allowed them to focus on their careers while women, some with advanced degrees and demanding careers, stepped out of the workplace to focus on their children.

Often in these families, men reported that their wives took a greater role in terms of child rearing. One father, whose wife had once worked outside the home, reflected on the fact that while his wife now performed the majority of housework, cooking, and other tasks to keep the house going, they had shared domestic work much more equally when she was employed. Quitting her job freed her to do more work inside the home and allowed him to focus his energy outside the home. Another father explained that he considered himself to be "support staff" in that he tried to do more housecleaning and grocery shopping to allow his wife to focus more attention on their children. While such a division of labor (greater focus on housework, less on child rearing) contrasts to that reported by other fathers, it still suggests that he takes a lesser role in the home than his wife. He explained his role with his children:

> Certainly it's a secondary role. . . . It's difficult because I tend to defer because she is around them much more, and she sets the ground rules. So very often they'll come to me and ask me something and I'll say, "You know what? You're going to have to ask your mom," because I don't want to say something to contradict something she's told them already. . . . So it does tend to be a very secondary role. . . . I think if she was working and we both saw them the same, I'm not sure what it would be.

This father felt that the role that he took with his children was secondary to that of his stay-at-home wife. He argued that because she was with their children more, she was responsible for setting the ground rules in the home and he was hesitant to tell his children something that might contradict what she had already said. While such intentions are helpful in terms of avoiding confusion, they also reflect this family's division of labor: the husband was responsible for work outside the home while his wife was responsible for most work inside the home. As he wondered, would roles be different if they both worked outside the home? For some dual-career couples, different roles were negotiated while in others traditional roles continued to reign.

Whereas traditional divisions of labor seemed to characterize marriages in which the wife stayed at home or worked part time, roles were less reified between couples where both husband and wife worked. Certainly, as discussed earlier, men typically performed less work than their wives. However, in homes with a stay-at-home mom or a mother who did not have the constraints of a standard 9-to-5, 40-hour workweek, both members of the couple knew that the wife was at home and could be relied on to attend to domestic matters. In fact, this was the primary reason many men gave that their wives stopped working: to take care of their children. In contrast, in dual-career couples, frequent negotiation occurred between husband and wife in terms of who was going to do what, both at work and at home.

Many fathers in dual-career couples discussed being in constant communication with their wives to figure out who would perform certain tasks. One father shared: "Every day, we're on the phone trying to figure out [who does what after work]: 'Where are you? What can you do? What can I do?' that kind of thing." He shared that their division of personal responsibilities depended on who had more pressing professional responsibilities that particular day. Another father shared that he and his working wife had a similar arrangement: "So if we did have to get home for anything, we would just call each other and negotiate, . . . [and] ask, 'What does your schedule look like? Can you shift things around?'" For this couple and many others, constant negotiation ensured that their children were always taken care of.

In earlier chapters, I discussed how fathers praised the flexibility of the faculty career for helping them balance work and family. Some fathers acknowledged that this flexibility allowed them benefits that their spouses working outside of the professoriate did not get. Such flexibility meant that some fathers needed to be more cognizant of their wives' needs, particularly on the weekends. One father described his experiences with his wife:

> It's kind of a negotiation, as so many things are, at least in my experience of marriage. By Friday night, she's just beat and so Saturday becomes a day when I can kind of handle the kids primarily. It's primarily me who has them on Saturday and so she can have some time to herself. Because it is a perk of an academic job that, you know, I get my own time. I'm working but I'm by myself and if I want to read the *New York Times* or whatever, watch a movie, I can. Her job doesn't allow that. And so . . . it's Sundays that I work and not Saturdays because that gives her a break and then Sunday, then I'll work. Even though she's very understanding and very supportive of my work it's hard. It's hard—it's exhausting for her.

This father reflected on the benefits that flexibility brings. Although he may have intense demands on his time, he also has the leisure to determine how to use his time and can opt to engage in self-care during the workweek. His wife, who works in a nonacademic position, does not have the same luxury.

Many fathers noted that the role that they take with their children differs from traditional male roles, and some avowed a commitment to coparenting. However, they also noted the trade-offs that come with this involvement. One father explained:

> I think one of the reasons that [my wife] and I kind of decided to get together right, we kind of saw in each other this commitment to doing things equally, sharing this whole experience—the work/family piece. I don't think anyone had any sense of how exhausting it would be to kind of divvy that up every day and kind of without clear expectations. I mean expectations are always being created almost week to week and you're kind of doing things a different way. So it's very flexible, but I remember my mom saying, "It's so great what you guys do!" And I'd say, "It's exhausting," like you fight more because you just have to kind of give and take more in a lot of ways.

This father noted the trade-offs that come with sharing in breadwinning and caregiving equally. Without firmly defined roles, both members of the couple regularly have to negotiate who is going to do which task. Other fathers noted the shift in roles, and both the costs and benefits they incurred for this shift:

> [My wife] wouldn't be married to somebody that didn't hold the same outlook as she does, which involved coparenting and coliving. You know what I mean. It's like that. This is a postgender division kind of reality here and so you know if sometimes I'll joke or something that like "my father never did this," she'll say, "Well, of course not." . . . So sometimes I'll go wow it would be nice to have a more standard guy in the 50s come home from work, stay at the office until 6 kind of day. . . . I don't really take that very seriously, but men have given up certain kinds of leisure that they once had and what we've gotten in exchange is the full membership in the parental theater, right? And sometimes you look at what you've gained—in other words, real intimacy with your kids and sometimes you look at what you've lost, which is . . . guys had it easy, and you know they didn't realize it then.

This professor and his wife both espouse a commitment to coparenting and both work full time outside the home. He reflected on the fact that gender roles have shifted considerably, suggesting that American society is in a postgender era. As the experiences of other faculty fathers suggest, such a claim may not be true, though certainly more men are sharing in child rearing, which suggests that norms of appropriate roles for men have shifted as well. And in exchange for such participation, men are able to form deeper relationships with their children. Such relationships may compensate for the leisure that men have relinquished by making a greater commitment in the home.

These portraits are not to suggest that all men who are in dual-career couples are committed to coparenting or that those with stay-at-home wives do not have meaningful relationships with their children. What these portraits make clear is that men whose wives do not work full time outside of the home have different demands on their time and different domestic responsibilities than men who are negotiating with a wife who also works full time. Couples who are able to fall back on a traditional division of labor may find that their roles are more clear, but yet, one might suggest that both man and woman suffer from being denied participation in the other sphere.

Conclusion

Men and women historically performed different types of labor: men worked in the professional sphere while women were relegated to the domestic sphere. Although these roles have shifted considerably over the past 50 years as more women have entered the workplace, traditional divisions of labor still maintain a stronghold in the home. As the literature indicates, women still perform more childcare and housework (Bianchi et al., 2000; Coltrane, 1996; U.S. Bureau of Labor Statistics, 2013). When men engage with their children, they are more likely to take a playful role. Some have suggested that fathers may be involved with their children in one of three ways: (1) engagement; (2) availability; and (3) responsibility (Lamb et al., 1985). While fathers' engagement and availability have increased, they still trail behind women with all three levels of involvement, and most particularly responsibility.

The experiences of faculty fathers echo the experiences of those outside the academy. First, men and women are likely to perform different tasks in the home. Men tend to gravitate toward activities that are fun: playing and roughhousing with their children, doing outdoors activities, and coaching sports teams. In contrast, women were reported as being more likely to be responsible for the details of the house; the mothers generally scheduled playdates, took children to the doctor, and made sure that homework was completed. They were also more likely to take their children shopping. Note the number of fathers who proudly stated that going to the mall was something they liked to avoid, underscoring with their insistence just how unmasculine shopping is. Women also were frequently sought out as children's confidantes and were the first point of contact when children were trying to navigate problems. Across families, while mothers and fathers participated equally in some tasks, they also split the performance of various tasks along gendered lines: men performed more physical and fun tasks while women performed the domestic duties. The fathers' experiences suggest that many were actively engaged with and available to their children, but they more often than not ceded responsibility duties to their wives (Lamb et al., 1985). Some fathers suggested that they left the planning to their wives because they were naturally better at it. However, as others have pointed out (Lorber, 2003; West & Zimmerman, 1987), organization and child rearing are not necessarily feminine skills, but rather women have acquired more experience with those skills over the course of their lifetime, thus making the division of labor in adulthood seem more natural.

While many married couples reported that they fell into these gendered roles, there were ways that additional factors, particularly the wife's employment status, shaped the provision of care in the home. Of the 70 fathers interviewed, 23 were married to women who stayed at home at least part time with their children. In those families, many of the men reported that they served a secondary role to that of their wives; since their wives were home more than they were, the women tended to maintain more responsibility for child rearing. Many men also discussed the decisions that the couple reached about how to manage having children; in many of these families, the women decided to give up successful careers to stay home with their children. Although some fathers suggested that they could have just as easily given up their careers, the number of women who gave up academic careers and other white-collar jobs suggests that these decisions were not gender neutral, but rather based on gender norms. And, in these families, gender norms were often reinforced through the division of labor.

In contrast, couples in which both parents worked outside of the home tended to evidence a shift in gender roles. Many fathers discussed the constant negotiation over who would take care of their children. Such negotiation was necessary because man and woman were working both outside the home and inside the home and could not call on a traditional division of labor to guide their actions. As several men pointed out, trading in their roles as sole breadwinners may have led to more work in the home for men, but it also allowed them to participate in their children's lives in ways that they had never been able to do before.

In many ways, the academic career embodies a series of contradictions. The structure of academic work brings flexibility that allows men to be more involved with their children than men working in other white-collar professions. Many fathers were able to coach their children's sports teams because they did not need permission to leave work at 4:00 P.M. Although these fathers might have been engaging in gendered activities, they were increasing their engagement with their children. However, academic work also assumes that the individual has few responsibilities inside the home. And, as national studies suggest, male faculty are far more likely to be in traditional sole breadwinner marriages than the U.S. population at large; 20% of all male faculty have a stay-at-home partner compared with 11% of the U.S. population (Schiebinger et al., 2008; U.S. Census Bureau, 2010). Clearly, something about academic work makes managing two careers difficult for families. Many fathers in this study suggested that their wives stopped working to attend to the needs of the children. Many fathers in dual-career couples reported the difficulties involved with negotiating childcare responsibilities with their wives. Life seemed easier for those couples that had identified a fixed (and gendered) division of labor. While the academy might create conditions for involved fatherhood, the nature and the expectations of the faculty career simultaneously reinforces traditional divisions of labor.

The conditions of work in the academy have implications for the conditions of work in the home. As I explored in the previous chapter, many fathers experienced a change in their productivity when becoming a parent, leading them to question their worth as an ideal worker. However, being a faculty member and a man has implications for men's work in the home. In particular, the gender norms that define academic work and are implicit in university structures expect that all faculty members can be ideal workers and leave caregiving duty to someone at home. For men, these expectations mean that they are supposed to adhere to norms of hegemonic masculinity eschewing nurturing activities. To do otherwise may lead to challenges to their identities as men. Until organizational structures and culture as well as gender roles change, both men and women will be expected to adhere to defined roles that constrain any behaviors that deviate from the norm.

The gendered division of labor has significant implications for men, women, and workplaces. Since gender norms still hold that women are more likely to stay home with children, employers lose human capital when well-qualified women leave the workplace to raise children. Note the number of women who left their careers to raise their children or who traded in one career for another that was more conducive to child rearing. Women are forced to make these choices because most workplaces are generally unforgiving of familial demands as they continue to depend on ideal worker norms. If society agrees that raising children should be given priority, then certainly workplaces should be structured in ways to allow both men and women to participate in the enterprise. However, ideal worker norms suggest that parenting does not factor into employee work, thus forcing many couples to make a decision about how to split their time. For men, the gendered division of labor excludes them from participating in their children's lives to the same extent as their wives. Even for men whose wives work outside the home full-time, traditional divisions of labor still reign, putting extra burdens on women and robbing men of important moments with their children. Although traditional gender norms remain entrenched in universities and among many who populate them, there have been shifts in how younger generations of academics conceptualize their identities as faculty and as fathers. I explore these shifts and the consequences they might have for the academy in the next chapter.

CHAPTER 7

Tenure versus Fatherhood

* — *

How Generation X Faculty Eschew the Ideal Worker

Seeking tenure is a stressful undertaking. And, as many parents can attest, raising children is stressful as well. Many assistant professors simultaneously contend with both major tasks. The norms of the academy expect assistant professors to work tirelessly to fulfill institutional expectations, often with little consideration for the personal demands on their time. And while historically many faculty were willing and able to make that sacrifice, the newest group of assistant professors—men and women alike—come from a generation less willing to prioritize work over family.

As I suggested in chapter 1, work/family issues have been labeled a woman's issue. And in part these assumptions are fair as research suggests that women typically perform more work in the home, even among academic couples (Mason & Goulden, 2004). However, gender roles are shifting, creating space for men to perform more caregiving in the home. At colleges and universities, this shift is particularly apparent in the most recent cohort of assistant professors. Whereas their senior counterparts may have been reticent to use family-friendly policies or to prioritize work over family, members of the younger generation are grappling more with their conflicting roles as academics and as fathers in a gendered university structure that places more value on the former role than the latter. In part, this shift may be attributed to the ascendance of those from Generation X to the ranks of the professoriate.

As I have discussed throughout this book, dominant societal norms suggest that men are to be breadwinners and women are to be caregivers. Such norms translate into the academy and inform faculty work. However, norms differ across generations. Full professors may espouse one set of norms

whereas assistant professors, as a cohort, may espouse another. It is the experiences of this younger group of fathers—and the ways that they navigate
their families and careers—that are the focus of this chapter. I argue that
many assistant professors, who most frequently come from Generation X,
reject traditional notions of faculty work to carve out ways to be involved
parents and, in the process, move closer to creating a new definition of
hegemonic masculinity that values both breadwinning and caregiving as
appropriate roles for men.

In this chapter, I draw on the experiences of 22 assistant professors
across the four universities. Like their tenured counterparts, the assistant
professors came from a variety of disciplines, including the humanities and
social sciences, science and engineering, and professional schools. All 22
men were married to women and all but three had wives who worked at
least 20 hours a week outside the home. The remaining three had wives
who stayed at home full time. Fathers had between one and three children,
ranging in age from infancy to high school.

After briefly describing the norms of the academy, I discuss the generations that currently populate the academy, focusing in particular on Generation X. While I go into depth shortly, Generation X faculty, more than
others who have come before them, place a higher emphasis on work/family
balance, a choice that has implications for the ways in which they navigate
their careers. As the experiences of these fathers suggest, even within the
work-driven culture of the academy and the extra pressure associated with
the pretenure period, faculty from Generation X are bucking the trend to
prioritize family over career and, in some cases, tenure.

Norms of the Academy

Academic work was founded on the notion that the scholar would give all
of his (or her) time to the enterprise. From Chaucer's characterization of the
scholar nearly a millennium ago to the professor in today's modern research
university, the stereotype is clear: academics devote all of their time to the
pursuit of knowledge. As I have made clear throughout this text, faculty
work is built on the norms of the ideal worker (Acker, 1990; Williams,
2000), which suggests that employees are always available to perform work,
typically putting in well over the standard 40 hours per week demanded of
a full-time position. As Schuster and Finkelstein (2006) found, while faculty
typically reported working 40 hours per week in 1984, more recently faculty
reported working an average of 49 hours per week. The authors also reported
that the proportion of faculty working more than 50 hours per week had
doubled from 23% in 1972 to 40% in 1998. As these data suggest, faculty

are indeed living up to the norms of the ideal worker, at least in terms of number of hours worked per week.

Ideal worker norms have come to define expectations for faculty work for men and women. Contributing to and informed by the norms of the ideal worker are the expectations that inform the quest for tenure. Typically, the assistant professor period is defined as a five- to six-year period in which scholars are expected to work nonstop to produce enough scholarship to earn tenure. While significant stress accompanies the tenure-seeking period, scholars have found that additional stress stems from a lack of clarity around tenure expectations (Austin & Rice, 1998; Eddy & Gaston-Gayles, 2008; Trower & Bleak, 2004). Furthermore, as tenure-track positions have decreased (Baldwin & Chronister, 2005; Sallee & Tierney, 2011; Schuster & Finkelstein, 2006), research expectations have increased (Austin & Rice; Schuster & Finkelstein; Trower, 2010). Faculty at research universities are increasingly being pushed to apply for external funding, which leads to additional stress. Achieving tenure seems to call for total devotion to work with little consideration of family responsibilities. Many of these norms are in direct contrast to those of Generation X, who compose the cohort of assistant professors in this study.

Norms of Generation X

Universities, like many workplaces, include representatives from many generations. From the emeriti faculty who represent the Silent Generation to the college students who compose the Millennial Generation, each group brings its own set of norms and values. Each generation's values are shaped by defining events that occurred during their youth and adolescence (Lancaster & Stillman, 2002; Zemke, Raines, & Filipczak, 2000). For example, given that the Great Depression shaped the Silent Generation, one might wonder whether the children growing up today will be similarly influenced by the economic downturn. In contrast, the Baby Boomers grew up in a time of record growth and optimism, leading those in this generation to espouse its own set of values.

Based on the work of Lancaster and Stillman (2002) and Zemke and colleagues (2000), I offer these brief summaries of the four generations that are found in colleges and universities today. The Silent Generation is composed of individuals born approximately between 1922 and 1943. Members of this generation came of age during the Great Depression and World War II and are most frequently described as hard-working, loyal, and unlikely to question the status quo. The majority of members of this generation have retired from colleges and universities, though some still represent the ranks of the senior professoriate. Baby Boomers (born between 1943 and 1962) compose the next generation and are frequently described as driven, team players, and possessing a desire to please. Well over 60 million Americans are classified as Baby Boomers; because of this population explosion, Baby Boomers often had to compete with many others for a limited number of jobs. As a result, many Baby Boomers internalized values of putting in long hours at work. Baby Boomers compose the majority of the professoriate, particularly at the associate and full levels.

Generation X is composed of individuals who were born between 1962 and 1980 and, in the most positive terms, its members are described as independent, creative, and adaptable. Members of Generation X developed their values in reaction to those of their parents; during their youth, the divorce rate tripled (Lancaster & Stillman, 2002), leading many in Generation X to prioritize family over work and, in the process, reject parts of the work ethic that defined previous generations. Most current assistant professors come from this generation. Finally, the Millennial Generation is composed of individuals born after 1980. Millennials typically maintain close connections with their parents, are good at multitasking, and are reliant on technology for communication and work. Millennials account for a small percentage of university faculty, but an ever-increasing percentage of the graduate student population.

Generational differences in values can lead to conflicts among members of different generations. For example, given that members of Generation X place great value on balancing work and family, they may find themselves at odds with Baby Boomers, who have built their careers on hard work and many hours in the office. As their experiences are the focus of this chapter, I provide a bit more detail on the values that define Generation X, highlighting in particular their emphasis on work/life balance, flexibility in work practices, the rise of dual-career couples, and coparenting and shifting gender norms.

Work/Life Balance

Scholars from both inside and outside the academy agree that members of Generation X value work/life balance more than any previous generation (Bickel & Brown, 2005; Helms, 2010; Howell, Servis, & Bonham, 2005; Lancaster & Stillman, 2002; Stone-Johnson, 2012; Trower, 2010, 2012; Zemke et al., 2000). Members of this generation are less willing to sacrifice family obligations for their career than their parents. Some speculate that this shift in values stems from the fact that many members of Generation X were raised in divorced parent homes or as latch-key kids, leading them to seek different ways to structure their own family lives. Perhaps in recognition of the importance of balancing personal and professional demands, many universities have implemented policies and practices that honor the family concerns of faculty. For example, Howell and colleagues noted that university hospitals have adjusted practices in recognition of these shifting values, such as by not scheduling meetings after 5:00 P.M. or on weekends. While such actions seem small, they represent a significant departure from the status quo in these environments, but, as the authors noted, are necessary in order to retain new generations who are more vocal about the importance of their nonprofessional lives.

Flexibility in Work Practices

Members of Generation X also seek greater flexibility in where they perform their work. As several have noted (Bickel & Brown, 2005; Helms, 2010; Lancaster & Stillman, 2002), they are less interested in "face time," or putting in hours in the office when they might be more productive at home. As Helms found in her study of 16 Generation X faculty, professors of this generation see putting in "face time" as "as a sign that they are not using their time effectively and productively—a weakness, rather than a strength, and something to improve upon" (p. 9). In contrast, more senior faculty may work on campus five days a week and expect their younger colleagues to do the same. Furthermore, members of Generation X suggest that they should be evaluated based on productivity and output, and not on the number of hours that they work (Zemke et al., 2000). In some ways, this emphasis on productivity complements the expectations around earning tenure that focus on publication output (whether defined as quality or quantity) versus time spent engaged in work. If Generation X faculty are adequately productive, they can structure their time to both be successful with tenure and involved with their children.

In some ways, faculty are able to distance themselves from the notion of "face time" as a result of changes in when and where they can perform their work. Faculty have the luxury of being able to perform their work nearly anywhere, particularly thanks to the increased use and availability of technology over the past several decades. Having access to journal articles online and e-mail from nearly anywhere means that faculty can and do have the flexibility to perform their work in their office, in their homes, or anywhere in between and at all hours of the night. While such flexibility brings great benefit, it also means that the workday never ceases. As many have suggested (Heijstra & Rafnsdóttir, 2010; Menzies & Newson, 2007; Rafnsdóttir & Heijstra, 2001; Walker, 2009), faculty now have the added burden of always being able to access work, which leads to increased expectations that faculty will be available to respond to queries from colleagues and students throughout the evenings and weekends. However, such expectations do not always sit well with members of Generation X who value the flexibility but distance themselves from the pressure to work at all hours of the day and night.

RISE OF DUAL-CAREER COUPLES

While this is not necessarily a value that characterizes Generation X, it is worth noting that, like some of their Baby Boomer predecessors, many Generation X faculty belong to couples in which both members of the couple work outside the home. As I noted earlier in this book, 36% of faculty have an academic partner while an additional 36% of faculty have an employed (but nonacademic) partner (Schiebinger et al., 2008). In other words, 7 out of 10 faculty members are in couples where both individuals work outside the home. Such demographics have implications for ideal worker norms. The fact that 70% of faculty are in couples in which neither parent stays at home challenges the traditional breadwinner/caregiver dichotomy.

COPARENTING AND SHIFTING GENDER NORMS

Today's man spends more time engaged in parenting responsibilities than ever before. As I discussed in chapter 1, according to time-diary studies, the amount of time men spend with their children has increased over the past several decades, from 26 minutes a day in 1985 to 1 hour a day in 1998 and to 1 hour and 45 minutes in 2012 (Sayer et al., 2004; U.S. Bureau of Labor Statistics, 2013). While these numbers are small, they suggest that men's involvement with their children is increasing and will continue to do so. In part this increase in time spent with children might be attributed to new definitions of the involved father. Whereas at one point, the involved father was one who provided for his children by being a breadwinner (Doherty et al., 1998; Emslie & Hunt, 2009; Marsiglio et al., 2000), today's involved father is more likely than before to engage in care and serve a more nurturing function once associated only with women. To a degree, societal expectations have shifted. While men still tend to perform less care and work in the home than women, many members of Generation X have eschewed traditional gender norms in favor of creating a more equitable division of labor in the home and more time with their children. However, such values put them at odds with the gendered norms of the academy that rely heavily on the ideal worker and gendered divisions of labor, in both the workplace and the home. Generation X faculty members find themselves in a peculiar situation. Members of this generation prioritize family over career and are more likely to share parenting duties between both members of the couple. Faculty in this generation are also less likely to value being physically present at the office if doing so does not facilitate productivity. And, as I soon discuss, this particular generation of faculty also reports being less willing to sacrifice their family for the demands of their careers, even for tenure. These values fly in the face of the traditional values of the academy, which depends on the norm of the ideal worker who is always available and always working and the breadwinner/caregiver dichotomy inherent in traditional notions of hegemonic masculinity. Fathers who give more weight to their roles as parents come into conflict with the continuous productivity required to earn tenure. However, the actions of the fathers in this study suggest that they are redefining hegemonic masculinity, at least within the university context, to position caregiver as a valued masculine identity.

Demands of Faculty Work

All of the assistant professors were well aware of the stresses that accompanied the pretenure period. As one faculty member in the social sciences summed up, "I don't know any junior faculty who's not exhausted all the time." For many, this exhaustion came from the constant pressures to publish and for those in the sciences to earn grants. As one scientist explained, "Everybody has to get grant money. Everybody has to make program managers happy. Everybody has to turn in a ridiculous number of grant proposals because the funding rates are so low." Another scientist who had recently become quite successful at securing external funding reflected on his first few years in the professoriate when he was struggling to get grants.

> My wife says that before I got these grants, I was trying to hit every single cycle [by constantly submitting grant proposals]. . . . Without the grants, basically you shut your life down. And, so that's a lot of pressure. And especially if you have grad students, you have postdocs and things like that. . . . So my wife always says that in the early years of my daughter that, you know, I was literally working every weekend. And so . . . she feels like I sort of missed out on that part of [our daughter's] development.

A third father reflected on the never-ending stress that was associated with seeking grants:

> This job, I often describe it as you are an athlete. . . . You are competing, but there is no age limit. So you just stay in that race until you retire or you're tired of it and you quit. Otherwise, no

matter how, you have to stay in the race and you are competing with people in Harvard, Yale, or in any place in the world to get that small part of the funding. That's very stressful, and research itself is very enjoyable, but it's kind of a business.

All of these faculty members' statements illustrate the concerns of many scientists who know that they need to compete with others across the country to bring in external funding in order to conduct their research and to support graduate students and postdoctoral researchers. And, in some cases, as with the second professor, there may be stress to work constantly, leading faculty to spend less time with their children than they (or their spouses) would like. However, as I discuss shortly, this pressure to work constantly seems to be the exception rather than the rule among many assistant professors.

In addition to the pressures to bring in grants, many faculty discussed the pressures they felt to publish. One first-year assistant professor in the sciences was already thinking about how to reach the number of publications suggested by his department chair, realizing that he had a lot of work to do while he got his lab established. "You're expected to produce a lot. That's kind of that overriding pressure," he said. "I went to a seminar last fall and they said for [our school] that [assistant professors are expected to publish 10 articles] during the pretenure years." He went on to say, "My department chair said anywhere between seven and above sometimes fits the bill depending on the quality of the journals that you publish in." This father said he spent a lot of time thinking about how to meet departmental expectations that his colleagues had for him and his lab. Another faculty member in the social sciences reflected on the nebulous expectations that accompany tenure:

> I don't think people necessarily try to scare you, but they do a good job of at least putting somewhat of a dark cloud that's always looming over the horizon and you're quickly getting towards it and you have to have X amount of publications, you have to have a book, you have to have two books, you have to have [it] all. You have to be active; you have to have service to the university. Your teaching, you have to have an amazing teaching record and create new classes. So what they want from you—it's sort of like the way graduate school was. They want to see how much you can handle without collapsing.

For this professor, the demands of earning tenure are exhausting and ever changing. He explained how the professor who earns tenure needs to have a number of outstanding publications, be a great teacher, and provide service to the university. No wonder another professor described all assistant professors as "exhausted." In part, this professor suggested, the heavy load is a type of hazing designed to test early career faculty. Those who pass will earn tenure while those who do not will find employment elsewhere.

Many universities build in a series of evaluation points during the pretenure period. At some institutions, faculty are evaluated every year whereas other institutions have a third- or fourth-year review as the sole pretenure evaluation. Two fathers in the same department discussed one assistant professor's rocky pretenure review that both attributed to expectations senior faculty place on productivity and a lack of consideration for family obligations, particularly for men. The assistant professor explained the outcome of his review:

> I had my third-year review last year and there were some worries in the department that I hadn't gotten enough published and I wasn't far enough along on the manuscript. And I wasn't in the room when they had this conversation but a lot of people came up to me after the vote, and they renewed my contract, and said that they had a really long conversation as a department about . . . wanting to be a department that supported men and women with kids. And apparently there was a little bit of a debate because there were some who sort of felt like, "Look, there's lots of people without kids who shouldn't be sort of thought of differently."

In this professor's review, the conversation quickly turned to whether someone's parental status should be taken into account in discussions of productivity. For some, ideal worker norms and the separation of gender roles continued to dominate, thus making the consideration of children irrelevant. This departmental discussion underscores the ways in which gender is enacted through interactions, as theories of hegemonic masculinity (Connell, 1995) and gendered organizations suggest (Acker, 1990). From what this assistant professor was told, his senior colleagues debated whether family responsibilities should even be a part of discussions about faculty work; for many, such obligations should not be considered.

A senior colleague in the department also recounted the same discussion in which many faculty were less concerned about the assistant professor's family demands, but more concerned about whether the professor was on track to earn tenure.

> There was an unusually extensive discussion and debate about whether or not his contract would be renewed, and it was quite striking because there was—the concern was whether or not the faculty

member would be able to have a book in press or to go to press by the time that he was up for tenure. On the other hand, . . . the teaching reports were really extraordinary, and his research reports were really extraordinary, and the book involved a large amount of archival research. . . . He had a book project and everybody was very enthusiastic about the book project. It was a groundbreaking project but he was sort of behind schedule for having the milestone line up with his tenure appointment. . . . I sort of had the impression that these third-year renewal contracts were relatively routine, . . . but a bunch of people were raising these concerns. . . . This person is also a father, and I know he works pretty hard at that role too, and I actually said something about that in the meeting and nobody—I don't think anybody responded directly to that.

This senior faculty member later went on to describe how some colleagues approached him after the meeting to thank him for bringing parenthood into the conversation. For many, that concern fell on deaf ears as many senior faculty in the department continue to expect that faculty are going to be very productive and have few family demands on their time. Given that until recently many assistant professors were able to focus on the demands of the faculty career to the exclusion of all other issues, such an expectation once made sense. For a variety of reasons, today's assistant professor is more likely to be juggling family demands with work. And, despite the expectations of senior colleagues and the norms of the academy that expect constant work and self-sacrifice, many assistant professors in this study suggested that they were unwilling to sacrifice family for their career.

Prioritizing Parenthood

While many of the professors realized what was required to earn tenure, they did not want their careers to take precedence over their families. Like many of their counterparts in the larger sample, the assistant professors were particularly appreciative of the flexibility of the faculty career that allowed them to attend to their children's needs when necessary. One scientist explained:

What I really appreciate most is the flexibility that this job entails. Obviously, when I'm teaching, that flexibility is somewhat limited, but not nearly [as much as] a 9-to-5 [job where] you're going to get docked your pay when you don't show up, so . . . I think that's huge too, 'cause you know, kids in daycare get sick all the time and, you know, so my wife and I split the days, so if our son has to come home, you know, she might take him in the morning and

I'll take him in afternoons. And, you know, I know not everybody has dual working parents, but . . . that's been a huge plus is having that degree of flexibility.

This father appreciated the ways that the flexibility of his work allows him and his wife to juggle caregiving responsibilities, particularly when their son is home sick from daycare. Such flexibility was pivotal, particularly when both members of the couple work outside the home. Flexible work schedules were noted by other faculty as being particularly useful for balancing parenting demands. As another professor explained, "I would say our department, in particular, is fairly kid-friendly. If you say, 'I gotta get the kids,' nobody has anything to say about it." For many fathers, the flexibility of their schedules gives them the freedom to determine when and where they perform their work.

However, this finding is not particularly unique to Generation X faculty. As I discussed in earlier chapters, academic parents from multiple generations have noted the benefit of flexibility that comes with a faculty appointment. What seems particularly unique about Generation X faculty is the degree to which they are willing to structure their work hours around the demands of their children and their lack of willingness to work nonstop. Although the demands of earning tenure seem to suggest that faculty should do whatever necessary to be successful, many participants limit the hours they work. While 14 of the assistant professors regularly worked at least some hours on weekends, many others were adamant about not working at all on Saturdays or Sundays. One assistant professor discussed his decision not to work after 5:00 P.M. or on weekends and some of the backlash he has received from senior colleagues as a result:

I've always really been strict about setting these hours. I don't work after 5 P.M. I don't work on weekends. My students know it. My colleagues know it. Whether they like it or not, [I] don't care. I've made my choice. I suppose if I hadn't made that adamant choice, then I would run into problems all the time, because I regularly . . . like last week was a great example. Last week, I didn't turn in two grant proposals that I wanted to write. Why? Well, 'cause I wasn't willing to work on it on the weekend or after 5 P.M. I could've written them. There were enough hours in the day. But, I just decided that . . . well, if I don't have enough time to do it, I don't have enough time to do it.

This professor has been very purposeful in setting boundaries on his time. He is fortunate in that he has also been very successful in bringing in grants.

When I asked him how his decision not to work on weekends was received by his colleagues, he responded:

> Some of the senior professors have said that they really don't think that that's appropriate, and I've pretty much told them that I would rather not get tenure than not know my kids. I guess not everybody can make that choice.

Although his senior colleagues may question his behavior, they also cannot argue that he is not meeting metrics for success in the department. This participant's behavior reflects the values of many Generation X faculty who are not willing to work the same types of hours that their parents might have. And, as this participant bluntly stated, he valued his family over earning tenure. While this father was unwilling to work weekends even in the event of a major deadline, other men discussed occasionally making an exception in order to meet a publication deadline.

Other assistant professors also placed boundaries on their work hours. A father on a different campus shared that he regularly only worked 40 hours per week:

> I hear stories about junior faculty who work 80 or 100 hours a week. I don't do that. I work about 40 hours a week and that's been successful for me. That's been effective . . . as far as the metrics that my department has laid out for me. I don't know how much more effective I would be if I worked double, but I simply can't. There just aren't enough hours in the day to keep my marriage intact and keep my kids happy. Forty hours is what I can do.

Like the previous father, this faculty member has also been immensely successful at bringing in grants. At another point in our interview, he mentioned that he had received so many grants that he was having a hard time figuring out how to spend all of the money. These two fathers' experiences indicate that one can be a successful academic while simultaneously placing boundaries on the number of hours one works, despite what norms of the ideal worker suggest.

Concern with working a 40-hour workweek echoed throughout other fathers' responses. Another faculty member in the sciences, who had recently stopped working on the weekends, shared his thoughts on how successful one might be working a standard workweek.

> There was actually a podcast on new investigators. . . . Their advice was, "You can do 40 hours a week, and you'll do okay. At

60 hours a week, you'll be successful." I know it's not a matter of, you know, it's not writing down time, it's what you do with that time. But, . . . I do think if I could definitely spend more time writing and doing things that I think would be important for my career development . . . if I didn't have kids.

Although the faculty member heard the message that working 60 hours a week was required for success in the academy, he was unwilling to make those trade-offs in the long term with his own career.

While many faculty placed boundaries on the number of hours they worked, still others found ways to be more involved in their children's care. Recall the faculty member who earlier praised the flexibility of the faculty career for allowing him to leave early to pick up his kids from school. Other faculty members discussed regular schedules in which they came into work late or left work early in order to spend time with their kids. One scientist left work at noon one day a week to take care of his young children. Another faculty member was typically on campus from 9:00 A.M. to 4:00 P.M.; his work hours were shaped by his son's daycare hours. Of particular interest, at the time of data collection, two assistant professors were engaging in substantial care of their young children during the workweek. One faculty member was taking advantage of an institution-sponsored release from teaching duties. He was home three days a week full time with his infant son and on campus from 9:00 A.M. to 4:00 P.M. the other two days. He was highly appreciative of the fact that his university provided some assistance so he could be home with his son, even if for a short period of time. The other faculty member was not receiving any accommodation from the institution, but still spent two days a week at home with his young son. As he explained, he and his wife wanted to avoid putting their son into childcare and so cobbled together care with the help of nearby family. He shared that he was not getting nearly enough research done, but he also commented that he was not as invested in his success as he had been before becoming a father. He was not alone in these sentiments.

Putting Work in Perspective

Several participants discussed how becoming fathers had changed their outlooks on their careers. The assistant professor discussed in the previous paragraph spent a great deal of time reflecting on how he had stepped back from some professional obligations since becoming a father.

Two years ago . . . I was really involved in our discipline at the national level, and I cared a lot about, you know, all kinds of discussions that were going on at the national level. . . . And I've probably like disappeared from a lot of different spaces. Like, that's bad for my chair. . . . There are issues that I just don't like care as much, because I like where things are now. I like the time that I've been with [my son] and, you know, it's kind of very indefinable, but . . . when you go home like last night, and he's like . . . he wakes up and he's just learning to walk, right? I'm trying to get him to walk like 15 to 20 feet, and you know, like when he walks a few steps more than the last time, like the joy on his face is both palpable and intoxicating.

This father explained how he was less invested in disciplinary issues on the national level and elsewhere in the interview discussed scaling back his research. Although he was confident in his tenure dossier, he also acknowledged that his department chair was not pleased with the ways he was choosing to spend his time as he was not meeting expectations of the ideal worker. However, this father was far more invested in watching his son develop and learn to walk and less interested in the opinions of his colleagues. He was not the only faculty member to discuss feeling torn between children and work. Much like the previous father, this social scientist was equally infatuated with his son: "My first priority is family. 'Cause I could just watch that kid. I could come home and he's different, you know what I mean? So I don't want to miss a second." As a result, this father found that he reprioritized his commitment to work and family:

I made a choice. I'm not going to be that person that works 24/7 writing. I just don't want to do it. I've seen professors when I was in grad school that were like that. I've seen a lot of professors that are divorced and, you know, I want to know my son. . . . I don't want to turn around one day and say, "Well I'm tenured now and he's 7 or 8 and he's got his own thing going on." . . . I just don't want to miss it. So it's—I mean the anxiety level [related to tenure] is just amazing when I think about it. But like I said, I did make a choice and so I'll roll the dice with tenure.

This father articulated a commitment to spending time with his son that supersedes his interest in earning tenure. While he is deeply invested in his scholarship, he is equally invested in his role as a father and is not willing to sacrifice family for career. These two fathers, like many others, seem to be redefining hegemonic masculinity to include an emphasis on caregiving while rejecting the demands of the ideal worker that form the foundation of academic work. Other fathers echoed these men's sentiments:

My idea of having a child was to actually also take care of it. You know that's a choice, but it seems like if you make this choice, that means somehow that you sacrifice your professional life and I find that kind of hard to swallow in a way. It shouldn't be that way. But academia is not a 40-hour-a-week job. If you do 40 hours a week, that's about a half time job, I guess. . . . But I refuse to let that take over the rest of my life.

This father echoed previous participants who shared the common belief that faculty need to work more than 40 hours a week to be successful. However, he rejected the notion that taking care of one's children is equated with a rejection of one's professional life and vice versa. Another father shared that because he prioritized his children above work, he would stay up late or get up early in order to get work done if he had other daytime commitments related to his children competing for his time. As he noted, "my legacy is what I leave with my family. It has nothing to do with what I do at work." This father, like so many others, represents a shift in the ways in which men think about their parenting responsibilities, underscoring this transition from men solely as breadwinners to a role in which men are free to prioritize their children's needs above those of their employer.

Chasing Gender Equity

Nearly all of the assistant professors—19 of the 22—were in dual-career couples. Of those, 12 had wives who worked full-time while 7 had wives who worked part-time, between 20 and 35 hours a week. Some of the assistant professors in the sample felt that this put them at odds with some of their more senior colleagues who they felt were less sympathetic to dual-career issues. Remarked one professor:

The impression I get from a lot of the sort of senior guys relative to work and family issues is that, . . . gosh, . . . a lot of them have nonworking spouses and exist in a world of domesticity that I can't imagine. And, I think that their sort of perspective on how . . . they don't quite see how [this city] and [state] can be problematic for people with spouses whose career aspirations exist beyond that sphere of domesticity.

He later went on to elaborate that his department chair shared with him that his wife had not been able to find meaningful work since moving to town two decades earlier. For this assistant professor and his wife, such an arrangement would not work because both seek meaningful professional careers. Many other participants remarked on the fact that due to this fairly traditional division of gender roles, their senior colleagues may have been less likely to engage in childcare, as did this father:

> Back in the day for men, it never was a problem because women were at home taking care of kids. Men had their careers—that I can see from my professors. They have all these books published, all these articles . . . great job done, great research. . . . I look at them and . . . how did they do it? And then I realize, of course, their wives were doing nothing—nothing in the sense of professional nothing. They were doing everything at home.

This professor pointed out that senior faculty came from a different generation when traditional gender norms were more acceptable. Men were free to excel in the academy precisely because they had a wife at home to care for their children. While few men longed for such an arrangement, they recognized that those with a stay-at-home wife had more time to focus on their work demands.

The fact that nearly all of the assistant professors were married to women who worked outside the home led many to engage in more childcare. Some noted that they frequently traded off childcare duty during the week and on weekends. Some men dropped off their children at school and their wives picked them up in the afternoon. Others noted that because both parents had such demanding careers that they had to carefully choreograph the time that they spent with their children and each other. One father was married to a medical resident, who was frequently on call at least one day each weekend, which meant that rarely did he and his wife find themselves in the same space with their young son. He described one recent day as an example:

> She was on call at the hospital and had been since Friday morning. She got off call at 10 o'clock in the morning on Saturday morning and I had just finished a big sort of push about a writing question and I had the day off and she was going to sleep for a good portion of the day. But she came to meet us at this local coffee shop on her way home and it was both really sweet and also really sad. My son was so excited to see her. But then it wasn't just being excited to see her, but he was excited to see the both of us. He was like hugging her and he is talking now, obviously, and he turned to me and said, "Daddy hug! Daddy hug!" I thought he wanted me to take him and he said, "No." He like hugged us both, and he put his arms around both of us and hugged us together and it was

so sweet and so nice. But also like this direct understanding that it was the fact of us both being there, and it's not like it never happens. But it was clearly suggestive of the fact that this was a special thing and it shouldn't be a special thing.

Both members of the couple have demanding careers—he as an assistant professor and she as a medical resident. Due to the lack of flexibility of his wife's job, the flexibility of his own, as well as his own interests in parenting, this father took an active role with their son. Particularly notable here is the fact that moments when all members of the family are able to be together are few and far between.

While being married to a medical resident brings its own challenges, some men were married to other academics, which brought both understanding about the demands of the job along with constant negotiation about who needed to get work done. Several men were married to women who were getting ready to go up for tenure. As one father explained, he and his wife frequently swapped childcare responsibilities over weekends or at night when the other needed to get work done.

> My wife and I kind of trade off working on the weekend to whoever has the most pressing deadline teaching, grading a stack of papers, some administrative task, or now reading admissions files or when writing we need to get done, we kind of trade off. I would try to take the kids over the weekend so that she could work on Saturday and Sunday and get something done or vice versa and the same thing would happen in the evenings when there are real work pressures you know. I would say, "Why don't you stay at the office. I'll get home and get dinner going and do bedtime and then you can stay."

When work demands encroach on family time, this academic couple shares in the division of labor in ways that do not always involve the mother as primary caregiver.

Other professors shared stories about how they carved out space to be involved fathers, despite feeling as if such actions were against the grain. The assistant professor who engaged in childcare two days a week regularly volunteered to be home with his son because his job was more flexible than his wife's. However, he also said that he tended to perform a lot more of the caregiving functions with their son.

> I still maintain like all the stuff that a man would do like doing the finances, and . . . taking care of the cars and the house and like all of the stuff that like my dad did. But, because I was very close to

my mom . . . [she] was a cook, . . . I still do the cooking and I do
a lot more of the actual watching him, and certainly the concern
for his health, say. Like that's way more me than it is for her.

While this father still divided roles into traditionally male and female,
he shared that he assumed roles associated with both genders. He later
stated that his experience was not idiosyncratic: "[My son] has a very distinct preference for me over [my wife]. . . . But, like one of my other colleagues, . . . his experiences are very similar to mine." Although childcare
has typically been labelled women's work, this father along with other men
in his department spend more time with their children than has traditionally been expected of men.

This father was not the only one to make a conscious effort to be
more involved with his children. Many fathers discussed how they tried to
be more cognizant of gender roles and share in the division of labor. One
father discussed his efforts to take an active role in childcare and housework:

It's almost equal I would say, and I think that she would agree to
that. . . . She definitely shoulders somewhat more of the burden,
maybe 60/40 or 70/30–ish, that kind of breakdown. But we definitely try to do as equal of sharing as we possibly can. And that's
a discussion that comes up a whole lot, is just how we're breaking
things down and how we're partitioning, because she feels . . . the
need to get her stuff done too.

This father tries to be more involved with childcare and other responsibilities, particularly because his wife is also employed and has her own
work responsibilities to fulfill. Another father shared that he felt that he
performed 50% of the work in the home, although his wife disagrees. "She
has complaints more on other house chores that she believes I don't do
enough, and maybe she's right. I don't know. I personally feel I do 50% if
not more, but she thinks sometimes that I don't." A few minutes later in
our conversation, the office phone rang and his wife was on the other end.
The father brought up our discussion with his wife:

Actually you called at such a good time. [I'm being interviewed
and] she's asking how you would be describing my work toward
the children, and I said even though you complain a lot about
other things in the house chores, you probably are content as far
as my work with the children goes, is that a right summary of the
thing? . . . Okay. Okay. I'll tell her. . . . She says I do less than
50% in housecleaning, but I do more than 50% at childcare.

This professor's wife corroborated the fact that he engages in substantial care in the home, performing more childcare and less housework than his wife. Engaging in such large amounts of childcare go against the norms of the ideal worker and traditional notions of masculinity. However, as should be clear from the experiences of these assistant professors, many members of Generation X reject both constructs in favor of developing new definitions of both.

However, many men also recognized that as much as they might do in the home, their wives often ended up doing more. One father acknowledged that while he tries to share in parenting duties with his wife, she inevitably shouldered more of the burden.

> It's really hard as somebody who is really trying to do the right thing professionally and also do the right thing at home. It's hard to do. I do also feel like it's worth saying that I, for as much as I could pat myself on the back as being an involved dad, and I do take a lot of pride in that . . . even today, I have an arrangement with my wife that I think is egalitarian, it's still hard. There's still kind of pressures on her that I don't experience.

This father, like many others, discussed feeling a tension between wanting to be successful at work and wanting to be successful at home. And despite making intentional efforts at coparenting, he recognized that his wife ultimately played a larger role with child rearing. These fathers, more than those who came before them, are charting new territory as hands-on fathers. While they recognize that their wives may perform more childcare, they are working hard to be involved with their children and challenge traditional gender roles.

Some fathers also discussed how they intentionally challenge traditional gender norms with their children. One father suggested that he and his wife do the same activities with their son because they wanted to teach him that particular tasks were not assigned to men or women.

> We don't want to teach him gender divisions. . . . He's now getting at that age where he goes, "Oh, girls do that," or, "Only boys will do that," and I explain to him it doesn't matter . . . that's just not a girl thing or a boy thing—even girls can do it. We pretty much do all things together. . . . We try not to create gender . . . engender activities.

This father and his wife were purposeful in rejecting traditional norms as was another father with his son and daughter:

> We definitely work hard not to push them into gender roles or
> something, and . . . they've just realized recently that there are "boy
> toys" and "girl toys." They're mostly into whatever we're going to
> play. I mean if we're doing wildfire, then they're both wild firemen.
> If we're playing house, then they're both playing house.

This father's children tended to play the same activities, regardless of
appropriate gender norms. And for their part, he and his wife tried not to
reinforce messages about gendered divisions of labor, which are implicit in
norms of hegemonic masculinity and the ideal worker. In sum, many fathers
reported straying from traditional notions of fathering as breadwinning but
not caregiving. Nearly all of the fathers were in dual-career marriages. And
many of the fathers engaged in a significant amount of childcare, arguing
that traditional gender roles should no longer apply. Whether their wives'
employment status influenced their beliefs on gender norms or whether
there is simply a relationship between the two is impossible to say. What
is clear, however, is that for this group of assistant professors, though they
value their careers, they place a premium on their identities as fathers and
take strategic action to perform both roles.

Conclusion

In what ways do the experiences of these 22 assistant professors illustrate the
tension between the norms of the academy and the norms of Generation X?
These fathers clearly understand that the academy is based on the norms
of the ideal worker (Acker, 1990; Williams, 2000), but they simultaneously
reject those norms in favor of those that are conducive to being a more
hands-on father. However, ideal worker norms inform the quest for tenure.
Assistant professors are expected to work for six years to put together a
tenure portfolio with high-impact research publications while teaching and
performing service, often to the exclusion of all other demands on their time.
Many professors acknowledged these pressures, such as the three scientists
who spoke about the never ending pressure to bring in grant money and the
other faculty member who talked about the hazing process associated with
earning tenure. All faculty understood the expectations that their colleagues
had about the type of work necessary to earn tenure.

Yet, at the same time, many of these fathers rejected these all-consum-
ing expectations associated with ideal worker norms. While most enjoyed
their work as faculty, they were unwilling to let their careers dictate the
rest of their lives and, in particular, their commitment to their families.
Such a focus on work/family issues is one of the hallmarks of members of

Generation X, who have earned a reputation for placing a greater emphasis on advocating for time with family than earlier generations (Lancaster & Stillman, 2002; Zemke et al., 2000). The experiences of these faculty fathers confirm this trend. A majority of the fathers discussed prioritizing their children over their work. Many participants limited the number of hours they worked. While many performed at least some academic work at night or on weekends, they spoke of trying to limit that time. Some fathers even refused to work outside regular business hours, such as the assistant professor who never worked after 5:00 P.M. or on weekends and made several choices throughout his career about what he could—and could not—accomplish, including not submitting grant proposals. Another assistant professor also was not willing to work more than 40 hours a week because he wanted to be present for his children. Faculty members were well aware of the impact that such choices could have on their careers. They discussed the common rhetoric that faculty work requires working 60 to 80 hours per week and yet many were unwilling to make such a sacrifice. Some acknowledged that such choices might have an impact on their careers while others felt that they were able to be quite successful by working fewer hours.

While the literature on Generation X underscores the value of face time, or being physically present at the workplace regardless of whether one is able to be productive there (Bickel & Brown, 2005; Helms, 2010; Lancaster & Stillman, 2002), such an issue did not seem to be of particular concern to faculty. This absence of discussion might be due to the nature of faculty work, which already provides a great deal of flexibility in terms of when and where faculty members perform their work. As I have discussed throughout, ideal worker norms are based on the expectation that employees are always available and working. Those norms, in turn, are founded on the separation of gender roles; men are available to be ideal workers because women are available to be caregivers (Acker, 1990; Williams, 2000). And yet, Generation X faculty are less interested in maintaining traditional gender roles. Several fathers talked about how they worked to challenge gender stereotypes with their children. Many others challenged gender stereotypes through the types of work they assumed inside and outside the home.

As others have written (Helms, 2010; Trower, 2010), Generation X individuals are more likely to be in dual-career couples and increasingly less likely to adhere to a strict division of labor inside and outside the home. Participants' experiences confirm this claim. All but three were in marriages in which both partners worked outside of the home. One could hypothesize that this increase in dual-career couples might lead to a shift in gender roles: because women are increasingly working outside of the home, men are therefore more likely to engage in more household work. Studies confirm such claims that men married to women whose partners work outside the home are more likely to perform household work than those with a stay-at-home wife (Coltrane, 1996, 2000; Cunningham, 2007). Many faculty estimated that they performed a significant amount of work in the home; one professor's wife even confirmed that he performed a greater share of childcare, though less housework, than she did. However, the picture is not yet one of gender equity. Of the 19 men with wives who worked, 7 wives worked fewer than 40 hours a week. For many, this was a deliberate choice to better allow the couple to manage the demands of career and family. Although men and women may both work outside of the home, women are still more likely than men to hold part-time positions. In part, the academy and other employers are to blame because jobs are still built on ideal worker norms and a separation of work and family.

To their credit, many of the fathers acknowledged that their wives maintained greater responsibility for their children. While many discussed the ways in which they tried to assume an active role in parenting, they also pointed out that their wives bore the greater brunt of child rearing. However, participants' behaviors suggest gender norms that value involved fathering. Recall the fathers who took time off to be with their young children, including the dad who discussed how "intoxicating" it was to watch his son learn to walk. Other dads discussed engaging in more care in the home and the degree to which they saw other men they knew doing the same. Many of these men reported that they would rather play active roles in their children's lives and risk not earning tenure.

In many ways, these men find themselves at odds with the culture of the gendered university (Acker, 1990). Many of them reject the gendered divisions of labor that are supposed to characterize life inside and outside the academy; rather than leaving the caregiving to their wives, they are interested in being involved with their children. Despite negative reactions from some senior colleagues who place greater premiums on academic work than family work, many of these assistant professors are charting a new path forward—one in which they are taking steps to redefine hegemonic masculinity—at least in the academy—to value caregiving and active fathering as much as crafting a career.

As has been said about each generation, the members of Generation X are trailblazers, not only making contributions to colleges and universities, but also simultaneously voicing a reticence to pursue academic work at the expense of their families. For these fathers who have voiced greater commitment to parenting, their actions suggest that gender norms are indeed shifting, which inevitably challenges the well-established norm of the ideal worker. Altering this limiting construct, which has been in place for centuries, is no small feat; yet doing so would ultimately lead to an academy that supports men and women alike in their pursuits of academic excellence and personal happiness.

CHAPTER 8

Redefining the Ideal

As should be clear from the experiences of the fathers discussed in this book, despite some shifts in policies and practices, the academy remains mired in gendered divisions of labor. Faculty are expected to be available to work long hours with minimal intrusions of personal demands on their time. Indeed, one might even suggest that ideal worker norms are becoming even more firmly entrenched based on increased expectations for faculty work and productivity. In the book's concluding chapter, I return to the ideal worker norms and hegemonic masculinity that I have considered throughout this text. I discuss the ways that ideal worker norms remain present throughout the university and consider why these norms are problematic. I also discuss how many of the fathers' actions challenge norms of the ideal worker and seek to redefine valued traits in hegemonic masculinity; ultimately, challenging both constructs will disrupt the gendered university. In the second half of the chapter, I offer suggestions to institutions that are interested in decentering gender norms on their campuses to help both male and female faculty lead productive lives inside and outside the academy.

The Entrenched Norm of the Ideal Worker

Throughout this text, men's experiences pointed to the ways that the norms of the ideal worker continue to influence how universities operate and, in particular, expectations about faculty work. Not only were faculty expected to always be working, but there was an accompanying expectation that fathers should separate their personal obligations from their professional lives. Although I discussed these competing demands throughout the book,

I review some of these challenges here before discussing why these expectations are problematic.

Ideal Worker: Always Available and Always Working

As the fathers pointed out, there is an expectation that the only way to
be successful in the academy is to work all the time. Many of the fathers
discussed the pressure they felt to work at all hours, including early in
the morning, late in the evening, and on weekends. One father described
exchanging e-mails with his colleagues at 10:00 P.M. Another father shared
what he learned from a podcast for new investigators in the sciences: working 40 hours a week is okay, but to be successful, an investigator needs
to work 60 hours per week. In part, these expectations are related to the
ever-increasing demands of faculty work. Faculty in the sciences and engineering along with an increasing number of other disciplines are expected to
secure external funding to support themselves along with graduate students,
postdoctoral researchers, and other staff. As some faculty explained, if they
do not bring these grants in, their research comes to a halt and their students have no funding. And, while many government agencies and private
foundations fund research, resources are finite. As an increasing number of
faculty compete for a decreasing amount of money, faculty feel pressed to
work more—both to submit an increasing number of grant applications and
to produce research to help increase their chances of being granted future
funding. As many fathers explained, if other faculty are working at all hours,
they, too, need to be working at all hours to be able to compete.

In addition to devoting an increasing number of hours to seeking
external funding, faculty reported that the university is placing demands
on their time outside of standard work hours. Some faculty complained
about meetings being scheduled before 8:00 A.M. and after 5:00 P.M., which
disrupted family time. Such practices are problematic, but have long held
sway in the academy. What is on the rise, however, is a shift toward offering
classes during nonstandard times, such as at night or on the weekend. Given
the increasing pressure that colleges and universities are under to recruit
and retain students, particularly in a context of declining state and federal
funds, many academic programs now offer courses at times that will appeal
to nontraditional students. These new teaching schedules may not always be
taken into account when setting meetings and other professional obligations.
A faculty member may teach a class until 10:00 P.M. but find that she or he
has other campus obligations to attend at 9:00 A.M., thus lengthening the
workday well past 8 hours. These after-hours teaching obligations not only
encroach on family time, but also place the onus on the faculty member
to find ways to care for his or her children. A faculty member who teaches

a 3:00 P.M. course can rely on childcare facilities; a faculty member who teaches a class until 10:00 P.M. typically cannot. Academic work continues to operate on the assumption that the faculty member does not have any personal obligations, has a spouse who is able to care for children, or has the financial resources to outsource that care. Implicit in these constructs, too, is an assumption about gendered divisions of labor. Faculty can be ideal workers precisely because they are not expected to be caregivers, thus reinforcing traditional definitions of hegemonic masculinity. Such expectations are problematic for men and women alike.

Although all of these changes are troubling, it is also worth pointing out that faculty occupy a relatively privileged position in society; tenure-line faculty at research universities have even greater privilege. Faculty have incredible autonomy in determining when and where they perform the majority of their work. Many fathers, in fact, noted the tremendous flexibility that the faculty career brings. Although a faculty member might work late into the evening, he might use a few hours in the middle of the afternoon to take care of his children. In contrast, a janitor for the university or even most administrative employees do not have the same luxury in determining when to perform their work, and they make considerably less money doing so. Characterizing faculty jobs as one of the least stressful in the United States, as one recent online survey did (Kensing, 2013), may not be accurate, but considerable privilege accompanies the considerable pressures. Despite these benefits, it is still important to challenge the expectations of the ideal worker for faculty—and indeed for all employees.

GENDERED DIVISIONS OF LABOR—AND LEAVE-TAKING

Colleges and universities now offer policies to help faculty navigate major life events, such as the arrival of a new child in the home. Faculty are eligible to take advantage of tenure-clock extensions, a reduction in teaching duties, and on some campuses a part-time tenure-track option for short periods of time. Despite the availability of these policies, many fathers across the campuses reported that they did not feel comfortable using them. One father in the sciences was told by senior colleagues that if he took a tenure-clock extension, he would be expected to produce additional scholarship to compensate for this accommodation. Another father recounted a story of a father who took a reduction in teaching duties, much to the chagrin of his colleagues, who felt that he had not yet earned the privilege to do so. Many men worried that taking advantage of institutional accommodations and devoting time to their children suggested that they were not "serious" about their work. Even men who reported engaging in a significant amount of care in the home, such as one father who made it a habit never to work at night or on weekends, did not plan to take more than two weeks off after the arrival of a new baby. For these men, reputation as an academic was equated with reputation as a man; having one identity challenged was linked for many with challenging the other. Given that men are expected to be breadwinners for their families, many were hesitant to access policies that they felt were intended for women. To do so would be unmasculine.

Although some men minimized their use of institutional accommodations, some reported using tenure-clock extensions and other policies. Nearly all of them reflected on the fact that using accommodations was uncommon for men and that they were, in some ways, pioneers. Many also recounted instances when their involvement with their children was remarked on by others, including their colleagues, chairs, and even strangers in the community. Although each of these men was trying to redefine hegemonic masculinity to value caregiving, others responded by reaffirming traditional gender roles. Such experiences underscore the ways in which gender is produced and reproduced through interactions with others (Acker, 1990; Connell, 1995; Connell & Messerschmidt, 2005). Like the fathers who were hesitant to take leave, these fathers also received messages that using policies was not valued for men. In contrast, there was no question in their minds that female faculty who became mothers were expected to use policies. Many fathers commented that a bias existed against caregiving by fathers whereas new mothers did not face a similar stigma. Although previous studies have indicated that both women and men feared bias from their colleagues (Colbeck & Drago, 2005), men have internalized beliefs about gender differences, which may keep them from accessing policies. This may be one of the significant challenges that universities face: reassuring men that they will incur no penalty for accessing institutional accommodations. Policies are available, but not everyone feels comfortable using them. Some men commented that since they did not face the physical demands of pregnancy and breastfeeding, their colleagues would look askance at them for taking significant time off following the birth of a child. Such differences point to the ways in which norms of the ideal worker are bound with gender norms and, in particular, hegemonic masculinity. The ideal worker depends on the division of gender roles—men as breadwinners and women as caregivers—and reifies notions of difference. As long as the ideal worker continues to guide practices in the academy, both men and women will have a difficult time breaking free of the norms that dictate acceptable behavior.

Some might express concern that men who access institutional accommodations will simply use that time to produce additional scholarship instead of spending time with their children. And, indeed, some theorists suggest that men may adopt new behaviors—such as those around involved fatherhood—as a way to simply perpetuate male domination (Demetriou, 2001).

In other words, as cultural norms shift to embrace more involvement from fathers, men may recognize that their overt behaviors need to shift as well, though in practice they may still leave the majority of care to women. Such duplicity is certainly a possibility. However, to assume that all men are out to game the system does a disservice to those who are interested in being involved with their children. Instead of mistrusting their employees, institutions that put faith in their faculty might find that as men's leave-taking patterns start to change, the reasons behind doing so might as well. Men might start taking leave because they value spending more time with their children, despite what dominant norms might suggest.

Problems with the Ideal Worker

As I have suggested throughout this book, the ideal worker is problematic for men, women, and the organizations for which they work. Ideal worker norms trap people into gender roles. Both men and women are disadvantaged by being relegated to a particular sphere: men to that of work and women to that of home. Both men and women face penalties for crossing boundaries. Men who are involved with their children are penalized. The number of men who avoided taking leave or using institutional accommodations points to the fact that child rearing is not a task expected to be performed by men because it is not a part of hegemonic masculinity. The men who classified themselves as equal caregivers with their wives noted that they incurred both benefits and penalties for becoming more involved with their children. While they might have given up the leisure associated with the male figure solely as breadwinner, as one man pointed out, they were able to form deeper relationships with their children. Although men may take steps to become more involved with their children, the current structures and demands of the academy prevent a true transformation of the paternal role.

Similarly, although not the focus of this book, women are also penalized by norms of the ideal worker. Women with children who work outside of the home have multiple responsibilities to fulfill: they have to be successful in the workplace and generally have to perform most tasks in the home. This second shift (Hochschild, 1989) puts extra demands on women that most men do not face. If many men are using their evenings and weekends to perform extra work while women are using that time to clean and shuttle children to activities, men are able to produce additional scholarship, thus widening the productivity gap between women and men. In addition, women who do not work outside the home are also penalized as many give up successful careers in order to raise children. Others may work part time to accommodate the demands of child rearing. While the fathers' narratives suggested that their wives voluntarily chose to stay home, women are socialized to believe that child rearing is a woman's responsibility and thus their choices may not have been voluntary as much as destined (Stone, 2007). When men opt to leave careers to stay at home full time, it is news; when women do so, it is expected.

And yet by opting out (or, phrased differently, being forced out), women are depriving colleges and universities and other employers of their expertise. This is one of two significant consequences of the ideal worker norm for institutions. Given the fact that workplaces are structured around the separation of work and family and the stubborn entrenchment of gender norms, many women give up careers in order to take care of children. Note the number of men who reported that their wives had once worked as teachers and lawyers and scientists, but had given up their careers to raise their children. There were still other wives who had sought academic careers, but their husbands had earned the tenure-track positions, thus relegating them to lecturer positions or forcing them to cobble together a series of adjunct jobs. Each of these exits from employment or from the careers of their choice robs workplaces of women's talent and ideas. It also signals tacit acceptance that men's careers take priority.

While women's forced absence from the workforce is problematic, the ideal worker norm is also troubling in that it suggests that the most productive employee is the one who works the greatest number of hours. Many studies have already debunked this assumption (Holman, Joyeux, & Kask, 2008; Perry-Smith & Blum, 2000; Shepard & Clifton, 2000; Shepard, Clifton, & Kruse, 1996). The experiences of some fathers in this study also underscore this claim. While many fathers felt that their productivity had declined after becoming parents, some reported that they were able to use their time more efficiently. For example, one father reported that the year he only worked 30 hours a week, he was able to produce five papers. He suggested that simply having time to step away from his work made him more productive. Perhaps if all faculty were encouraged to maintain more sensible work hours, they would find that both their personal lives and professional lives would benefit.

Challenging the Status Quo

Although ideal worker norms and hegemonic masculinity remain engrained in campus culture, the stories that the fathers shared indicated that such norms are being challenged. The gendered division of labor is no longer absolute and many are questioning the hierarchy of work over family and the rigid separation between the two spheres. Norms of hegemonic masculinity are shifting, albeit slowly. While fathers were once expected to provide for their children by being breadwinners, today's father, particularly at the university, is more likely to engage in some child rearing. And dismantling the ideal worker goes hand-in-hand with redefining hegemonic masculinity. Each construct relies on the other and shifts in one cannot help but affect the other.

Of course, not all men are interested in redefining either construct, as some profit from both. In this study, a handful of men reported that their wives performed all the work in the home. At the other extreme, some men reported that they fulfilled more typically feminine functions by attending to nearly all of their children's needs. Between these two positions were men who struggled daily with how to balance the demands of their career with the demands of child rearing, and how to share equally in those duties with their wife. Men across the disciplines and across campuses reported that they were involved with their children in many ways: driving them to and from school and after-school activities, coaching sports teams, cooking dinner, helping with homework, doing bedtime routines, and the list goes on. Some men, most often in the social sciences and humanities, even reported that they frequently left work midafternoon to pick their children up from school; many returned to their work later in the evening after children had gone to bed. These fathers took advantage of the flexibility of the faculty career to allow them to be more involved with their children than they might have been if they had worked in other professions. Many fathers who worked in professional schools noted that working as faculty in the law school or the business school afforded them the opportunity to be more engaged with their children than their colleagues outside academia. All of these fathers made deliberate choices in how to spend their time; for many, these choices involved spending more time with their children.

In addition, evidence suggests that the newest generation of faculty is more likely to struggle with balancing the demands of work and family (Helms, 2010; Trower, 2010). Although one might expect that pretenure faculty would be more likely to prioritize their careers over their children, many of the fathers suggested that they would be willing to give up tenure if the relentless pursuit of job security would cost them significant relationships with their children. Contrast this attitude with those of more senior faculty who reported that they had put in long hours, particularly in the pretenure years, and had missed out on some events in their children's lives. One tenured professor suggested that he owed his success to the fact that his wife had not worked outside of the home during his assistant professor days. I turn to these shifting employment patterns shortly, but what is particularly critical is this shift in values among Generation X faculty. For this group of faculty, academic work is important, but prioritizing personal life is as—if not more—important. Such attitudes suggest that this generation does not necessarily subscribe to the idea that being successful necessitates working long hours. Similarly, this group of men appears to challenge traditional norms of hegemonic masculinity by engaging more with their children.

Ideal worker norms and hegemonic masculinity are also being challenged in the degree to which universities no longer emphasize a separation between work and family. As I have discussed throughout, although they may not be comprehensive or assist faculty with all major life demands, many campuses now offer accommodations in recognition of childbirth, illness, and other significant personal events. In addition, faculty across many of the campuses reported that children were frequently included in department events. In some departments, fathers occasionally brought their children in to work. While the types of work performed by humanities and social science faculty was more conducive to bringing children into the workplace, fathers in numerous disciplines reported that their chairs and other colleagues affirmed their responsibilities to their children. Such support underscores the degree to which gender is created and re-created through interactions. Men whose other male colleagues suggest that caregiving is a valued part of the masculine identity will most likely adopt different behaviors than men in departments with colleagues who suggest that caregiving is best left to women. As Acker (1990) pointed out, interactions reinforce identities. The experiences of some fathers suggest that being an ideal worker is no longer equated with rejecting caregiving responsibilities. The experiences of many of these fathers suggest that both sets of norms are indeed shifting.

Finally, ideal worker norms and hegemonic masculinity are being challenged in that many couples no longer are characterized by the gendered division of labor between husband and wife. Only 10 of the 70 fathers interviewed were married to women who stayed home full time while an additional 13 had wives who worked only part time outside of the home. Given that two out of three couples now contend with dual-career issues, the traditional division of labor has to change. If both husband and wife have to fulfill the demands of the workplace, the division of labor in the home must shift as well. Faculty fathers married to women who work in nonacademic careers may find that they perform additional work, given that their work hours allow them a bit more flexibility with their time. A faculty member, for example, has the flexibility to leave work at 4:00 P.M. whereas someone working in a traditional office job does not necessarily have the same luxury. In some ways, the flexibility the faculty career affords men greater latitude to be more involved with their children. Until recently, men had not taken advantage of this flexibility. The experiences of men in this study suggest that many are engaging more with their children, frequently blurring the lines between work and home.

Disrupting norms of the ideal worker and hegemonic masculinity has greater implications than simply changing faculty lives and workloads. Given that the ideal worker is built on traditional divisions of labor that simultaneously reinforces hegemonic masculinity, disrupting norms of the ideal worker also challenges norms of the gendered university. Recall that Acker (1990) pointed out five ways in which universities might be gendered, through: (1) constructions of divisions along lines of gender; (2) organizational symbols; (3) interactions; (4) the ways that interactions inform differences in individual identity; and (5) the ways that differences in identities shape organizational structures. The ideal worker underscores differences along lines of gender, namely through the division of labor in the home. The man can be successful because his wife is working in the home. However, as has been established, such a division no longer holds true. Few couples adhere to a traditional division of labor and more women work outside the home. In addition, men perform more work inside the home than in the past. While women may still perform more childcare and housework, the distinction between a man's sphere and a woman's sphere is slowly disappearing. Second, if the ideal worker is no longer defined as one who is always working, the traditional symbol of the productive academic needs modification. Perhaps the ideal worker is one who works reasonable hours and spends time with his children or cultivates personal hobbies. By challenging the notion that men and women should perform different tasks and disrupting the notion that family-friendly policies are reserved for women's use, the ideal worker norm loses its strength. This leads to a gradual erosion of the gendering of universities. Several other factors contribute to universities' gendered nature. For example, until the sciences and engineering reach gender parity, universities will remain gendered. Of course, reaching gender parity is not the same as reaching gender equality. Rather, until behaviors and practices that favor men over women are eradicated, universities will remain gendered. Challenging the ideal worker and the associated gendered norms that undergird it can help to create a university that does not marginalize parenting and that creates a space where both men and women can lead healthy and productive lives as parents and professors. Throughout this book, I have discussed how the four campuses profiled helped faculty navigate work and family. In the remainder of the text, I turn my attention to practical suggestions aimed at helping male and female faculty craft healthy professional and personal lives.

Creating Supportive Campuses

Transforming campuses requires attention to both structural and cultural factors. As Kossek and colleagues (2009) suggested, structural work/life supports include policies and practices, including challenging the practice of employees working more than 40 hours per week or outside of standard work hours. Cultural work/life supports pertain more to changing attitudes and behaviors of those on campus, or to use Schein's (2004) typology, changing organizational values and assumptions. An employee who receives messages from all members of the organization—from leaders and coworkers—that personal lives are valued as much as professional lives may be more likely to find ways to prioritize family and disrupt the norm of the ideal worker. Unless cultural support exists, structural supports will be inadequate in terms of transforming organizational culture. I offer suggestions aimed at both categories, beginning by discussing structural supports and concluding with actions that different campus agents, including presidents and department chairs, might take to support fathers and disrupt the ideal worker, hegemonic masculinity, and, in the process, the gendered university. Given that the focus of this text has been on fathers employed at research universities, my suggestions are targeted at these institutions. Those employed at other types of colleges and universities may find some suggestions helpful for their campuses.

STRUCTURAL SUPPORT

Earlier in the book, I discussed the types of policies that are typically available at research universities, including tenure-clock extensions, release from teaching duties, dual-career hire programs, and childcare centers. I discuss these policies and resources because they were most relevant for fathers and offer additional suggestions that emerged from these fathers' experiences.

Tenure-clock extensions. One of the easiest policies for any institution to provide is a tenure-clock extension. With the exception of obligating the institution to pay the faculty member's salary for an additional year, the extension carries no cost. Institutions have a number of options in determining the details of the tenure-clock extension. The experiences of faculty fathers suggests that tenure-clock extensions should be (1) automatic; (2) given to both men and women; and (3) available more than once in a pretenure period. Many of the fathers in this study suggested that they were hesitant to take advantage of any institutional policies. Making the tenure-clock extension automatic for all faculty who welcome a child into the home (either through childbirth or adoption) helps to remove the stigma some men may associate with requesting accommodation. For example, if a faculty member adds a new child to his or her insurance, such information might be automatically communicated to the vice provost's office, thereby triggering an automatic extension. Other possibilities include the faculty member and chair submitting paperwork close to the child's arrival.

The vice provost's office should also note—and communicate—that being entitled to the extension of the tenure clock does not obligate the faculty member to take it. Faculty should be encouraged to file for the clock extension and then make a decision whether they want to use it as they approach the end of the original tenure period. Many fathers in this study reported comfort in knowing that they had filed the extension, regardless of whether they ultimately chose to use it. The policy should also clearly communicate that men and women are eligible to use the extension. Some policies specify that a parent needs to have a substantial caregiving role in order to be eligible to use the policy. While regulating a parent's degree of involvement is impossible, including such language may encourage fathers to be more involved. In addition, given the rise of dual-career couples, if both parents are faculty members, both should be eligible to take the clock extension because both of their lives (and productivity) will certainly be affected by the new arrival.

Institutions might consider offering faculty who have multiple children during the pretenure period more than one extension of the tenure clock. In all likelihood, most parents will not opt to extend the clock more than once, but offering this flexibility sends the message that the institution recognizes the demands of parenting. Finally, the policy should clearly articulate that faculty are not expected to produce additional scholarship in exchange for the extension of the clock and provide instructions for how tenure and promotion committees should view the possible gap in scholarship.

Modified duties. Colleges and universities might also offer a release from teaching duties to new parents. Such policies generally involve releasing a faculty member from all teaching duties for a semester to allow him or her to channel the energy not being devoted to caring for a newborn toward research productivity. In addition, faculty are expected to continue to fulfill committee obligations, including working with students on dissertations. Most policies stipulate that faculty must take the release within the first year of the child's arrival into the home. Like the tenure-clock extension, modified duties should be available to men and women. The language of the policy might again stipulate that the parent must provide a substantial amount of care in order to be eligible for a release. Campuses that are truly interested in disrupting norms of the ideal worker and redefining hegemonic masculinity might also make modified duties automatic following the birth of a child. Doing so will again help to reduce the stigma of using it.

If both parents are faculty, each should be eligible to take advantage of modified duties. Some campuses specify that if both parents are faculty, only one is eligible for a release from teaching. If constrained by such rules, many families will opt to have women use the policy, given the entrenchment of gender norms. Allowing each parent to access the policy will prevent families from having to make difficult decisions and will encourage men to take more active roles as parents. Most campuses do not put a limit on the number of times an individual is eligible to use modified duties. In addition to offering modified duties for the arrival of children, institutions might also offer such policies for faculty contending with other significant life events, such as a major illness of a child or caring for elderly parents or spouses. Allowing faculty to access modified duties across the lifespan signals that institutions understand that navigating personal demands is not just an issue when children are born, but rather is an ongoing journey.

Offering a formal modified duties policy is important. However, as the vice provost at Western University shared, providing central funding for the policy is critical in terms of gaining acceptance across campus. Departments generally need to hire adjunct faculty as replacements for the absent professor for a semester. Regardless of a department's size, such costs can add up; for small departments, such costs can be disastrous. If a university is able to offer funds for an adjunct, this removes the financial burden on the department and the psychological burden on the faculty asking to take leave. While their experiences were not the focus of the study, institutions might also consider offering similar releases for full-time clinical faculty. Given that more universities now rely on nontenure-line faculty to staff their courses, these benefits must not be solely offered to tenure-line faculty, thereby further perpetuating a two-tier system. Institutions might consider how to help clinical faculty also cope with major life demands; providing some release from teaching duties is one way to do so.

Dual-career assistance. Given that two out of three faculty members are married to someone who works full-time outside the home and one out of three is married to another academic (Schiebinger et al., 2008), it is critically important that institutions provide job placement assistance to a faculty member's partner or spouse. Providing assistance not only serves as a strong recruitment and retention incentive for the faculty member, but also helps to reduce the stress the family might experience in seeking employment for the partner or spouse. While some campuses might provide such assistance on an ad-hoc basis, campuses should be encouraged to create a formalized office and publicize their presence on the web and through other means. Such an office might provide all spouses with a list of available jobs, both on campus and in the surrounding community. Many campuses now belong to higher education recruitment consortiums (HERCs), which are a group of campuses in a geographical area that share job announcements and other resources to support job seekers. A dual-career office might also offer assistance crafting cover letters and resumes and coaching on interviews; alternately, such assistance could be offered in partnership with the campus career center.

While many of the fathers were grateful to the universities for finding some employment for their wives who were interested in academic careers, more often than not, these positions were not tenure-line positions. Instead, wives were hired as lecturers, as adjuncts, and in temporary visiting positions. Such assistance offers only a short-term solution and does little to help close the gender gap. Although certainly costly, institutions might consider hiring both husband and wife into tenure-line positions, assuming both are qualified. Doing so will provide more meaningful employment for both and reduce the possibility that faculty will leave to take a job elsewhere. Given the difficulty of managing dual-careers, couples who are both employed will be more likely to stay at their institution, thus saving the university the cost of launching a search for a new faculty member.

Establish a central work/life office. Having a work/life office on campus will accomplish multiple goals. First, it provides a way to consolidate all work/life resources into one place. In addition, the office can serve as a clearinghouse for information ranging from institutional policies on parental leave to family-friendly resources in the surrounding community. Just as an LGBT student center signals that a campus supports nonheterosexual students and a women's center signals support for gender issues, a work/life office sends a message that the institution values employees' personal lives.

The work/life office might offer gender-specific programming, such as a fathers' group. Many men whom I interviewed mentioned that they were far less likely to talk to other men about parenting because there was no opportunity to do so. Creating groups, particularly for new dads, might help to eliminate that stigma. Such groups might also serve as an opportunity for men to talk about parenting as a valued part of the masculine identity. Additionally, such groups might allow fathers from various racial and ethnic backgrounds to provide support to one another. Given that the ranks of the professoriate do not yet reflect the diversity of the United States, some men may find that they are the sole men of color in their departments. Parenting groups might provide a source of support for fathers of color to discuss the additional cultural concerns that come with raising children in an environment that is both gendered and raced.

Childcare. Faculty on every campus I visited complained about a lack of space in childcare centers. Chances are that no campus will ever be able to accommodate all interested faculty, staff, and students. To accommodate the needs of the campus community, many campuses also offer referrals to off-campus childcare centers. In exchange for providing these referrals, some campuses, like Midwestern University, offer professional development to these childcare providers. In this way, the university is able to extend its expertise into the community while also providing additional resources for employees looking for childcare. Such a creative solution takes advantage of local resources, which is related to the next point.

Given that institutions are also now extending the hours that they expect faculty to teach from during standard work hours to evenings and weekends, universities need to consider what types of support to offer in exchange. A single parent with a young child, for example, may have a difficult time teaching evening courses. Campuses might consider offering extended hours in their childcare center to accommodate the needs of faculty teaching after hours. Alternately, campuses might also maintain a list of licensed childcare providers who are available as in-home babysitters. Regardless of solution, institutions must also consider the cost that individual families will bear in finding childcare after hours. Not only can the financial cost be prohibitive, but so too are the emotional costs to parents and their children.

Take context into account. Campuses might develop policies and programs with the needs of the local community in mind. Some campuses in expensive real estate markets offer housing assistance to faculty and executive level staff. The University of California–Berkeley, for example, has price-controlled condominiums that sell for far less than the $750,000 average home price in the area. Such a benefit makes sense at that university in ways that would not be needed in lower-priced housing markets such as for faculty at Iowa State University. However, Iowa State might provide free snow removal for a year for new faculty whereas such a benefit would be of no use to Berkeley faculty. Context matters and matching resources to the environment makes sense. For example, campuses should be encouraged to develop their academic calendars in conjunction with the local school district. Ensuring that the university's spring break matches the local schools' spring break allows parents to minimize conflict and, indeed, spend more time with their children. Finally, campuses might also develop partnerships with other area colleges or local community agencies, like Midwestern University has done with local childcare providers. Such partnerships might allow the university to provide more resources for their employees.

Offer creative solutions. Many of the previous suggestions have become relatively standard on campuses. Campuses should be encouraged to think beyond obvious solutions, such as the possibility of offering snow removal to new faculty in chilly climates. For example, Lehigh University offers new faculty parents $6,000 grants to spend whatever way they want, including on hiring housecleaners or paying for childcare. The institution lets the individual faculty member determine what assistance would be of most help in navigating personal and professional demands. Other institutions, such as Princeton University, offer grants to pay for childcare while a faculty member attends a conference. Work/life support need not solely take the form of a tenure-clock extension or modified duties. Campuses can help faculty be successful in both their personal and professional endeavors in a variety of ways.

Provide support for faculty work responsibilities. In addition to offering support for professors' personal lives, institutions should not neglect their responsibility to help faculty succeed professionally. Based on these fathers' experiences, four types of support seem particularly critical: (1) Given the increasing importance of grants and external funding, institutions must provide support to *help faculty prepare grants*. While many institutions offer assistance with budgets, faculty would certainly benefit from additional assistance with drafting the many documents federal agencies require. Institutions might also maintain a repository of grants that have been successfully funded in the past and allow faculty to view the various components of each of the proposals. (2) Institutions should *implement formal mentoring systems*, particularly for early career faculty. Navigating the expectations of tenure is difficult. Campuses might match a new assistant professor with a tenured professor in the department or in a related department. Such partnerships will develop to fit the needs of the individual, but could include a range of activities, including answering questions about university procedures to providing feedback on written manuscripts to perhaps coauthoring articles together. Such mentors could also serve as an informal source of support around work/life issues. If institutions want new faculty to be successful, they should provide as much support as possible. (3) Universities might *offer seed money* to allow faculty to explore ideas without risking professional consequences. Given that many participants discussed their hesitation to pursue risky lines of inquiry out of concern for their families and careers, such funds would allow exploration of potentially productive ideas. Such grants would reinforce the idea that universities should be sites of inquiry and exploration. (4) Campuses might also offer *faculty writing retreats* that provide uninterrupted time for faculty to get writing done. Given how many fathers discussed missing sustained blocks of time to engage in intellectual thought, providing a quiet place (with perhaps free snacks and lunch) may allow faculty to accomplish writing projects that they need to get done. These suggestions underscore that being sensitive to a professor's work/family demands entails providing support in both realms. While these policies and programs offer one type of support, cultural transformation will only come through changing the attitudes and behaviors of everyone on campus.

CULTURAL SUPPORT

Simply having policies in place does not mean that men will feel comfortable using them. Instead, all members of a campus community—including the president, deans, department chairs, and other faculty—must send messages that attending to both work and life concerns is valued for men and women. I offer targeted suggestions to each of these groups as to what actions they might take to support faculty parents.

Presidents and deans. The president's actions set the tone for the entire institution. Presidents who frequently call attention to work/family issues will run a different campus than those who frequently encourage their faculty to work longer hours. Just as the president plays an important role in shaping institutional culture, deans play a central role in shaping the culture of individual colleges and schools. Here are a few ways that presidents and deans might promote a family-friendly campus:

1. *Make frequent statements in support of work/family issues.* If an issue is not discussed, it does not matter to an institution. Presidents and deans should be encouraged to regularly reference the importance of work/family issues in speeches and statements. Such statements might include a reminder of the policies available along with encouragement for male and female faculty to use existing policies. Statements are only the first step in promoting a family-friendly culture, however; they must be backed up with action.

2. *Direct funding toward family-friendly initiatives.* While making verbal statements of support is important, providing financial resources to support family-friendly initiatives sends an even stronger message that faculty's personal lives are valued. Presidents might direct money toward a central replacement teaching fund for faculty who use modified duties or to hire a full-time staff person to coordinate work/family issues. Similarly, deans might also be encouraged to direct financial resources to meet faculty needs. Since each campus has a unique culture, initiatives must be tailored to fit the needs of faculty and staff. Regardless of context, supportive rhetoric needs to be backed up with financial support.

3. *Publicize family-friendly initiatives.* While the president should articulate the importance of work/family issues in statements, the institution should also regularly distribute information about

campus policies. Such publicity might feature male and female faculty who have used policies and discuss the benefits of having done so. Including men in publicity materials indicates that such policies are not targeted solely at women and have been used by men, which might help reduce the stigma some men feel in accessing institutional supports.

4. *Host events that are inclusive of families.* Universities and the individual colleges that compose them might host semiannual events for employees and their families. Such events might be as simple as a family movie night or as elaborate as a campuswide open house, complete with educational and social activities. Such events reinforce the message that the campus is supportive of employees' personal lives while also opening the campus to the wider community.

Department chairs. Although the president and the dean set the direction for the institution and college, culture is enacted at the department level. Department chairs play a pivotal role in translating rhetoric into action. They can support male and female faculty who are navigating personal and professional concerns in several ways.

1. *Support the use of family-friendly policies.* If an institution provides a tenure-clock extension or modified duties, department chairs should support faculty who wish to use the policies. Given the number of men who reported negative interactions with their chairs over using institutionally available policies, clearly not all faculty find themselves in supportive situations. And beyond simply supporting faculty who want to use the policies, chairs should be knowledgeable about the policies and share information about the policies with faculty. If a faculty member shares that he is going to be a father, the chair should provide details about how the faculty member can access institutional accommodations and take steps to provide the necessary paperwork to do so.

2. *Talk about family.* Although families and children are not frequently physically present in departments, they can be present through discussion. Chairs might make a habit of asking their faculty about their children. Several fathers reported being moved when their chairs showed interest in their families. When possible, department chairs should also talk about their own children to send the message that families are valued

and not something to be hidden. Chairs can further promote a pro-family culture by proudly displaying family photos and children's artwork in their offices and on their doors. Visual symbols send important messages and, in this case, disrupt the separation between work and family.

3. *Host family-friendly events.* Some fathers noted that their departments frequently hosted events that were inclusive of partners and children. While not all departments need to order a bounce house for parties, department chairs might organize annual parties with activities designed to appeal to those with children. Providing opportunities for faculty to socialize outside the workplace might help increase collegiality inside the workplace. Family-friendly events are particularly important to those with significant caregiving responsibilities because many may be forced to forego attending these events in order to care for their children. Welcoming children to department socials may allow more faculty to attend and reduce conflict or stress around doing so.

4. *Schedule meetings during standard work hours.* Given the flexibility built into faculty work schedules and the fact that many faculty have responsibility for getting their children to or from school, department chairs might schedule department meetings and seminars beginning no earlier than 9:00 A.M. and ending no later than 5:00 P.M. Such start and stop times respect faculty members' family responsibilities and still leave many hours in the day for meetings. In addition, departments in which faculty frequently teach in the evenings should also strongly consider not holding early morning meetings. A faculty member who teaches until 10:00 P.M. should not be asked to attend a 9:00 A.M. meeting.

5. *Conduct workshops on family-friendly issues.* Department chairs might consider bringing in individuals from the campus work/life office or other administrators who can talk about institutional policies and accommodations. In addition, faculty search committees should also undergo training to learn about the types of resources the campus offers and the types of questions one can and cannot ask prospective candidates. Although the law prohibits search committee members from asking whether a candidate has children, members can still share information about family-friendly resources in a way that both highlights all that the campus has to offer and does not require the candidate to reveal his or her parental status.

6. *Facilitate conversations on work/family issues.* In many departments, fathers reported that family concerns often went unspoken. Department chairs might consider facilitating regular conversations with all faculty about the demands that parenthood places on faculty. In addition to signaling that such concerns are valid, such conversations serve multiple functions by (1) indicating that family concerns should not be silenced and (2) helping male and female faculty to understand the unique demands that each group faces.

Senior faculty. Senior faculty play an important role in assistant professors' career trajectories and in shaping departmental culture. A chair who supports faculty with children can be undermined by faculty who do not value finding a balance between work and family. To help create a supportive climate, faculty members might be encouraged to do the following:

1. *Talk about family.* Just as the department chair should be encouraged to talk about his or her children, so too should senior faculty talk about their own children. Faculty might also be encouraged to display family photos and children's artwork and to share stories about their children's activities. Making children present through conversations is an important way to signal that personal lives are valued.

2. *Use institutional accommodations.* Research suggests that senior male employees play an important role in shaping the degree to which men feel able to access parental leave; a man is more likely to use institutional accommodations if more senior men have accessed such accommodations before (Bygren & Duvander, 2006; Haas & Hwang, 1995, 2009). Tenured faculty should use family-friendly policies, such as modified duties, to signal to assistant professors that doing so is valued in the department.

3. *Advocate for and support early career faculty.* Senior faculty should also be encouraged to support assistant professors who are contending with significant professional and personal obligations. Senior faculty might encourage assistant professors to use family-friendly policies and explain that they will incur no penalty for doing so. At the very least, senior faculty should be instructed not to share misinformation with faculty, such as suggesting that faculty must produce extra scholarship to compensate for a tenure-clock extension. All faculty must be

informed about available institutional accommodations and the ramifications that their use has for a department and individual professors' careers.

4. *Create a culture that supports personal and professional achievements.* Given that faculty spend much of their life engaged in work, their colleagues can become like a second family. Faculty might consider recognizing major milestones, such as the birth of children. Faculty might organize baby showers for expectant fathers and mothers or provide meals for new parents. Similarly, faculty should also provide support during tragic life events, such as serious illness or death. One father was particularly appreciative of the fact that his colleagues stepped in to teach his classes for him when his infant daughter died. Small actions send important messages that faculty are valued for more than just their professional contributions to the department. However, faculty should also be recognized for their professional achievements. Celebrating success is important.

5. *Role model good balance.* The faculty career can easily consume an individual's life. And, as has been established in this text, the faculty career is built on the norm of the ideal worker in which faculty work at all hours. Senior faculty might take an active role in challenging this norm by role modeling more reasonable engagement with their careers. For example, faculty might not send e-mails to their colleagues in the evenings or on weekends. If such e-mails are necessary, they should clearly indicate that a response is not needed. Sending e-mails after hours indicates that senior faculty are working, which may lead assistant professors to feel that they should be working too.

6. *Make tenure expectations transparent.* A perennial complaint among assistant professors is the lack of clarity in tenure expectations. Most departments are hesitant to give precise guidelines regarding how much scholarship a faculty member needs to produce in order to earn tenure. Departments, instead, argue that they seek to evaluate "quality" instead of "quantity." While certainly it is understandable that publication in a field's top-tier journal might hold different weight than publication in a third-tier journal, departments can and should be encouraged to provide written guidelines to faculty about the range of research, teaching, and service expected for a successful tenure

dossier. Clarifying these expectations may help faculty regulate the amount of time they need to work to allow them to have a better balance between work and home.

Certainly campus agents might take other actions to develop policies to support their male and female faculty. Whatever the policies or actions might be, they should attend to both the personal and professional lives of faculty and the ways that gender roles are currently inherent in divisions of labor. They should also take context into account. What works at Eastern University may not work at Midwestern University. This by no means gives institutions an excuse not to implement family-friendly policies. Rather, it provides an additional challenge for each institution to develop comprehensive policies and programs that help meet the unique needs of its faculty.

I began this book by suggesting that universities have an opportunity to play a pivotal role in challenging ideal worker norms and hegemonic masculinity to ultimately dismantle gendered organizational norms. It is time to acknowledge that faculty have lives outside the workplace and, more importantly, that those lives matter. It is also time to acknowledge that the current division of work has ramifications for women, men, and the workplaces that do (or do not) employ them. If all institutions provide support—not just via policies, but through cultural transformation—to faculty navigating work and family concerns, everyone benefits. Men will gain by being more involved with their children's lives; women will gain by being able to regain their place in the workforce; universities will gain from the contributions of these two groups. Society will benefit by being one step closer to dismantling gender norms to create a society where all men and women are given the opportunity to succeed.

References

Acker, J. (1990). Hierarchies, jobs, bodies: A theory of gendered organizations. *Gender & Society, 4*(2), 139–158.

Armenti, C. (2004). May babies and posttenure babies: Maternal decisions of women professors. *Review of Higher Education, 27*(2), 211–231.

Association of American Universities. (n.d.). *About AAU.* Retrieved from http://www.aau.edu/about/default.aspx?id=58.

Austin, A. E. (1990). Faculty cultures, faculty values. *New Directions for Institutional Research, 68*, 61–74.

Austin, A. E. (2002). Preparing the next generation of faculty: Graduate school as socialization to the academic career. *Journal of Higher Education, 73*(1), 94–122.

Austin, A. E., & Rice, R. E. (1998). Making tenure viable: Listening to early career faculty. *American Behavioral Scientist, 41*(5), 736–754.

Bailyn, L. (2003). Academic careers and gender equity: Lessons learned from MIT. *Gender, Work and Organization, 10*(2), 137–153.

Baldwin, R. G., & Chronister, J. L. (2005). What happened to the tenure track? In R. Chait (Ed.), *The questions of tenure* (pp. 125–159). Cambridge, MA: Harvard University Press.

Becher, T. (1994). The significance of disciplinary differences. *Studies in Higher Education, 19*(2), 151–161.

Becher, T., & Trowler, P. (2001). *Academic tribes and territories: Intellectual enquiry and the culture of the disciplines* (2nd ed.). Buckingham, UK: Society for Research into Higher Education and Open University Press.

Bellas, M. L., & Toutkoushian, R. K. (1999). Faculty time allocations and research productivity: Gender, race and family effects. *Review of Higher Education, 22*(4), 367–390.

Bergquist, W. H. (1992). *The four cultures of the academy:* San Francisco, CA: Jossey-Bass.

Bianchi, S. M., Milkie, M. A., Sayer, L. C., & Robinson, J. P. (2000). Is anyone doing the housework? Trends in the gender division of household labor. *Social Forces, 79*(1), 191–228.

Bickel, J., & Brown, A. J. (2005). Generation X: Implications for faculty recruitment and development in academic health centers. *Academic Medicine, 80*(3), 205–210.

Bird, S. R. (1996). Welcome to the men's club: Homosociality and the maintenance of hegemonic masculinity. *Gender & Society, 10*(2), 120–132.

Blair-Loy, M., & Wharton, A. S. (2002). Employees' use of work-family policies and the workplace social context. *Social Forces, 80*(3), 813–845.

Bok, D. (2003). *Universities in the marketplace: The commercialization of higher education.* Princeton, NJ: Princeton University Press.

Brandth, B., & Kvande, E. (1998). Masculinity and child care: The reconstruction of fathering. *Sociological Review, 46*(2), 293–313.

Britton, D. M. (1997). Gendered organizational logic: Policy and practice in men's and women's prisons. *Gender & Society, 11*(6), 796–818.

Bulanda, R. E. (2004). Paternal involvement with children: The influence of gender ideologies. *Journal of Marriage and Family, 66*(1), 40–45.

Bygren, M., & Duvander, A. (2006). Parents' workplace situation and fathers' parental leave use. *Journal of Marriage and Family, 68*, 363–372.

Carrigan, T., Connell, B., & Lee, J. (1985). Toward a new sociology of masculinity. *Theory and Society, 14*(5), 551–604.

Clark, B. R. (1987). *The academic life: Small worlds, different worlds.* Princeton, NJ: Carnegie Foundation for the Advancement of Teaching.

Colbeck, C. L., & Drago, R. (2005). Accept, avoid, resist: How faculty members respond to bias against caregiving . . . and how departments can help. *Change, 37*(6), 10–17.

Cole, J. R., & Zuckerman, H. (1987). Marriage, motherhood and research performance in science. *Scientific American, 256*, 119–125.

Collinson, D. L., & Hearn, J. (2005). Men and masculinities in work, organizations, and management. In M. S. Kimmel, J. Hearn, & R. W. Connell (Eds.), *Handbook of Studies on Men & Masculinities* (pp. 289–310). Thousand Oaks, CA: Sage.

Coltrane, S. (1996). *Family man.* New York: Oxford University Press.

Coltrane, S. (2000). Research on household labor: Modeling and measuring the social embeddedness of routine family work. *Journal of Marriage and Family, 62*(4), 1208–1233.

Comer, D. R., & Stites-Doe, S. (2006). Antecedents and consequences of faculty women's academic-parental role balancing. *Journal of Family and Economic Issues, 27*(3), 495–512.

Commission for Women. (2010). *Results of the 2010 campus work-life climate survey.* Knoxville: University of Tennessee Commission for Women.

Connell, R. W. (2006). Glass ceilings or gendered institutions? Mapping the gender regimes of public sector worksites. *Public Administration Review, 66*(6), 837–849.

Connell, R. W. (1995). *Masculinities.* Berkeley: University of California Press.

Connell, R. W., & Messerschmidt, J. W. (2005). Hegemonic masculinity: Rethinking the concept. *Gender & Society, 19*(6), 829–859.

Coser, L. A. (1974). *Greedy institutions: Patterns of undivided commitment*. New York: Free Press.

Craig, L. (2006). Does father care mean fathers share? A comparison of how mothers and fathers in intact families spend time with children. *Gender & Society, 20*(2), 259–281.

Crompton, R., & Harris, F. (1999). Attitudes, women's employment, and the changing domestic division of labour: A cross-national analysis. In R. Crompton (Ed.), *Restructuring gender relations and employment: The decline of the male breadwinner* (pp. 105–127). Oxford, UK: Oxford University Press.

Cunningham, M. (2007). Influences of women's employment on the gendered division of household labor over the life course: Evidence from a 31–year panel study. *Journal of Family Issues, 28*(3), 422–444.

de Zilwa, D. (2007). Organisational culture and values and the adaptation of academic units in Australian universities. *Higher Education, 54*, 557–554.

Demetriou, D. Z. (2001). Connell's concept of hegemonic masculinity: A critique. *Theory and Society, 30*, 337–361.

Deutsch, F. M., Lussier, J. B., & Servis, L. J. (1993). Husbands at home: Predictors of paternal participation in childcare and housework. *Journal of Personality and Social Psychology, 65*(6), 1154–1166.

DiMaggio, P. J., & Powell, W. W. (1983). The iron cage revisited: Institutional isomorphism and collective rationality in organizational fields. *American Sociological Review, 48*(2), 147–160.

Doherty, W. J., Kouneski, E. F., & Erickson, M. F. (1998). Responsible fathering: An overview and conceptual framework. *Journal of Marriage and Family, 60*(2), 277–292.

Drago, R., Colbeck, C., Stauffer, K. D., Pirretti, A., Burkum, K., Fazioli, J., et al. (2005). Bias against caregiving. *Academe, 91*(5), 22–25.

Eddy, P. L., & Gaston-Gayles, J. L. (2008). New faculty on the block: Issues of stress and support. *Journal of Human Behavior in the Social Environment, 17*(1–2), 89–106.

Elliott, M. (2008). Gender differences in the causes of work and family strain among academic faculty. *Journal of Human Behavior in the Social Environment, 17*(1–2), 157–173.

Elliott, M. (2003). Work and family role strain among university employees. *Journal of Family and Economic Issues, 24*(2), 157–181.

Ely, R. J., & Meyerson, D. E. (2000). Theories of gender in organizations: A new approach to organizational analysis and change. *Research in Organizational Behaviour, 22*, 103–151.

Emslie, C., & Hunt, K. (2009). "Live to work" or "work to live"? A qualitative study of gender and work-life balance among men and women in mid-life. *Gender, Work and Organization, 16*(1), 151–172.

Erickson, S. K. (2012). Women Ph.D. students in engineering and a nuanced terrain: Avoiding and revealing gender. *Review of Higher Education, 35*(3), 355–374.

Fairweather, J. S. (2002). The mythologies of faculty productivity: Implications for institutional policy and decision making. *Journal of Higher Education, 73*(1), 26–48.

Finkel, S. K., Olswang, S. G., & She, N. (1994). The implications of childbirth on tenure and promotion for women faculty. *Review of Higher Education, 17*(3), 259–70.

Fothergill, A., & Feltey, K. (2003). "I've worked very hard and slept very little": Mothers on the tenure track in academia. *Journal for the Association of Research on Mothering, 5*, 5–19.

Fox, M. F. (2005). Gender, family characteristics, and publication productivity among scientists. *Social Studies of Science, 35*(1), 131–150.

Gerstel, N., & Gallagher, S. K. (2001). Men's caregiving: Gender and the contingent character of care. *Gender and Society, 15*(2), 197–217.

Haas, L., & Hwang, P. (1995). Company culture and men's usage of family leave benefits in Sweden. *Family Relations, 44*(1), 28–36.

Haas, L., & Hwang, C. P. (2007). Gender and organizational culture: Correlates of companies' responsiveness to fathers in Sweden. *Gender & Society, 21*(1), 52–79.

Haas, L., & Hwang, C. P. (2009). Is fatherhood becoming more visible at work? Trends in corporate support for fathers taking parental leave in Sweden. *Fathering, 7*(3), 303–321.

Hasselback, J. R., Reinstein, A., & Schwan, E. S. (2000). Benchmarks for evaluating the research productivity of accounting faculty. *Journal of Accounting Education, 18*, 79–97.

Hecht, I. W. D., Higgerson, M. L., Gmelch, W. H., & Tucker, A. (1999). *The department chair as academic leader.* Phoenix, AZ: American Council on Education and Oryx Press.

Heijstra, T. M., & Rafnsdóttir, G. L. (2010). The Internet and academics' workload and work-family balance. *Internet and Higher Education, 13*(3), 158–163.

Helms, R. M. (2010). *New challenges, new priorities: The experience of Generation X faculty.* Report for the Collaborative on Academic Careers in Higher Education. Cambridge, MA: Collaborative on Academic Careers in Higher Education.

Hochschild, A. R. (1989). *The second shift: Working parents and the revolution at home.* New York: Viking Press.

Hofferth, S. L. (2003). Race/ethnic differences in father involvement in two-parent families: Culture, context, or economy? *Journal of Family Issues, 24*(2), 185–216.

Hollenshead, C. S., Sullivan, B., Smith, G. C., August, L., & Hamilton, S. (2005). Work/family policies in higher education: Survey data and case studies of policy implementation. *New Directions for Higher Education, 130*, 41–65.

Holman, C., Joyeux, B., & Kask, C. (2008). Labor productivity trends since 2000, by sector and industry. *Monthly Labor Review, 131*, 64–82.

Howell, L. P., Servis, G., & Bonham, A. (2005). Multigenerational challenges in academic medicine: UC Davis's responses. *Academic Medicine, 80*(6), 527–532.

Hunter, L. A., & Leahey, E. (2010). Parenting and research productivity: New evidence and methods. *Social Studies of Science, 40*(3), 433–451.

Kazura, K. (2000). Fathers' qualitative and quantitative involvement: An investigation of attachment, play, and social interactions. *Journal of Men's Studies*, 9(1), 41–57.

Kensing, K. (2013). The 10 least stressful jobs of 2013. Careercast.com. Retrieved from http://www.careercast.com/jobs-rated/10–least-stressful-jobs-2013.

Kezar, A., (2001). *Understanding and facilitating change in higher education in the 21st century*. San Francisco, CA: Jossey-Bass.

Kezar, A., & Eckel, P. D. (2002). The effect of institutional culture on change strategies in higher education. *Journal of Higher Education*, 73(4), 435–460.

Kimmel, M. S. (2001). Masculinity as homophobia: Fear, shame, and silence in the construction of gender identity. In S. M. Whitehead & F. J. Barrett (Eds.), *The masculinities reader* (pp. 266–287). Cambridge, UK: Polity Press.

Kossek, E. E., Lewis, S., & Hammer, L. B. (2009). Work-life initiatives and organizational change: Overcoming mixed messages to move from the margin to the mainstream. *Human Relations*, 63(3), 3–19.

Kuh, G. D., & Whitt, E. J. (1988). *The invisible tapestry: Culture in American colleges and universities*. ASHE-ERIC Higher Education Report, No. 1. Washington, DC: Association for the Study of Higher Education.

Kyvik, S. (1990). Motherhood and scientific productivity. *Social Studies of Science*, 20(1), 149–160.

Lamb. M. E., & Lewis, C. (2004). The development and significance of father-child relationships in two-parent families. In M. E. Lamb (Ed.), *The role of the father in child development* (4th ed., pp. 272–306). Hoboken, NJ: Wiley.

Lamb. M. E., Pleck, J. H., Charnov, E. L., & Levine, J. A. (1985). Paternal behavior in humans. *American Zoologist*, 25, 883–894.

Lancaster, L. C., & Stillman, D. (2002). *When generations collide*. New York: HarperCollins.

Lansford, J. E., Bornstein, M. H., Dodge, K. A., Skinner, A. T., Putnick, D. L., & Deater-Deckard, K. (2011). Attributions and attitudes of mothers and fathers in the United States. *Parenting: Science and Practice*, 11(2–3), 199–213.

Leavell, A. S., Tamis-LeMonda, C. S., Ruble, D. N., Zosuls, K. M., & Cabrera, N. J. (2012). African American, White and Latino fathers' activities with their sons and daughters in early childhood. *Sex Roles*, 66(1–2), 53–65.

Lim, S., & Lim, B. K. (2003). Parenting style and child outcomes in Chinese and immigrant Chinese families: Current findings and cross-cultural considerations in conceptualization and research. *Marriage & Family Review*, 35(3–4), 21–43.

Liston, D. D., Griffin, M. M., & Hecker, J. M. (1997, March). *Living with the Family Leave Act of 1993: Case studies of women in academe*. Paper presented at the annual meeting of the American Educational Research Association, Chicago, IL.

Lorber, J. (2003). "Night to his day": The social construction of gender. In P. S. Rothenberg (Ed.), *Race, class, and gender in the United States: An integrated study* (pp. 54–65). New York: Worth Publishers.

Lorber, J. (1998). Symposium on R. W. Connell's Masculinities: Men's gender politics. *Gender & Society*, 12(4), 469–477.

Lundquist, J. H., Misra, J., & O'Meara, K. A. (2012). Parental leave usage by fathers and mothers at an American university. *Fathering, 10*(3), 337–363.

Manchester, C. F., Leslie, L. M., & Kramer, A. (2010). Stop the clock policies and career success in academia. *American Economic Review, 100*, 219–223.

Manville, J. (1997). The gendered organization of an Australian Anglican parish. *Sociology of Religion, 58*(1), 25–38.

Marsiglio, W., Amato, P., Day, R. D., & Lamb, M. E. (2000). Scholarship on fatherhood in the 1990s and beyond. *Journal of Marriage and the Family, 62*, 1173–1191.

Martin, J. (2002). *Organizational culture: Mapping the terrain.* Thousand Oaks, CA: Sage.

Martin, J. (1994). The organization of exclusion: Institutionalization of sex inequality, gendered faculty jobs and gendered knowledge in organizational theory and research. *Organization, 1*(2), 401–431.

Martin, P. Y. (1998). Symposium on R. W. Connell's Masculinities: Why can't a man be more like a woman? Reflections on Connell's Masculinities. *Gender & Society, 12*(4), 472–474.

Masland, A. T. (1985). Organizational culture in the study of higher education. *Review of Higher Education, 8*(2), 157–168.

Mason, M. A., & Goulden, M. (2002). Do babies matter: The effect of family formation on the lifelong careers of academic men and women. *Academe, 88*(6), 21–27.

Mason, M. A., & Goulden, M. (2004). Do babies matter (Part II)?: Closing the baby gap. *Academe, 90*(6), 10–15.

Mason, M. A., Goulden, M., & Wolfinger, N. H. (2006). Babies matter: Pushing the equity revolution forward. In S. J. Bracken, J. K. Allen, & D. R. Dean (Eds.), *The balancing act: Gendered perspectives in faculty roles and work lives* (pp. 9–30). Sterling, VA: Stylus Publishing.

Mason, M. A., Wolfinger, N. H., & Goulden, M. (2013). *Do babies matter? Gender and family in the ivory tower.* New Brunswick, NJ: Rutgers University Press.

Matta, D., & Knudson-Martin, C. (2006). Father responsivity: Couple processes and the coconstruction of fatherhood. *Family Process, 45*(1), 19–37.

McBrier, D. B. (2003). Gender and career dynamics within a segmented professional labor market: The case of law academia. *Social Forces, 81*(4), 1201–1266.

Menzies, H., & Newson, J. (2007). No time to think: Academics' life in the globally wired university. *Time & Society, 16*(1), 83–98.

Merriam, S. B. (1998). *Qualitative research and case study applications in education.* San Francisco, CA: Jossey-Bass.

Misra, J., Lundquist, J. H., & Templer, A. (2012). Gender, work time, and care responsibilities among faculty. *Sociological Forum, 27*(2), 300–323.

Mohrman, K., Ma, W., & Baker, D. (2008). The research university in transition: The emerging global model. *Higher Education Policy, 21*, 5–27.

Nakhaie, M. R. (2009). Professors, ideology and housework. *Journal of Family and Economic Issues, 30*, 399–411.

National Center for Education Statistics. (2005). *2004 national study of postsecondary faculty report on faculty and instructional staff.* Washington, DC: U.S. Department of Education.

National Center for Education Statistics. (2010). *Table 276: Degree-granting institutions and branches, by type and control of institution and state or jurisdiction (2009–2010)*. Washington, DC: Integrated Postsecondary Education Data System.

O'Laughlin, E. M., & Bischoff, L. G. (2005). Balancing parenthood and academia: Work/family stress as influenced by gender and tenure status. *Journal of Family Issues, 26*(1), 79–106.

O'Meara, K. A., & Campbell, C. (2011). Faculty sense of agency in decisions about work and family. *Review of Higher Education, 34*, 447–476.

Park, S. M. (1996). Research, teaching, and service: Why shouldn't women's work count? *Journal of Higher Education, 67*(1), 46–84.

Perna, L. W. (2001). The relationship between family responsibilities and employment status among college and university faculty. *Journal of Higher Education, 72*(5), 584–611.

Perry-Smith, J. E., & Blum, T. C. (2000). Work-life human resource bundles and perceived organizational performance. *Academy of Management Journal, 43*(6), 1107–1117.

Pleck, J. H., & Masciadrelli, B. P. (2004). Paternal involvement by U.S. residential fathers: Levels, sources, and consequences. In M. E. Lamb (Ed.), *The role of the father in child development* (4th ed., pp. 222–271). Hoboken, NJ: Wiley.

Pribbenow, C. M., Sheridan, J., Winchell, J., Benting, D., Handelsman, J., & Carnes, M. (2010). The tenure process and extending the tenure clock: The experience of faculty at one university. *Higher Education Policy, 23*, 17–38.

Quinn, K. (2010). Tenure clock extension policies: Who uses them and to what effect? *NASPA Journal About Women in Higher Education, 3*(1), 182–206.

Rafnsdóttir, G. L., & Heijstra, T. M. (2011). Balancing work–family life in academia: The power of time. *Gender, Work & Organization, 20*(3), 283–296.

Russell, G., & Hwang, C. P. (2004). The impact of workplace practices on father involvement. In M. E. Lamb (Ed.), *The role of the father in child development* (4th ed., pp. 476–503). Hoboken, NJ: Wiley.

Sallee, M. W. (2011). Performing masculinity: Considering gender in doctoral student socialization. *Journal of Higher Education, 82*(2), 187–216.

Sallee, M. W. (2008). *Socialization and masculinities: Tales of two disciplines*. Unpublished doctoral dissertation, University of Southern California, Los Angeles.

Sallee, M. W., & Pascale, A. B. (2012). Multiple roles, multiple burdens: The experiences of female scientists with children. *Journal of Women and Minorities in Science and Engineering, 18*(2), 135–152.

Sallee, M. W., & Tierney, W. G. (2011). The transformation of professors of education. *Journal of the Professoriate, 4*(1), 1–38.

Sax, L. J., Hagedorn, L. S., Arredondo, M., & Dicrisi, F. A., III. (2002). Faculty research productivity: Exploring the role of gender and family-related factors. *Research in Higher Education, 43*(4), 423–446.

Sayer, C. L., Bianchi, S. M., & Robinson, J. P. (2004). Are parents investing less in children? Trends in mothers' and fathers' time with children. *American Journal of Sociology, 110*(1), 1–43.

Schein, E. (2004). *Organizational culture and leadership* (3rd ed.). San Francisco, CA: Jossey-Bass.

Schiebinger, L., Henderson, A. D., & Gilmartin, S. K. (2008). *Dual-career academic couples: What universities need to know.* Stanford, CA: Michelle R. Clayton Institute for Gender Research.

Schuster, J. H., & Finkelstein, M. J. (2006). *The American faculty: The restructuring of academic work and careers.* Baltimore, MD: Johns Hopkins University Press.

Seagren, A. T., Creswell, J. W., & Wheeler, D. W. (1993). *The department chair: New roles, responsibilities, and challenges.* ASHE-ERIC Higher Education Report, No. 1. Washington, DC: George Washington University.

Shelton, B. A. (1990). The distribution of household tasks: Does wife's employment status make a difference? *Journal of Family Issues, 11*(2), 115–135.

Shepard, E., & Clifton, T. (2000). Are longer hours reducing productivity in manufacturing? *International Journal of Manpower, 21*(7), 540–553.

Shepard, E., Clifton, T., & Kruse, D. (1996). Flexible work hours and productivity: Some evidence from the pharmaceutical industry. *Industrial Relations, 35*(1), 123–139.

Slaughter, S., & Rhoades, G. (2004). *Academic capitalism and the new economy: Markets, state, and higher education.* Baltimore, MD: Johns Hopkins University Press.

Smith-Doerr, L. (2004). Flexibility and fairness: Effects of the network form of organization on gender equity in life science careers. *Sociological Perspectives, 47*(1), 25–54.

Smithson, J., & Stokoe, E. H. (2005). Discourses of work-life balance: Negotiating "genderblind" terms in organizations. *Gender, Work and Organization, 12*(2), 147–168.

Stack, S. (2004). Gender, children and research productivity. *Research in Higher Education, 45*(8), 891–920.

Stake, R. E. (1994). Case studies. In N. K. Denzin & Y. S. Lincoln (Eds.), *Handbook of qualitative research* (pp. 236–247). Thousand Oaks, CA: Sage.

Stone, P. (2007). *Opting out? Why women really quit careers and head home.* Berkeley: University of California Press.

Stone-Johnson, C. (2012). Not cut out to be an administrator: Generations, change, and the career transition from teacher to principal. *Education and Urban Society.* Available online at 10.1177/0013124512458120.

Taylor, B. A., & Behnke, A. (2005). Fathering across the border: Latino fathers in Mexico and the U.S. *Fathering: A Journal of Theory, Research, and Practice About Men as Fathers, 3*(2), 99–120.

Thompson, C. A., Beauvais, L. L., & Lyness, K. S. (1999). When work-family benefits are not enough: The influence of work-family culture on benefit utilization, organizational attachment, and work-family conflict. *Journal of Vocational Behavior, 54*, 392–415.

Thompson, L., & Walker, A. J. (1989). Gender in families: Women and men in marriage, work, and parenthood. *Journal of Marriage and Family, 51*(4), 845–871.

Tierney, W. G. (1988). Organizational culture in higher education: Defining the essentials. *Journal of Higher Education, 59*(1), 2–21.

Tierney, W. G., & Bensimon, E. M. (2000). (En)Gender(ing) socialization. In J. Glazer-Raymo, B. K. Townsend, & B. Ropers-Huilman (Eds.), *Women in higher education: A feminist perspective* (2nd ed., pp. 309–325). Boston: Pearson Custom Publishing.

Tierney, W. G., & Rhoads, R. A. (1994). *Faculty socialization as cultural process: A mirror of institutional commitment.* ASHE-ERIC Higher Education Report, 93(6). Washington, DC: George Washington University, School of Education and Human Development.

Trower, C. A. (2010). A new generation of faculty: Similar core values in a different world. *Peer Review, 12*(3), 27–30.

Trower, C. (2012). Gen X meets Theory X: What new scholars want. *Journal of Collective Bargaining in the Academy,* (1), Article 11. Retrieved from http://thekeep.eiu.edu/jcba/vol0/iss1/11.

Trower, C. A., & Bleak, J. L. (2004). *Tenure-track faculty job satisfaction survey. Gender: Statistical report.* Cambridge, MA: Harvard Graduate School of Education.

U.S. Bureau of Labor Statistics. (2013). *American time use survey: 2012 results* (USDL-13-1178). Retrieved Oct. 1, 2013, from http://www.bls.gov/news.release/pdf/atus.pdf.

U.S. Census Bureau (2010). *Current population survey, 2010 annual social and economic supplement.* Washington, DC: U.S. Census Bureau.

Van Maanen, J., & Schein, E. H. (1979). Toward a theory of organizational socialization. In B. M. Staw (Ed.), *Research in organization behavior: An annual series of analytic essays and critical reviews* (pp. 209–264). Greenwich, CT: JAI Press.

Walker, J. (2009). Time as the fourth dimension in the globalization of higher education. *Journal of Higher Education, 80*(5), 483–509.

Waltman, J., & August, L. (2005). *Tenure clock, modified duties, and sick leave policies: Creating "a network of support and understanding" for University of Michigan faculty women during pregnancy and childbirth.* Ann Arbor: University of Michigan Center for the Education of Women.

Ward, K., & Wolf-Wendel, L. (2012). *Academic motherhood: How faculty manage work and family.* New Brunswick, NJ: Rutgers University Press.

Ward, K., & Wolf-Wendel, L. (2004). Academic motherhood: Managing complex roles in research universities. *Review of Higher Education, 27*(2), 233–257.

Waters, M. A., & Bardoel, E. A. (2006). Work-family policies in the context of higher education: Useful or symbolic? *Asia Pacific Journal of Human Resources, 44*(1), 67–82.

West, C., & Zimmerman, D. H. (1987). Doing gender. *Gender and Society, 1*(2), 125–151.

Williams, J. C. (2010). *Reshaping the work-family debate: Why men and class matter.* Cambridge, MA: Harvard University Press.

Williams, J. (2000). *Unbending gender: Why family and work conflict and what to do about it.* Oxford, UK: Oxford University Press.

Wolf-Wendel, L. E., Twombly, S., & Rice, S. (2003). *The two-body problem: Dual career couple hiring policies in higher education.* Baltimore, MD: Johns Hopkins University Press.

Wolf-Wendel, L. E., & Ward, K. (2006a). Academic life and motherhood: Variations by institutional type. *Higher Education, 52,* 487–521.

Wolf-Wendel, L. E., & Ward, K. (2006b). Faculty life at comprehensive universities: Between a rock and a hard place. *Journal of the Professoriate, 1*(2), 1–21.

Wolf-Wendel, L., Ward, K., & Twombly, S. (2007). Faculty life at community colleges: The perspective of women with children. *Community College Review, 34*(4), 255–281.

Yin, R. K. (2009). *Case study research: Design and methods* (4th ed.). Thousand Oaks, CA: Sage.

Youn, T. I. K., & Price, T. M. (2009). Learning from the experience of others: The evolution of faculty tenure and promotion rules in comprehensive institutions. *Journal of Higher Education, 80*(2), 204–237.

Zemke, R., Raines, C., & Filipczak, B. (2000). *Generations at work*. New York: AMACOM.

Index

Acker, Joan, 11–13, 29, 53–55, 213.
    See also gendered organization
Active Service/Modified Duties. *See*
    modified duties
Administration, Central, 66, 70–72,
    76–78, 84–86, 90
    And role in supporting family-
        friendly policies, 71, 76–77,
        220–221
Adoption Leave, 75
Artifacts, 12, 58, 59, 88–92, 125–127
    Behaviors, overt, 59, 126
    Language, written and spoken, 59,
        89
    Physical environment, 59, 88–89, 126
    Social environment, 59, 127
    Symbols, 59
    Technology, 59, 125–126
Assistant professors
    And ideal worker norms, 36–37
    And stress of pre-tenure career, 6,
        183, 187–190, 200
Assumptions, 12, 58, 59, 92–96,
    127–132

Baby Boomers, 184
Becher, Tony, 97, 98, 101

Breadwinners, Men as, 8, 9, 50, 53, 54,
    151, 153, 179, 209, 211
    See also ideal worker, hegemonic
        masculinity
Breastfeeding, 38–39, 73
    And lactation support, 20

Caregiving
    And activities performed with
        children, 160–163, 211
    As oppositional to masculine
        identity, 2, 40, 54
    And societal expectation that wife
        serves as caregiver, 35, 36
    Time spent engaged in care, 3, 14,
        104–105, 112, 157–158
    Types of activities that men perform
        more, 158, 163–167
    Types of activities that women
        perform more, 157–158, 167–171
    Women perform more caregiving, 37,
        42–44, 157, 167–168
Childbearing leave, 18, 75
Childcare
    Backup, 19–20, 83
    Center(s) on campus, 65, 70, 76, 84,
        217–218

Children included in department events, 67–68, 79–80, 109, 116, 123

Children present on campus, 109, 116, 124

Coach for sports teams, 163, 166–167, 177

Colleagues, Role of, 223–225
  And discussions about parenting, 107–108, 122–123, 223
  And negative interactions around work/family issues, 85, 124
  And social support, 64–65, 108–109, 122
  In policy use, 44, 45, 47, 55, 62, 90–91, 107–109
  See also department chair

Connell, R. W., 8–10, 30 See also hegemonic masculinity

Cost of living, 63–64, 69

Commute to campus, 64
  And presence of children on campus, 67–68
  And relationship to collegiality, 64, 65, 67–68

Complicit masculinity, 9, 30. See also hegemonic masculinity

Culture, departmental, 66–68, 72, 73, 78–70, 86–88
  No discussion of family-friendly issues needed, 114
  Supportive of mothers only, 113–114

Culture, disciplinary, 97–102, 125–132, 212
  Structure of work, 98–99, 104–105, 112–113, 119–121, 125–126
  See also humanities and social sciences, sciences and engineering, and professional schools

Culture, organizational, 12–13, 58–60, 70–72, 213–214
  Culture as decentralized, 84–86
  Levels of culture, 12, 58–59. See also artifacts, assumptions, and values

Demetriou, Demetrakis, 9–10, 208

Department chair, Role of, 100, 105–107, 114–115, 121–122, 221–223
  In policy use, 61–62, 67, 72, 78–79, 106, 114–115, 121–122, 221
  Support of, 78–79, 105–107, 114, 115

Division of labor, 160, 163–180, 211
  And employment status of married couples, 7, 69, 158–159, 171–177, 178–179, 195–199, 212
  And negotiation of tasks, 174–176, 197
  And relationship to traditional gender roles, 69, 73, 163–171

Dual-career assistance programs, 20, 70, 76, 83–84, 216–217

Dual-career couples, 65–66, 69–70, 75, 82, 83–84, 186

Eastern University, 22–23, 63–68
  Administration, central, 66
  Culture, departmental, 66–68
  Employment status of spouse, 64–65
  Institutional location, 63–65
  Policies, family-friendly, 65–66

Faculty work, 6–7, 182–183
  And flexibility, 6, 31–33, 104–105, 119–120, 124–125, 185–186, 190–191, 207, 211
  And work/life issues, 13–16

Gender
  As biologically constructed, 38–39
  Created through interaction, 10–11, 50, 53, 189, 208, 212
  See also gender norms, hegemonic masculinity

Gender composition of organization, 99–100, 126–127
  And relationship to policy use, 99–100, 126–127

Gender norms, 2, 3, 8
  And child rearing, 38–40, 164, 165, 166, 170–171, 171–178, 186, 197–199, 213

And policy use, 4, 41–52, 59
  See also breadwinning, caregiving,
    hegemonic masculinity, ideal
    worker
Gender roles. *See* gender norms
Gendered organization, 10–12, 13, 29,
    52–56, 91–96, 130–132, 202, 212,
    213
  And relationship to hegemonic
    masculinity, 11–12, 29–30, 52, 55
  And relationship to ideal worker
    norms, 11, 29, 30
Generation X, 184–187, 201–202
  And flexibility in work practices,
    185–186, 193
  And work/family balance, 184–185,
    191–195, 197–199, 211–212
Generations
  Characteristics of, 183–184
  Differences between, 124, 192,
    195–196, 211–212
  See also Silent Generation, Baby
    Boomers, Generation X, and
    Millennial Generation
Grants
  Importance of, 6, 98, 112–113,
    125–126, 187–188, 206
  Institutional assistance for, 219

Hegemonic masculinity, 8–10, 30, 53,
    91–96, 127–132, 153, 210–213
  And breadwinning, 8
  Dependent on context, 9
  In opposition to femininity, 8–9
  And relationship to scholarly
    engagement, 153
  And subordinated masculinities,
    9–10
History of policy use by men, 46–47,
    61, 62, 87, 89, 223
Hours worked, 33–34, 104–105,
    112–113, 133, 137–139, 145–147
  Mornings or evenings, 33, 137–138
  Weekends, 33–34
  Placing boundaries on work hours,
    191–193, 201

Humanities and social sciences,
    102–110, 127, 129, 130–131
  Structure of work, 104–105
  Support of chair, 105–107
  Support of colleagues, 107–109

Ideal worker, 8, 29, 52–53, 91–96,
    127–132, 153–154, 182–183,
    205–213
  And conflict with caregiving, 133–135,
    145–147, 193–195, 201–202, 207
  And conflict with scholarly work,
    140–141
  And gender norms, 8, 209–210
  And hours worked 33–37, 192–193,
    210
  And policy use, 45
Involved father, 2, 8, 12, 30, 31, 36,
    40, 50, 54, 95, 131, 163, 179, 186,
    197, 202, 208
  And conflict with ideal worker, 66,
    73, 98, 121, 134
  See also caregiving and gender norms
Involvement in children's activities,
    31–33
  See also coach for sports teams, out-
    door activities, play with children
Involvement typology, 158

Location, Institutional, 63–65, 69–70,
    74–75, 81–82, 88–89, 218–219
  And employment opportunities, 65,
    69–70, 82
  As family-friendly, 69–70, 74–75,
    81–82

Men's careers taking priority, 172–174,
    179
Methodology, 21–26
  Demographics of participants, 23–25
Midwestern University, 22, 80–88
  Administration, central, 84–86
  Culture, departmental, 86–88
  Employment status of spouse, 82
  Institutional location, 81–82
  Policies, family-friendly, 82–84

Millennial Generation, 184
Mimetic conformity, 57
    Modified duties, 18–19, 70, 75,
        82–83, 215–216
    And financial cost, 19, 77–78

National Study of Postsecondary
    Faculty (NSOPF), 98–99, 133, 135

Organization, Characteristics of a
    Father-Friendly, 60–62
    See also role of department chair,
        role of colleagues, history of policy
        use by men
Outdoor activities, 165–166, 177

Parental leave. See childbearing leave
Partner hiring program, See dual-career
    assistance programs
Patriarchy, 9, 10, 30. See also
    hegemonic masculinity
Play with children, 158, 163–165, 177
Policies, Family-friendly, 17–21, 65–66,
    70, 75–76, 82–84
    See also adoption leave, childbearing
        leave, dual-career assistance,
        modified duties, part-time tenure
        track, tenure-clock extension
Policy use, 40–52, 207–209
    And bias avoidance, 14–15, 44–45,
        48–52, 62, 207–208
    Belief that universities have no
        responsibility to provide assistance,
        41–42, 63, 66
    And career penalties, 48, 50–51, 66,
        207
    And masculinity penalties, 48–50,
        73, 207–208
    By men, 44–47, 78
    Misinformation about eligibility,
        43–44, 45, 77
    Targeted toward women's use, 42–44,
        71–72, 72–73, 77, 208
Pregnancy leave. See childbearing leave
Productivity, 15–16
    Career penalties, 141–143

Impact of children on hours worked,
    137–139, 145–147, 148–149, 152
Impact of children on research
    output, 135–137, 139–147,
    152–153, 189–190
Impact of children on scholarly
    engagement, 138–139, 147–151,
    153
    Measurements of, 135–137, 185
    Reduction in travel, 144–145
Professional schools, 117–125, 130, 131
    Structure of work, 119–121
    Support of chair, 121–122
    Support of colleagues, 122–124

Release from teaching duties. See
    modified duties
Replacement teaching fund, 77–78
Research, 6, 34, 98–99, 112–113,
    125–126, 128, 129, 130, 135
    See also productivity
Research universities, 6–7, 57
    And provision of family-friendly
        policies, 16–17

Schein, Edgar, 12–13, 58–60. See also
    organizational culture
Sciences and engineering, 110–117,
    129–130, 131
    Structure of work, 112–113
    Support of chair, 114–115
    Support of colleagues, 115
Search committee training, 21, 83, 85,
    222
Second shift, 39, 209
Silent Generation, 183–184
Socialization to organizational roles,
    100, 127
Southern University, 22, 68–73
    Administration, central, 70–72
    Culture, departmental, 72–73
    Employment status of spouse, 70
    Institutional location, 69–70
    Policies, family-friendly, 70
Spousal hiring program. See dual-career
    assistance programs

Stay-at-home wives, 7, 24, 69, 75,
    82, 93, 155–156, 159, 171–175,
    178–179, 182, 196, 202, 210, 212
    And the ideal worker, 54, 124
    See also employment status of spouse,
    gender norms
Subordinated masculinities, 9–10. See
    also hegemonic masculinity

Teaching, 6, 15, 16, 34–35, 98–99,
    104, 114, 115, 120–121, 128, 135,
    148, 149, 206–207, 222
    And conflict with caregiving, 35, 45,
    107, 121, 130, 207, 218
    And interactions with own children,
    162, 199
    See also disciplinary culture and
    structure of work and after-hours
    work obligations
Tenure-clock extension, 17–18, 40–41,
    65, 70, 75, 82, 214–215
Tenure track, part-time, 19, 65, 76

Trowler, Paul, 101
"Two body problem," 20. See also dual-
    career couples

Universities as catalysts for change,
    4–5, 208–209

Values, 12, 58, 59, 92–96, 127–132

Western University, 22, 73–80
    Administration, central, 76–78
    Culture, departmental, 78–80
    Employment status of spouse, 75
    Institutional location, 74–75
    Policies, family-friendly, 75–76
Women. See caregiving, policy use
Work obligations, after-hours, 34,
    120–121, 126, 206–207, 222
Work/family conflict, 2–3, 133–135
    Issues unique to women, 14, 15,
    38–40
Work/family staff, 76, 84, 217

www.ingramcontent.com/pod-product-compliance
Lightning Source LLC
Chambersburg PA
CBHW021526210326
41599CB00012B/1392